JUST BEGINNING

ELISA MASSELLI

Translated into English by:
Liz Huamaní Alejo
Lima, Peru, November 2020

Just Beginning
Original Tittle in Portuguese:
"*Apenas começando*" © Elisa Masselli

Reviewers:
Amar Espinoza Vega
Luisa F. Arias Novoa

World Spiritist Institute

Houston, Texas, USA
E–mail: contact@worldspiritistinstitute.org

Just Beginning

Synopsis:

When going through difficult times, we feel that everything is over and that there is no more hope or a way forward. How many times do we feel that we need to make a decision, despite not always knowing what the best option would be?

Julia, after being in a relationship with an engaged man, felt that it was all over and had to make a decision. For this, she had the affection of spiritual friends who would have had to postpone important projects on the spiritual realm that would help them evolve. Out of love, they will postpone projects, be reborn and die, only to help her in her redemption and evolution, and, mainly, to help her understand that: when we think that everything is over, truthfully, for God, it is JUST BEGINNING.

Just Beginning

Just Beginning

About the Medium

Born on 9/11/1943, Elisa Masselli was a poor girl, but never unhappy. Her mother had the theory that "a child needed to play, because when she grew up, she would have a lot of problems, so her mother was responsible for the household chores." During her childhood she always played a lot. At 17, her sister Nair, who raised her, fell into a deep depression until she attempted suicide twice. After several hospitalizations, her sister committed suicide by hanging herself in the shower. That destroyed everything she had learned about God. However, she soon met a man who gave her the book "*Our Home*" (*Nosso Lar*) by André Luiz. As she loved reading, she fell in love with the book and its content, and said: "I started reading, and I fell in love. Perhaps, because it was what I wanted to hear, that my sister maybe was not in a good place, but that she was not alone and that at any moment she could be rescued and have a new opportunity to reincarnate. I read that book quickly and Mr. José brought me the entire collection of André Luiz's books. When I finished reading them all, I was in love with everything I had read, so I began to attend the Spiritist Federation of the state of São Paulo. "

In 1964, she married Henrique, who died in 1984. "I suffered a lot when I saw my husband's suffering, because for everyone and especially for me, he did not deserve to suffer the way he suffered,

Just Beginning

but I had learned that everything was always fine and that God was the one who knew why things happened, so I didn't despair. "

In 1991, without knowing why and how, she began to hear voices and one of them had told her that she would have to write novels with teachings. For psychiatry, this was nothing more than a psychotic crisis. After a turbulent phase of depression and doubts, she came up with the idea of writing a book, which began to take over her thoughts, so she decided to write just as a hobby. Little by little the story emerged. "I couldn't believe that I was writing a story like that. I cried and laughed while writing. When it was ready, I sent it to the editor of Dona Zibia Gasparetto. Title: 'When the past doesn't pass.' In that moment she remembered what some voice had told her: "The name does not matter, what matters is that you write." Thus, the writer Elisa Masselli was born.

Just Beginning

Index

FOREWORD 9
1.– Surprise 11
2.– Time of decision... 19
3.– Discovery 26
4.– Words of comfort.. 33
5.– An incredible story 40
6.– The rebeginning... 70
7.– The recipe for unhappiness.................................... 84
8.– The power of money 91
9.– Life begins again... 119
10.– Life begins again... 125
11. Unexpected Situation 129
12.– Taking note 133
13.– The story of Julia... 145
14.– Taking action... 187
15.– Fatal decision 195
16.– Act of despair.. 207
17. – Friendly visit.. 225
18. – The dream 242
19. – Spiritual help... 255
20.– Eulalia.. 273
21.– A true story 289
22.– The dance 302

Just Beginning

23.– New life 322

24.– The ceremony 337

25.– The delivery 356

26. – The wait 366

27.– The rudeness 376

28.– Free will 399

29.– Sensation on the skin 414

30.– The clarification 422

Epilogue 436

Just Beginning

FOREWORD

Every time I start writing a book, I never know how the story will go on; I know it will come in pieces.

One morning, as I was almost waking up, as always, I heard the voice of a man saying:

– "An abandoned woman."

I woke up, knowing in advance that my next story would be about an abandoned woman. I smiled and began to write.

As I always do, I didn't bother to think about what the story would be like, or its characters, because I knew they would come. Not just the story, but, in my opinion, the most important thing: the teachings on spirituality. When I write, I don't care too much about the form or the story itself, I just write.

However, it was different with this book. At one point, after finishing a chapter, I stopped to think. I know several people who, like me, have often been tempted to abandon the Doctrine and others who have actually abandoned it. The reason was, is and will always be the same: consciousness and unconsciousness.

As I was always conscious and saw that the people next to me said they were unconscious, I thought they were lying, just "acting". I often stopped going to the spiritist houses, although I still believed in the Doctrine and tried to live it in the best possible way and apply it to my life without having to go to these spiritist

Just Beginning

houses and lie about a mentor, which I did not think I had to do. But, for one reason or another, I always came back. During one of those times that I stopped going, I was waking up and heard a man's voice:

– "What matters is the message." I fully woke up and thought:

– That is it! It does not matter in which way the messages get across, what matters is that they get across.

From that moment on, I no longer cared who transmitted them or how, whether by books or by words. I just started to make the most of them. At the time, I never imagined that I would write one day. When I wrote my first book, I didn't think for a minute that this wonderful story was mine. I was sure it was a product of intuition. I knew and I know that, due to my lack of education, I cannot write a story like that or the others that came later. People ask me the name of the mentor who writes with me. In fact, I can't say because I don't know. I could, if I wanted, make up any name and no one would dispute it, but it wouldn't be the truth.

I think my mentor doesn't want to identify himself, because if he wanted to, he would. And on any morning, as I always do, I would wake up hearing his name. After this book, my concern became less or almost null, because I understood, through the book, the enormous work that the spiritual realm has to carry out with the mediums so that they believe and surrender.

Today, I am sure that the most important thing is the MESSAGES, no matter how they get across. Therefore, I can only say: if you, spiritist or not, believer or not, feel like writing, WRITE; if you feel like talking, TALK; if you feel like composing a song, COMPOSE; receiving and thanking with affection the INTUITION or, if you prefer, the INSPIRATION that comes, facilitating, substantially, the life of the spiritual realm. Because, in the end, what really matters is the MESSAGE.

Elisa Masselli

Just Beginning

1.– Surprise

Suzana opened her eyes and extended her arm to the side of the bed where Anselmo slept. He was not there. She smiled and thought: He, as always when he's angry, left without saying goodbye.

She turned and looked at her watch: I'm late, I need to get up and go to work. Today's the big day! She got up and, as she dressed, thought: "I don't understand why Anselmo is so nervous about my work. He doesn't understand that I have a career and that I need to take care of it... "

In a few minutes she was ready to go. Before that, she passed by Rodrigo's room, who was peacefully sleeping. She smiled and went to the kitchen. Edit was at the Kitchen

– Good morning, Edit.

– Good morning, Mrs. Suzana.

While having a cup of coffee, Suzana asked:

– When Anselmo left, were you already awake?

– Yes, he had a coffee and left quickly. He didn't look good.

Suzana smiled:

– I know, but don't worry. Tonight, when I return with good news, his bad mood will pass.

Just Beginning

– Hopefully, Mrs. Suzana. I don't like it when you argue and neither does Rodrigo. He gets angry.

– He didn't witness our argument. He was already asleep.

– Good, I don't think he needs to witness it. The child senses when something is wrong.

– Maybe you're right, I'll pay attention, but this will all pass. I need to go now.

– Are you going to have that cup of coffee, aren't you going to eat?

– No, Edit, I have to go.

– You need to eat...

Suzana smiled, took the bag and left. She called the elevator, which was slow to arrive. In the garage, she got into her car, this year's model, started the engine, sped up, and left.

On the road, while driving, she thought: "I don't understand why Anselmo gets so nervous and argues almost every day. He knows that I am working and that my work takes up most of my time. However long I stay in the office, it never ends. I love my job."

As she drove, in a traffic jam, she thought: "last night, when I arrived, he was watching a movie on television. As soon as I entered, I went over, kissed him and said: Good evening, Anselmo."

He looked at me, fell silent, and looked back at the movie he was watching. That got on my nerves.

– I'm saying good night, Anselmo!

– You know I don't like to talk when I'm watching a movie.

I know he doesn't like to talk, when he's watching a movie, yet I still went up to him and gave him a kiss on the cheek.

Just Beginning

– I know you don't want to talk right now. I'll see if you have something to eat.

To my surprise, he turned off the television, got up and said: – We need to talk, Suzana! I was waiting for you to get here.

– Not now, Anselmo. I'm dead tired. Today was a hard day. I'm going to shower, eat something and go to bed. I need to sleep...

He, unable to hide his annoyance, said: – This is precisely what we have to talk about.

– I know what you're going to say. So I'd rather not speak now. We will leave it for another time.

– You always say that! You always want to talk another time! However, that times never comes!

– Please, Anselmo...

He, looking me straight in the eye, almost yelled: – I can't wait any longer! Our marriage no longer exists!

– I do not understand what you say. We have been married for six years. How can you say that this marriage does not exist?

– It doesn't exist, Suzana! We hardly see each other! You only care about your job!

Furious, I yelled: I have to care about it! Everything I have depends on my job, the life we lead!

– Thanks to this job, we live in an apartment like this and we have the best car of the year!

– Because of this job, we don't have to worry about bills to pay or food we need to buy!

– Thanks to this job, Rodrigo can attend one of the best schools! How do you want me not to care about my job?

– I know that this is all important to you, but for me, the most important thing is to have a family!

Just Beginning

– The most important thing is getting home from work, being able to have dinner and talk with my wife, but she's never there.

– It doesn't even look like you're my wife! You are a stranger, a roommate! I'm sick of everything and I'm leaving! So far, I'm not satisfied with your attitude. Annoyed, I kept shouting: – What do you want?

– Do you want me to stop working?

– No, Suzana! I want you to find a job where you don't have to stay so late!

Where you can start at eight o'clock and leave at six in the afternoon, like almost everyone does! I want to have your presence!

I want to have a woman at home I can talk to and even go out with!

That hasn't happened in a long time, you're always tired!

– You don't know what you're talking about, Anselmo! If I work the way you say, my salary will go down a lot and that's not what I spent my life studying for, preparing myself for the future!

– My salary is not so low, Suzana! We don't need to live in a fancy apartment like this, we can live in a smaller one, yet still live like a royal family!

I couldn't take it anymore and started laughing:

– What are you saying? That with your salary, we will go back to living in a two–bedroom apartment, like the one we lived in when we got married?

– Why not, Suzana? At that time, we had a simpler but happier life.

– We talked a lot, we made plans. – That's right, we made plans! We wanted to have children, improve our lives, live in a better place, have a good car! We have achieved everything we dreamed of! I don't understand why you are complaining!

– I waited thirty–five years to have my first child! I did it because I wanted him to have it all! Of course!

– Effectively, he has everything, he just doesn't have a mother!

– What are you saying?

– What you heard! I take him to school and pick him up in the afternoon. When you get here, he is already asleep.

– He thinks that the teacher or the maid is his mother! He doesn't know you as his mother, Suzana!

– You are the one who, on the weekends, takes him out for a walk and gives him everything he wants, much more than he really needs! – Upon hearing that, I couldn't take it anymore, I left the room and went to my room.

"I am not happy with what he thinks of me! He didn't say it, but if he wants to go, so be it! I don't need him or anyone! I have my job and today is going to be the big day! With the purchase of our company by a multinational, in this meeting that will take place, I will probably become president of the company, here in Brazil, and I will grow even more.

My dreams are not over yet. "

She arrived at the company's entrance. The guard at the guardhouse smiled and opened the entrance, where she, speeding up the car, entered.

She parked the car in her assigned spot. She looked at the watch on her wrist, smiled, and went down.

As she walked into the lobby, she thought, I'm glad I got here on time. Because of the traffic, I was afraid of not getting here on time. I still have a few minutes left to get ready.

Just Beginning

My future depends on that meeting. I'm glad I arrived on time.

She entered and, when she passed by the reception, a girl who was sitting in front of a computer said: – Good morning, Mrs. Suzana.

– Good morning, Helena.

– Mrs. Suzana, I have a message for you.

– Message? Which one?

– Dr. Santana asked me to ask you, before going to the meeting, to head to HR.

– HR? Why?

– I don't know. I'm just relaying the message.

– Okay, thanks.

She headed for the elevator. Worried, she thought: what's going on? Maybe it's because I didn't take my vacation or, who knows, I'm going to get a raise... Eager, she got to a room. She knocked lightly and came in.

As soon as she came in, a lady approached her: – Good morning, Suzana.

– Good morning, Judit. I got a message to come here. What is it about?

– Unfortunately, I don't have good news, Suzana.

– What happened, Judit?

– Dr. Santana asked you to sign this letter of resignation.

– What? Resignation?

– Yes...

– It can't be! He couldn't have done that! What happened?

Just Beginning

– I don't know, Suzana. You know Dr. Santana. He does not say much. Helena, his secretary brought me the letter and said that it had to be relayed to you.

– It can't be! I will talk to him!

– Helena also said that today he will not be able to talk with you because he is preparing for a very important meeting.

He said you were supposed to go home, and when he had the time, he would let you know.

– I know about that meeting. I also prepared for that! What happened, Judit?

– I don't know, Suzana. I am also intrigued. You are one of his main advisers. I really don't know... – Suzana, unable to help it, began to cry.

– This can't be happening, I must be dreaming...

Judit, saddened, took Suzana's hand and said: – I know this is a difficult moment, but it is just a moment, Suzana. In the end everything always works.

– How can it work, Judit? It never crossed my mind that this could happen!

– I thought that with the purchase of the company by another, my position would improve! As you said, I was the main advisor of Dr. Santana! I really need this job! I just bought an apartment, without a job, how will I be able to pay the installments?

– Don't worry, Suzana. You have the ability and you will soon find a new job and, who knows, even better than this one. We don't know anything about our life. We think we have control, but in the end, we don't have any control.

– God is the one who knows what is best for each one of us and nothing happens without his permission.

Just Beginning

Upon hearing that, Suzana became possessed: – What planet are you from, Judit? Do you really think I can find another job with a better salary than the one I get here? That's impossible!

– Impossible, why?

– The country is facing difficult times. It's in recession!

– You know there are not many spots for people with a resume like mine! What am I going to do?

– You can't do anything now, Suzana. I suggest you go home and hand your life over to God.

– He certainly knows what you need and will show you a way. Have faith my friend...

– For those of you who are employed, it is easy to think so, but for me, it is a horror! God is not worried about me, He has a lot to do! You don't know what I need, I know!

Judit smiled, but stayed silent.

Suzana, with nothing further to say, said goodbye and left.

In the garage, she got in the car and desperately sped up and drove aimlessly.

Just Beginning

2.– Time of decision

Meanwhile, Anselmo arrived at the company where he worked. Before going in, he went to a coffee shop across the street. Standing still at the main entrance, he glanced at one of the tables. A girl was sitting at the table, and when she saw him, she smiled.

He smiled too and went to the counter, ordered coffee, bread with butter, and walked over to where the girl was sitting. He sat down.

– Good morning, Julia!

– Good morning, Anselmo. You're late today. Something happened?

– Nothing happened, it was just the traffic.

– Is everything okay at your house? Did you talk to her?

– No. Nothing's okay, Julia. I tried to talk to Suzana, but, as always, I couldn't.

– She is very focused on her job and a possible promotion.

– You need to make a decision, Anselmo. We cannot continue as we have so far.

– I also think that this situation cannot continue, but you have no right to blame me for anything.

– Why not? We have been together for over two years!

Just Beginning

– You don't have to change, Julia. I say this because, when we started, you knew that I was married and had no intention to leave my family. I remember that I made it very clear. I didn't lie to you.

She looked at him incredulously and he continued: – You know I can't abandon my son.

– He's still very young...

– You don't want to break up with her just because of your son or because you still have feelings for her?

– Where did you get that idea from? Of course it's because of my son!

– Someone said that a married man always says this, that he does not abandon his wife because of his children, but he is lying.

– Do you like to lie? Why?

– Just lying. When he no longer likes his wife, he cannot bear to live with her anymore, he provides all the assistance for his children and leaves the house. When the man uses his children as an excuse, he actually wants to keep both.

– That is not true! You know how much I like you, but my son is very important. He was born because I wanted him, it's not fair that he grows up far from me! I've always told you how important he is to me!

– I know, but after so long and the way you complain about your wife, I thought that would change.

– It may happen that I leave my house, but you have to wait. I need to think very carefully before taking such a measure. I don't want to traumatize the child.

– You say you like me...

– I like you, Julia, but you must be patient. We will still be together.

Just Beginning

– Are you sure?

– Of course I am. If I didn't have you by my side, I couldn't bear the life I'm living.

– It's okay. That's all I've been doing... waiting for you...

He smiled: – If we weren't here, I'd kiss you, but since I can't, I think we'd better go to work. She, getting up, also smiled and said: – You're right. Let's go to work. It's time.

Hand in hand, they walked towards the company. Before entering, he shook her hand slightly and got in. She smiled, shook his hand, crossed the street and joined the company where she worked.

The company he worked for was in the food business. He had been working there for fourteen years.

– He started as an assistant and was now manager of the sales department. His salary was good.

– Not even a third of Suzana's, but with that salary they could have a good life.

As soon as he entered the office, Anselmo sat down. Two young men followed him. They were sellers who were under his supervision.

He replied to both of them, made some calls. He looked at a photo frame, where there was a photo of Suzana and Rodrigo. Sadly, he thought: My son, I love you very much, but I think I will be forced to leave the house.

There is no way to continue living with your mother. She became a stranger to me.

Without him knowing it, there were two figures, a man and a woman. She looked at him and he smiled, then she brought her hands to Anselmo's head, who, without knowing why, remembered the day he met Suzana.

Just Beginning

What's going on? Why do I remember that day? I think I'm missing that time. When we got married, we loved each other and had many dreams, but over time I changed, Suzana changed and everything changed. The phone rang, he answered. It was a customer who made a complaint.

He handled the situation and the satisfied customer hung up. He thought again: until now, because Suzana is the way she is, I have been involved with several women, but for none of them did I feel what I feel for Julia. She is wonderful.

Marta, his secretary, came in, signed some papers and he thought again: our marriage has become a routine.

She works, I work.

Despite everything she has acquired, she always wants more. For me, what is important is adventure, seduction.

– What happens now, Marta?

– Dr. Alfredo asked you to come to his office now.

– I can't get out of here now! I am welcoming the sales reps!

– I told him that, but he said it had to be now.

– Do you know what's going on?

– No, I don't know. He seemed very anxious. You'd better go, and if any sales rep comes in, I'll ask them to wait.

– Good, I'll see what he wants. He must be a bomb about to explode. He hardly talks to me... – She smiled: – It's true, but the news can be good.

– Hopefully. I'm leaving and if someone comes, ask them to wait.

Intrigued, he got up and went to the director's office. He couldn't imagine what it was about, but due to the urgency, it seemed important.

Just Beginning

He took a few steps and stopped in front of a door. He waited a few seconds, then he knocked and entered.

Behind a table, a man who was seated stood up: – Good morning, Anselmo, I am glad you came soon. I really wanted to talk. Take a seat.

Still confused, Anselmo pulled up a chair and sat down.

Smiling, the gentleman said: – I know you don't understand what is happening, nor the reason for calling you.

– I confess it's true. I can't imagine what it could be.

– You have been working in this company since you were very young. You went through various departments, you learned all about them, but you only really found yourself when you went to work in sales. You proved to be a great salesman and then an excellent sales manager. Today I can guarantee that, thanks to you, we have the best sales team to exist.

– Our salespeople, influenced by you, feel motivated and valued, so they do a good job.

– Thank you, sir, but I must point out that they are excellent.

– That's because you knew how to choose the best ones.

– Thanks again, but I still don't understand the reason for being here.

– As I said, we have the best sales team to exist, however, the same does not happen at our branch in Recife.

– We are having losses and we need to reverse this situation. Anselmo looked at him and asked: – What are you trying to say?

– Do you see how smart you are? I'm trying to say exactly what you are thinking. We had a board meeting and decided to make you a proposal.

– What proposal?

Just Beginning

– We need you to go to Recife for a year or two, or less, until you can put together a sales team as good as the one we have here.

Anselmo, a little dizzy, got up and almost shouting, asked:
– To Recife?

– That's right. Don't worry, you will get a raise and an allowance to rent a house.

Anselmo sat down again: – I can't, sir. I have a life here. My wife works in a large company and has a good position. She won't want to move.

– We know you will have some problems relocating, but with the salary you will receive, you will be able to live very well.

– I don't know. I can't answer now, sir. I need to talk to my wife, but I have to warn you that it will be very difficult to convince her to move.

– Why this indecisiveness? After all, you are the man of the house!

– Today's times are not like yours. Today, men are no longer the man of the house.

– Today women have their jobs, their careers and can live in peace without the presence of a man by their side.

– My wife makes three times more than me. It's not just about money. She has a career.

– She is fighting to become president of the company.

– Yes, but you also need to grow professionally, and this is a great opportunity.

You need to think about your professional future.

Let's do this: you can go out now, go see your wife, take her out to lunch, and during lunch, give her the news.

Just Beginning

– Tell her how important it is for you to accept this invitation. As soon as you have an answer, let us know. We are in a hurry.

– Ok, I will do it.

He left the room. Outside, he thought: it really is a great opportunity, but I know it will be difficult for Suzana to accept it. If it were with Julia, I know there would be no problem, but with Suzana there is no possibility.

I can't do what Dr. Santana suggested. I need to think about what I'm going to say to her. He looked at the watch on his wrist and kept thinking: it was almost time for lunch.

I'll meet Julia and, during lunch, I'll tell her what happened. Let's see what she says.

3.– Discovery

Meanwhile, Suzana had been driving without a destination for quite a while. With one hand, she wiped away the tears that kept falling. She couldn't understand or accept what had happened: how did it happen?

For almost ten years I was totally devoted to the company. I worked every day until dawn so that all the work was done.

I have always been an exemplary employee.

How can Dr. Santana say goodbye, now that I thought I had gotten to where I always wanted? I thought I was going to be president of the company! This cannot be happening! I must be dreaming! Dreaming, no! Having a nightmare!

She stopped the car at a traffic light. Very nervous she thought: I need to talk to Anselmo. I know he won't believe what happened. I don't know what to do. Maybe he'll have an idea.

The traffic light turned green and she continued towards Anselmo's job.

The time for lunch has come. Anselmo took his wallet and left. When he got to the street, Júlia, smiling, was waiting for him.

He approached her and, also smiling, kissed her forehead. Together and holding hands they walked to the restaurant where they ate every day.

Just Beginning

At the same time, Suzana was driving down the street. She was looking for a place where she could park the car.

She saw when Anselmo left the company's place. She tried to call but he didn't pick up. She was petrified when she saw him approach Julia, kiss her face and walk hand in hand in the opposite direction. Furious, she stopped the car in the middle of the street and thought: What is happening here? Who is that woman?

The cars behind were honking their horns. Suzana, out of control, sped up the car and kept looking for a place to park.

After driving a few meters, she found a place by the sidewalk, where she could stop.

She quickly parked the car and got out and, in a hurry, almost running, she went to the nearby restaurant. Very nervous, she thought: They must have gone there for lunch!

She got in and, even from the entrance, she could see Anselmo and Julia talking. He began to tell her about the invitation he had received.

Suzana entered and approached them:

– Anselmo, who is this woman?

Upon seeing her, Anselmo turned pale. Julia felt her heart racing and she could barely breathe. After a few seconds, he managed to say: – Suzana! What are you doing here?

– That doesn't matter now! I want to know, who is this woman?

Anselmo looked at Julia and realized how nervous she was. Stammering, he replied: – It's Julia, a friend from work. He looked back at Julia and continued: – Julia, this is Suzana, my wife.

Furious, Suzana said in a loud voice: – Friend from work? You don't have to lie. I saw when you ran into each other and when

Just Beginning

you kissed her on the forehead and then when you walked together hand in hand!

– It's not what you're thinking, Suzana... but... what are you doing here?

Before answering, Julia, hearing what he said, got up and, without saying anything, tried to leave, but Suzana grabbed her by the arm and shouted: – Where do you think you are going, young lady?

The shout was so loud that the people who were also having lunch looked at them.

With a push, Julia managed to get rid of Suzana's hands and, embarrassed, she quickly left.

Anselmo, ashamed, grabbed Suzana's arm tightly and softly spoke: – Let's get out of here, Suzana, people are enjoying the scene you're making.

She, out of control, shouting, said: – Scene? Of course I'm making a scene! I found my husband making out with another woman, what did you want me to do? Besides, I don't care what people think!

I'ts good to know you're a scoundrel!

Anselmo got up and said: – Suzana, let's get out of here. We will talk at home and everything will be clear.

– No, let's not get out of here! We'll stay! I want everyone to know who you are!

He, nervous, continued: – If you want to you can stay, but I'm leaving! When you're calmer and ready to talk, I'll be home!

Before she could say anything, he left the restaurant.

She stood there, looked around, and realized that everyone was looking at her. Embarrassed, she left and went to the place

Just Beginning

where she had parked the car. She got in, started the engine, sped up, and left.

As she drove, she thought: What is happening to my life? Everything is falling apart!

First it was my job and now this! What an awful day! In the morning, I shouldn't have gotten out of bed.

The figures that were next to Anselmo, were now next to her and smiled, and at the same time, without knowing why, Suzana remembered her mother.

What would she say about what is happening in my life? She smiled and continued thinking: as if I didn't know.

Surely she would say: – Don't worry, my daughter. When things are not how we like them to be, for some reason, we just have to stop and try to figure out what is wrong, because if we don't do that, life will manage to show us.

I never took what she said very seriously and every time she said something like that I answered back:

– It may be like that for, but not for me. I know very well what I want out of life.

I have full control over it. I will achieve everything I ever dreamed of.

– I hope you can, Suzana. I hope you can...

Suzana remembered her mother's smile and also smiled: Was she right? I'm starting to think that she was. Until yesterday I had my life under control, my job, my husband.

It is not like that today. What am I going to do? Why did I go to that restaurant? How did I make such a scene? Why couldn't I control myself? I am an educated person, an executive!

Mom, what am I going to do with my life? After exposing Anselmo, I need to act, but what should I do?

Just Beginning

You said we have the chance to choose the path we want, but which path should I choose? I don't know, I don't know. H ow to make a choice, now that I have nothing else and no way to choose? A woman's figure extended her hands and said: – We always have a way, my daughter, we always have a choice.

Suzana didn't hear her, but she felt a breeze on her face. She kept thinking: After everything that happened, the only option is to abandon Anselmo! I cannot accept his betrayal!

One of the figures looked at the other, then at Suzana and nodded from side to side, saying:

– No, Suzana! That is not the best option!

Suzana continued driving.

Anselmo, ashamed, left the restaurant, went to the company garage, where his car was. He got in, started the engine and left.

As he drove, he thought: it's all over now. Suzana won't forgive me. Sometimes I felt that way, but deep down I didn't want to. Júlia is right, I love my son, but I can't deny that I love Suzana too. Now there is no turning back. She won't accept what she saw. If I knew before that she would not agree to leave her job to go with me, now I am sure. I didn't want it to be like this.

Since he was nervous, he drove slowly and thought: I don't understand how Suzana showed up like that. I never imagined this could happen, much less today, such an important day for her. The day that she would be promoted. Did she suspect my relationship with Julia?

No, that couldn't have happened. She didn't have time to think about something like that.

Always worried about work, she hardly looked at me. Did someone tell her? I don't know. One thing I'm sure of, our marriage is over.

Just Beginning

He stopped at a stoplight and, while it was red, he remembered Julia.

She was nervous and embarrassed. After all, at the time, at the restaurant, there were people from my company and from hers.

Surely the comments must be many. They can reach her boss' ears and she may even lose her job. This is not fair.

Stopped at the stoplight, he kept thinking: I don't feel like going home. I don't know what's going to happen or what I'm going to say to Suzana.

The traffic light turned green and he kept thinking: Instead of going home, I'm going to call Julia to see how she's doing. With the end of my marriage, I will be free. I will ask her to go with me to Recife. Will she accept?

He passed a square and saw a public telephone. He stopped the car and got out.

He looked around and saw a bakery, he thought: There, they probably must have a calling card. He went to the bakery. He bought the card and went to the phone.

He dialed Julia's office's number. A young woman replied:
– Hello!

– Please, I need to speak to Julia.

– She is not here.

– She is not?

– No, she didn't come back after lunch.

– All right, thanks.

He hung up the phone: she must have been so embarrassed she didn't have the courage to go back to work. Did she go home? I'll call her and find out.

Just Beginning

He was about to dial the numbers, but he thought: I think it's best not to call her but to speak to her in person. She must be nervous and she may not answer the phone.

He got back in the car and drove to Julia's house. He knew the way very well, because it was there where once or twice a week he spent happy times.

4.– Words of comfort

Júlia, ashamed and crying, left the restaurant. She walked to the corner, where she stopped a taxi.

As soon as the taxi stopped, she got in and kept crying. She cried nonstop and so desperately that the driver, a concerned man, asked: – Did something serious happened, young girl? Is anyone in your family sick?

She realized where she was and, wiping her eyes with her hands, not knowing what to say, lied:

– I'm fine, it's just a problem at work. I got fired

– He started laughing –. That's no reason to cry like that. There is a lot of work out there and you will soon find another job, and sometimes it may be better than the one you lost. There is no problem without a solution. There's always an exit.

Life sometimes plays a trick on us, I think it's to test us, but soon everything will be fixed.

She, crying again, said: – There is no solution for my life. I don't know how I'm going to keep on living. Everything is over.

– I am very sad.

– I'm noticing that you were very hurt, but it doesn't matter. Trust in God, he always shows us the way to go.

Just Beginning

– God has nothing to do with what happened to me. I'm a fool, I believed in those who didn't deserve it. I made a huge mistake!

– Girl, in my experience, you are not crying because of work.

She, trying to stop crying and not knowing why she trusted that man who could be her father, said:

– You're right. They didn't fire me, what happened to me was much worse. And It was my fault.

Although I knew it could happen, I believed that I was different from all other women, but I am not!

– You're blaming yourself, but you shouldn't, because there are no mistakes or successes. There are only lessons that we live day by day. This is part of our growth. When we go through difficult times, we feel and think that the world will end, but that's not true. Later, afterwards, we will see that what seemed to be so bad, the end of the world, was the best thing that could have happened to us, and we almost always laugh at having suffered so much for nothing.

She wiped her eyes again. She looked at that strange man who seemed to know what she was feeling. She asked: – Do you really believe what you're saying?

– I think so. I have lived a lot and I have been through a lot. Today, when I remember everything, I see that every time I thought everything was lost, something happened or someone came to help me, in that difficult moment.

– I understood that we are never alone, girl. We always have friends by our side that we don't even know they exist, who help us walk in this land of God. I believe that God always finds a way to send us a message, and for that, He uses people we don't even know.

Just Beginning

– So, like it is happening with you now? Do you think God is using you to help me? He began to laugh: – No, girl! Who am I to be used by God? I'm just a taxi driver.

– Everything I said was to calm you down!

The figures, when they heard that, smiled and illuminated them. He continued: – Those who always help us are our spiritual friends.

– Spiritual friends?

–Yes.

– I don't understand what you're saying... it's very complicated...

It's not complicated. Too bad we can't keep talking.

– We arrived at your address. Who knows, one day we will cross paths and we can continue our conversation.

– I would love to keep talking to you, but, as I said, we arrived.

She paid and got out of the car. After getting out, smiling, she said: – Thank you, sir. Our conversation helped me a lot. The man, also smiling, said: – God bless you, girl. I hope everything goes well in your life.

He sped up and drove away.

Julia watched the car disappear and thought: Who is this strange man? He seemed to know what was going on with me.

She entered the building where she lived and took the elevator. She went up to the fifth floor, took a keychain from her bag, picked a key, opened the door, and entered.

As soon as she entered, she found Sueli, a friend who shared the apartment with her.

Just Beginning

– Sueli, as soon as she saw Julia enter, scared, she asked: – Julia, what happened? at this time at home? Ju lia, trying to hide it, replied: – Nothing happened, Sueli.

– How come nothing happened? Your eyes are red. Have you been crying?

Without answering, Julia started crying again. Sueli, intrigued and concerned, asked: – What happened, Julia? Why are you not at work?

– I will never go back to work...

– Why? Were you fired?

Julia went to the bedroom and sat on the bed.

– All right, Sueli. I know you won't leave me alone until you know what happened. Sit here on the bed.

I'll tell you what happened. So, you will tell me if I am right to be desperate and if I can go back to work... – Sueli, scared by the expression on her friend's face, sat down and waited.

Julia recounted everything that had taken place and ended by saying: – He lied to me, Sueli! He never had any intention of leaving his wife! He's a scoundrel!

When she heard that, Sueli got up from the bed and, staring at her friend, said: – Wait a minute, Julia!

– I know how this romance began and Anselmo always said, from the beginning, that he would never abandon his son, because his father abandoned his mother with four young children.

– He always said that he had a very difficult childhood and that he didn't want the same to happen to his son!

You can't blame him for wanting to be with his son, for not wanting to disband the family!

– Are you against me, Sueli?

Just Beginning

– No, Julia. I am on the side of truth. He never lied to you. He was always very clear!

– He said that, but when we were together, in our times of love, he always said that I was a perfect woman. The one who understood him and made him happy! He said there was no other like me!

Although he didn't say it, he implied that one day he would stay with me. I had hope, but because of what happened today, I see that there is none. I was really stupid! I see today that I wasted a lot of time waiting for him to leave his wife, to stay with me forever.

– You fantasized, you imagined something that never existed, Julia. He never said he would do that. Regarding work, why did you say you'd never go back?

– After everything I told you, do you think I can go back to work?

– Why not? You like what you do and the salary is very good. You will hardly find another job like this.

– Sueli! Didn't you hear what I said?

– Of course I heard, but I still don't understand why you can't go back to work.

– Everything I told you happened at lunch, at the restaurant where almost all my co-workers were having lunch and who, up until now, didn't know. Everyone is laughing at me! How can I go back, Sueli?

– By returning as if nothing had happened. Do you think you are the only woman who has stupidly dated a married man? I assure you that you are not only one. Many have done so already and many others will.

– I can't face them...

Just Beginning

– Sure you can. Tomorrow, go to work and when you arrive, say hello to everyone, smile like nothing happened. I assure you that even if they are thinking about something, they won't dare talk to you.

– Even if they don't talk to me, they will surely be thinking.

– And what? You are just an employee; nobody has anything to do with your private life.

– Come to think about it: let him who is without sin cast the first stone. I assure you that everyone will hide their hands very well. You don't owe anything to anyone.

– I always thought so too, but now I see that it was not true.

– The opinion of others does matter, I am ashamed.

– You have nothing to be ashamed of, as I said; you are not the first nor will you be the last to get involved with a married man.

– I always knew it, but with him it was different. It seemed like he really liked me.

– Now that it's over, I don't know how I'm going to keep on living without him! I don't know, Sueli! He is the reason why I live.

– During these two years that we were together, I lived only for him. My life without him is meaningless... I'd rather die... – desperate, she started crying again.

Seeing her cry, Sueli started laughing. Julia, outraged, asked: – Why are you laughing, Sueli?

Are you happy with my despair?

– No, Julia! I'm not happy with your despair, I just see myself in you.

– I didn't understand, see yourself in me?

– That's right. We have lived together for a long time. We have talked about many things, but never about my past.

Just Beginning

— That's right. We never talk about the past, do you have any past history? — Sueli laughed again: — Of course, Julia and who doesn't?

Julia stopped crying: — Do you want to talk about that?

— Do I want to? I don't want to, but I feel like this is the moment.

— I'm anxious.

— Well, I'll tell you what happened to me, but first, let's have some tea. You are very nervous —. Julia smiled: — I think you're right. I really need some tea.

Sueli, smiling, said: — Let's go to the kitchen and, while I make tea and something to drink, I will tell you my life.

5.– An incredible story

In the kitchen, Sueli put water in a pot, brought it to the fire and sat down, then she began to speak:

– Today you see me happy with Eduardo, but it wasn't always like that. I lived in Rio de Janeiro with my parents and my two brothers.

I was the princess of the house. They all took care of me and did what I said. I was happy. My parents are wonderful, but they have always cared about people's moral and decency. At eighteen I finished high school, I really wanted to go to college.

I didn't really know what I wanted to be, but whatever it was, I needed to be prepared to face an entrance exam.

For that, I needed to keep studying. Although I was not poor, my parents had no way to pay for college. I needed to try a federal university. At the same time I wanted to continue my studies, I felt a strong desire to have my own money, I decided that I would work and study as well. At first, my father did not accept the idea and said:

"You don't need to work outside, Sueli. You have everything you need to continue studying.
Your mother never worked and when you get married, you won't work either. You will have to take care of your family. "

Just Beginning

– That was everything I didn't want, Julia. Without thinking, I said:

"I need to work outside. I don't want to spend the rest of my life at home, taking care of the family.

Why don't you want that?

It's a worthless job, Mom.

Do you think that taking care of the family, raising and educating children is a useless job?

No, mother, of course raising a child is wonderful, but I think a woman needs something more.

I want to work outside, have my own money. I don't want to stay at home working hard without getting paid. "

I knew my mother was hurt, Julia, but I thought:

"No, I don't want to be like you!

I want to have my own life, be my owner! I don't want to live for the good of others. "

I thought that, but didn't say it. I didn't want to hurt my mother, Julia. I hardly managed to convince them.

My father and my brothers accepted, but my mother imposed a condition:

– "You can work outside, but only if you continue studying.

How can I work and study at the same time, Mom?

I don't know how you are going to do it, but that is my condition. You said you don't want to take care of home and family, well, for that to happen, you will have to have a profession to be able to choose whether you want to stay at home or not.

I want you to know that I do not regret having stayed at home taking care of you. For this same reason, I want you to study and have the option to choose the life you want. "

Just Beginning

When I heard that, I was ashamed, Julia, because I realized that my mother knew how I felt about her.

I felt that she was hurt and devalued and that was what I least wanted. I just smiled, kissed her and went to my room.

– You can't deny that your mother was wise. You are today a respected chef. Don't forget that this is a man's profession!

– That is true, but that will change as time goes by. I believe that soon women will perform the same functions as men.

– I'm taking the first steps. However, we are not talking about my mother, we are talking about my past, my history.

– You're right, go on.

– After a lot of searching, I got a job in a restaurant as an assistant.

My mother agreed, because I would work at night and would have all day to study. I started as an assistant, but in a short time, with a lot of dedication I had the chance and became a waitress. I loved waitering people, so the tips were high.

Over time, I fell in love with all of that and convinced myself that I wanted to work in a restaurant my whole life. I would come to work early to help the chef and learn how to prepare and present dishes.

I discovered that there was a school that trained people to work in hotels and restaurants.

I decided to study at that school. Searching, I discovered that the available spots were limited, so I studied in the afternoon and worked at night. I had the mornings to rest. I studied and worked hard. In less than a year, I was ready to try going to school. I was in another city, far from where I lived, so I needed to have money not only to pay for school and buy the necessary materials, but also to support myself. I knew my family would help me, but

Just Beginning

they couldn't pay all the expenses. So, knowing the difficulties I would have, I wrote a letter to the school in which I talked about my situation and the immense desire I had to study. In the end, I applied for a scholarship.

I knew it would be difficult, but it was worth a try.

I sent the letter and waited for an answer.

Did you get the scholarship, Sueli?

I was waiting for the answer, Julia, but life is not always as we imagine it.

– What happened?

– One night, when entering the room, where meals were served, I noticed that several men entered and sat at one of the tables that were in my area. I was happy because, due to the number of men, I knew the tip would be high.

I served the table in the best possible way. They ate, drank, and talked.

When they finished eating, I presented the bill and as I had predicted the tip was high, which made me very happy.

Everyone got up and I was waiting for them to leave. They all left, however, one of the men stayed behind, gave me a card and said: – You are very beautiful, I wish I could see you again somewhere else so we can talk.

This card has my name and my phone number. When you have time, call so we can meet.

I took the card and as soon as he was gone, I smiled and threw it away.

Why did you do that?

I can't deny that I was impressed. Tall, dark, in his thirties and with a beautiful smile, but I was used to it. Many customers gave me cards or just wrote their phone numbers, but I never called

Just Beginning

and they never came back to the restaurant. After a few days, when I had already forgotten about him, one night, to my surprise, he returned alone and sat down again at one of the tables in my area. I was surprised to see him back and as it was my duty, I walked over and, smiling, I handed him the menu.

He took it, looked, and in a few minutes made his order. I served the food and walked away to assist the other tables.

When he finished eating, he motioned for me to go to his table.

As soon as I approached him, smiling he said: – The food was very good. Can I have the bill, please?

Also smiling, I walked away and came back a few minutes later, bringing the bill to him in an appropriate book.

He looked and put the money: – You can keep the change.

Thank you, sir.

I was walking away when he said: – Wait a minute.

I looked at him puzzled. He asked: – What's your name?

Sueli, I replied embarrassed.

Do you have a boyfriend? Are you married?

No!

This is very good, because from tonight on you will be my girlfriend and then my wife.

When I heard that, thinking it was a joke, I started laughing. He continued: – Why are you laughing, do you think I'm kidding?

You must be kidding.

I have never been so serious in my life.

I kept finding it amusing and went to wait another table, Julia.

After serving the table, I looked back at the one he was at.

Just Beginning

He was gone. It was just after midnight when a friend and I, also a waitress, left.

To my surprise, he was there, in a car, waiting for me. As soon as he saw me, he got out of the car, approached me and, smiling, said: – How is my future wife?

I couldn't help laughing, Julia. He, who seemed angry, asked: – Why are you laughing? Don't you believe what I'm talking about?

From his tone of voice, I thought he was being honest and I replied: – I don't know if what you're saying is true, but we can't talk today. It's late and I have to go home. Maybe another day, another time.

Get in the car, I can take you home.

I felt uneasy, not knowing what to do. He insisted: – Get in the car, don't be afraid.

My intentions with you are the best possible. I really want you to be my wife!

I looked at my co–worker, Débora. She was also looking at me with eyes wide open.

In a trembling voice, I replied: – No, thank you. My colleague and I share the taxi every night. We live close.

All good. I can take you both. Come in!

No thanks. Look, a taxi is coming.

A taxi came up. I made a sign with my hand and he stopped.

When we were getting in, he, holding my arm, said: – Okay. I understand that today it is late, that you don't know me and that you should go home. I want you to know that I am being honest. We need to talk, get to know each other better. So tomorrow, at two in the afternoon, I'll be waiting for you at that square.

Just Beginning

Not knowing what to do or say, Júlia, I got into the taxi and Débora followed suit.

As soon as we got in, Debora, laughing, asked: – What was that, Sueli? This man seems to be in love!

I was nervous and shaking, Julia. My heart was beating hard.

Nervous, I said: – In love? He looks crazy, Deborah!

No, Sueli! He is really interested in you and besides, you can't deny that he is very handsome.

Are you going to see him tomorrow afternoon?

Are you crazy, Sueli? Of course not! I don't know him!

That's why you should go.

No! I'm scared!

Scared of what? What do you think he can do to you at a square in the middle of the day? Go find him and find out if what he's saying is serious. You have nothing to lose. He, apart from being handsome, because of his car, seems to be rich.

I wouldn't think for a second.

I do not know. I'm confused.

Don't think too much! Go see him just to see how far it all goes.

If you want, I'll be watching you from afar, and if he does something different, I'll go rescue you.

You can't miss this chance to find someone, Sueli. You only think about working and studying.

You are young, you need to think about other things too.

I looked at her and smiled. She lived on a street before mine.

As soon as the taxi stopped in front of her house, before getting out, she smiled and said: – See you tomorrow, Sueli.

Just Beginning

Do not miss this opportunity.

See you tomorrow, Débora. I'm going to think.

As soon as the taxi stopped in front of my house, the door opened, Julia. It was my mother who never used to sleep before I got home.

I got out of the taxi and went into the house.

Good night, Sueli. Is everything alright?

Good night mom. Everything is fine, as always.

Thank goodness. Drink your tea and go to bed. I can't be happy with you working so late.

You need to get another job.

We went to the kitchen. Every night she made tea and toast for me to eat before going to bed.

I had tea, ate toast, and went to bed. As soon as I went to bed I started thinking about that strange man:

"Débora is right, he is really attractive. Could it be that he is not just playing? I don't know, he seemed honest. I don't know if I'm going to meet him... if I go and he's not there. On the other hand, it is worth it to see what happens.

I do not know what to do."

Julia, who listened attentively, drank some more tea and, anxiously, asked: – What did you do, Sueli, to meet him?

Sueli laughed.

– You're very curious, aren't you, Julia?

– Of course I am! I've never heard such a story!

– I'll continue, Julia:

– The next day, as soon as I woke up, I thought about him again. His face, his smile, but mainly his eyes that were beautiful. I

Just Beginning

spent the whole morning wondering what to do. After lunch, I changed my clothes and left.

My mother was not surprised, because I used to leave for school every day. Since I lived near the square and near the restaurant where I worked and since it was during the day, I was walking.

At every moment, I wondered if I would go to school or to the square. Finally, I decided: I will go to the square and, if he is not there, there is still time for me to go to school.

I kept walking and as soon as I got to the square, I saw that he was sitting on one of the benches.

I started shaking and tried to escape, but it was too late. He also saw me and, getting up, walked towards me.

I was terrified, not knowing what he was going to say when he arrived. He got closer: – I'm glad you came, Sueli!

I was afraid you wouldn't come!

I, shaking, silent, took the hand that he extended to me.

Sit here, we have a lot to talk about. I don't know anything about you, just that you're beautiful and that you work at that restaurant. What else do you do?

I sat down and, without knowing why, I felt good and began to speak. I told him about the school and my plans for the future.

That I would like to work in restaurants and that I wanted, one day, to be a renowned chef.

He smiled and said: – I'm glad to know that you like to cook, because I like to eat.

Even if you are not a renowned chef, you will cook for me and our children.

Aren't you going too fast?

Just Beginning

Not! As soon as I saw you, I knew you were the woman of my life. With whom I want to spend the rest of my days.

I started laughing, Julia. We went to a cafeteria and, while we had a snack and a soda, he told me that he owned a shoe factory and had forty employees.

That his grandfather had started that factory, transferred it to his children and then to his grandchildren. That they had been in the market for a long time, so they had a good clientele. We talked a lot. When we left the cafeteria, I saw Débora sitting on one of the benches in the square and she smiled at me. I also smiled and we kept walking. We spent the whole afternoon talking.

When it was time to go to the restaurant, he said: – Since you work at night, the best thing we can do is meet in the afternoon.

I can't, I need to go to school.

You can be absent once or twice a week.

I don't know... I need to study...

He kissed my forehead and said: – What you need is to be my wife!

I started laughing again: – You have to be kidding.

I'm not kidding and I'll show you!

Since that day, Julia, we started meeting two or three times a week.

Every time he came to see me, he would bring a bouquet of yellow roses, and when we weren't seeing each other, he would send them to the restaurant.

We walked, we went to the movies, to the cafeteria or we just sat on a bench in the square, simply talking or going, with the car to a deserted street, exchanging kisses and trading caresses, nothing more.

Just Beginning

Little by little I fell in love with him and before long I just wanted to be with him all the time.

We used to go out on weekdays. On the weekends, he always had an excuse for not coming to see me, because he needed to work, travel to visit clients, or go to a family lunch that he couldn't miss. I was so in love that I didn't care. I never suspected what he was talking about.

– You really didn't suspect, Sueli?

– No, Julia. Haven't you heard that when we are in love we don't see beyond our noses?

Today I can assure you that this is true. For me, everything he did and said was correct and true.

– So what happened?

– It had been almost six months since we met, when one afternoon, at the square, he took out a keychain with several keys from his pocket and gave it to me.

– What keys are these, Nilson? I asked intrigued.

– They are yours.

– Mine? I'm not understanding.

– I bought a house where we can live after we get married. I want you to go there to see and choose the furniture you want to buy.

– Choose?

– Yes, what's the surprise, didn't I always say that we were getting married?

– You did, but I didn't think it would be that fast. I didn't even tell my family that I'm dating you.

– I think it is better, for now, not to tell them. When the house is ready, I will talk to them and I can take your parents to see

Just Beginning

the house, so they have no way of not consenting to our courtship and then our marriage.

– Did he, Sueli?

– He did. So I told you that Anselmo never lied to you. You always knew he was married. Julia's eyes watered again and a tear took shape.

Seeing that, Sueli nervously said: – If you're going to cry again, I'll stop telling what happened to me! Julia quickly wiped away the tear that had taken shape: – I will not cry. What did you do, Sueli?

– What do you think I did? It was the happiest day of my life. All I wanted was to see the house that would be mine!

I opened my arms and hugged him with all my strength. After the hug, he, smiling, asked: – Are we going to the house?

– Of course!

– We got in the car and left. The house was in a neighborhood close to where I lived.

– We entered a street where there were beautiful houses and they all had a garden. I was more and more delighted.

– He stopped the car in front of a house painted very light green with the windows painted white.

– On the left side, there was a wide hallway and at the end, you could see a garage that had a large wooden door.

– I looked at the house and asked: – Is this it?

– Yes, do you like it?

– It's beautiful!

– You haven't seen it inside! Do we go in?

– Let's go! – I answered, amazed.

Just Beginning

– We entered through the living room door and I was even more impressed, Julia, because the living room was huge, much bigger than the one my family lived in. The house had only two rooms, but they were large. He took me by the hand and led me to see the room that would be ours. Excited and curious, I followed him. He opened a door and I could see a room, it was huge!

– I felt that my eyes were shining with happiness. We went to see the kitchen, the bathroom and the yard. We went into the house again.

– He hugged me, asked: – What do you think, did you like it?

– I was so moved that I couldn't answer. Tears were flowing down my face.

– He hugged me and kissed me lovingly: – You don't need to cry. This house is ours and we will be very happy here.

– We left the room and he opened another door. There was another room.

– A little smaller than the previous one, but still big.

With his arms on my shoulder, he laughed and said: – You will choose the furniture for the whole house, except for this one.

– Why?

– Because this will be our son's room. Since we do not know if it will be a boy or a girl, we must wait for the child to be born.

Julia couldn't help it: – Wow, Sueli, how beautiful!

– Seriously, Julia! I couldn't believe it happened.

– It drove me crazy with happiness, but let me continue, because if it takes a little longer, I won't be able to finish. These memories make me feel really bad.

– You're right, Sueli. You must have suffered a lot, but how did you find out he was married?

Just Beginning

– We went back to the living room. Although the entire house was empty, there was a worn sofa in the living room.

– He looked at the sofa, then at me and said: – The former owner left this sofa, but said he will come and get it soon.

– It doesn't matter, Nilson. I'm very happy to keep it here.

– He smiled, hugged me again and made me take a seat.

– He started kissing me and hugging me with the same affection I was used to. The caresses became stronger and, in a few minutes, I surrendered myself to him with great happiness. Even though it was my first time, it felt great, because I loved him and was sure that we would get married.

Julia, holding the cup, drank the tea immediately. She couldn't help it and said: – He was an actor, Sueli!

Yes, he was, Julia, and luckily for him, he got what he wanted.

– What happened next, Sueli? Did he disappear?

No, Julia. After that day, we started meeting at the house and went shopping for furniture.

– I chose everything I wanted and before long, the house was beautiful, with furniture and even curtains.

– We bought bedding, table linen and towels. I was the happiest woman in the world. I had a beautiful house that would be mine and a man that I loved and who loved me too.

Júlia sighed deeply: – You lived incredible and happy moments, right, Sueli?

– Yes, I did, but in the end it was not worth it, because the moments of sadness were also incredible and I don't wish on anyone, not even on my worst enemy, what I went through.

– What happened after that?

Just Beginning

– One afternoon, I was at the house when he arrived. As always, we hugged, kissed, and ended up in the bedroom and surrendered ourselves to love. When we finished, I asked: – When are we getting married, Nilson?

I didn't notice it that day, Julia, but when I remembered everything, I also remembered that he turned pale and that it took him a while to answer: – At this time it is not possible...

Why not?

I love you, but I have some problems to solve. Another day, we will talk again.

As always, I believed what he said and didn't mention it anymore. A little more time passed.

We continued meeting two or three times a week. I was waiting for him to say that he wanted to meet my family so we could organize the wedding, but that didn't happen.

Every time I brought it up, he changed the conversation. It started to bother me.

Then, some time later, I insisted: – We can't go on like this, Nilson. The house is ready, we can already schedule the wedding. I can't stand it anymore without telling my family how happy I am. I'm going to make a meeting for next Sunday, go there and talk to everyone. I am sure that despite the shock and surprise, they will be happy to know that we already have a home.

He was looking at me silently, Julia. After a while, I saw that his eyes were red, full of water and a tear was flowing down his face. Scared, I asked: – What's going on, Nilson? Why are you crying?

He hugged me and let the sobs out of his throat.

I asked him again: – What is it, Nilson?

Just Beginning

He didn't answer and kept crying. I pulled away from his arms, held his hands and, looking directly into his eyes, I asked: – Are you going to tell me the reason for this crying?

He sat on the sofa, lowered his head onto his lap and, without looking at me, said: – I know you will never forgive me, Sueli, but everything I did was because I love you so much and I did not want to lose you...

Lose me, why? Raise your head, Nilson! Look at me!

I didn't mean to lie to you, but as soon as I saw you, I felt like you were the woman of my life, the one I had been looking for for so long. I didn't want to lose you!

Stop repeating this, Nilson, and tell me what is happening!

In a trembling voice between sobs, he said: – I can't go to your house to talk to your parents, because I can't marry you.

Why can't you do it?

I'm already married...

Hearing that, I let go of his hand, walked away and yelled: – Married? How could you do this to me?

How could you lie to me like this?

I was afraid to tell you and that you would abandon me! If that happened, I don't know what my life would be like!

Your life? What will happen to mine, Nilson? What did you do to me?

I'm sorry, Sueli, but I can't lose you, please forgive me.

Forgive you? How can I forgive you after being lie to in this way?

You are right to be so upset and I deserve everything that you can speak and think about me, but please hear the reason why I hid my status from you.

Just Beginning

Your status? There is no status! You're married, period!

I'm not married, I'm married, but I won't be for long.

I was nervous and started to leave the house, Julia. He grabbed me by the arm: – Don't go, Sueli!

Let me tell you why I was silent. You need to know the whole truth...

He hugged me tight and made me sit, Julia.

– He continued speaking: – I've been married for five years. I have a four-year-old boy. Everything was going well, until a year ago.

My wife had a lot of pain in her stomach, we went to the doctor and it was discovered that she had cancer in an advanced stage. The doctor called me and said that she would have a maximum of one year to live. He asked me if I wanted him to tell her.

I said no, because she would suffer a lot with this news. I decided to stay by her side, providing all possible comforts.

That is what I did and what I am doing. I can't abandon her.

Meanwhile, I met you. I soon realized that you could be my wife and mother to my son.

He is beautiful and once you meet him, you will fall in love with him. She is very sick. The doctor said that there was nothing else to do for her, death can happen at any time. It can be in a day, a week, but it won't be longer than six months.

I can't abandon her, Sueli. I love you and want you to be my wife, but I also love and respect the mother of my son, the woman with whom I had a wonderful time. Be patient, wait a little longer.

Soon we will be able to get married and start a life of happiness and without lies...

Just Beginning

Julia was speechless: – After everything he said, did you have the courage to leave him, Sueli?

No, Julia. He seemed so honest that I had no way to escape. I was so in love that I couldn't imagine my life without him.

Sueli realized that Julia was going to start crying again, she spoke quickly: – He opened his arms and I, crying, curled up.

– After hugging and kissing me several times, he said: – You will not regret having forgiven me, Sueli.

I will make you the happiest woman in the world!

– What did go wrong, Sueli? Why are you not together?

– Because I learned that when we are on the wrong path, life takes care of bringing us back.

– I'm not understanding...

– From that day on, everything was as it was before. Some days during the week, we met at that house.

He asked me to stop going to school because, due to his wife's illness, he didn't know when he could come to see me.

I, infatuated and stupid, accepted everything he said. I stopped attending school and stayed home every afternoon, expecting him to show up at any moment.

That took months. Every time we met, he would tell me about that woman, about how much she was suffering and how much he suffered to see her that way, that she did not deserve so much suffering.

– Poor man...

– I thought so too, and often asked God to take her soon, not only to stop her suffering, but to be able to marry him and fulfill my happiness.

– Did you think that, Sueli? How awful! – Sueli laughed.

Just Beginning

– You're right, it was awful and I'm really sorry, I just don't understand. Why are you making that accusatory face, Julia?

– Wishing someone's death is horrible, Sueli –. Sueli kept laughing.

– What are you laughing at?

– The falsehood of everyone.

– I don't understand what you say.

– It's very simple, Julia. Can you swear that you never wanted Anselmo's wife to die so that you could stay with him forever?

Julia looked at Sueli as if she didn't understand: – What are you talking about, Sueli?

– I will repeat the question: did you never wish the death of Anselmo's wife so that you could stay with him forever?

Be honest not with me, but with yourself. Don't be concerned about wishing it, as all lovers do. The only hope of being with the man they love is for his wife to die and I can assure that everyone, without exception, has already thought about it, even if it's only once and just for a minute.

– You're being very harsh, Sueli!

– Am I, Julia? Am I not being honest? Can you really swear you never had that thought? – Julia was silent, just thinking.

Sueli laughed again: – Do you see that you cannot answer immediately, Julia? Because you had that thought, even if it was just once.

– I don't know what to say...

– Don't worry about it. You were not the first and you will not be the last.

– That's right, Sueli, but I still don't understand why you haven't been with him until today...

Just Beginning

– As I said, life takes care of showing us what we need to see and getting us back on track.

– I became more dependent on him every day and lived according to everything he said and asked for.

On the weekends, I knew he would not come to see me. At Christmas, New Years and all the long vacations the same thing happened, I spent my time just thinking about him, how he might be suffering being away from me.

One Saturday, before leaving the restaurant, Débora, my friend, invited me to have lunch at her house, since it was her mother's birthday and it would be a special lunch. As I had nothing to do and knew that Nilson would not come, I agreed.

She gave me the address and, very early on Sunday, I left the house and went to see Débora.

She was married and lived close to my home, with her family in a nearby neighborhood.

Her husband worked as a driver in a bus company, so that day he would be working and could not go to lunch. I met her and together we took a bus. As the bus moved, we talked.

I talked more, telling her about Nilson's wife's illness. The bus stopped at a square. We got off.

The day was sunny, many parents went for a walk and played with their children. As soon as I got off the bus, I saw about forty meters away, Nilson with a ball in his hands, it looked like he was going to throw it at someone. I looked closely and saw that in front of him was a little boy who was smiling, waiting for the ball. Nilson threw the ball and the boy ran to catch it.

I smiled and was happy to see him play with his son. This was an opportunity to meet the boy.

Just Beginning

I walked towards him. As I approached, and before Nilson saw me, the boy ran to the other side.

I followed him with my eyes and, terrified, I stopped. He went to meet a woman who, with open arms, waited for him to approach.

Nilson went towards her, too. As soon as he arrived, he gave her a kiss on the cheek and the three of them walked towards me.

I was petrified, paralyzed, not only because he was with his wife and child, but, much more, because she was pregnant.

As soon as he saw me, I noticed that he turned pale, but he pretended not to see me. He passed by without looking at me and went to a restaurant that was over there. I didn't know what to do.

I stayed there, I stopped, until Débora approached: – What was that, Débora? What was Nilson doing with that woman? Didn't he say she was sick?

Let's go, Sueli. It's time for lunch. My parents are waiting.

I'm sorry, Débora, but I am not in a condition to have lunch or be with other people.

I need to be alone and think about everything that happened.

You can't be alone, Sueli. Come home, my family is very excited and you will be distracted.

I can't, Débora. I need to be alone. Take this gift to your mother, give her my apologies, and tell her that one of these days I will have lunch with her.

Okay, if that's how you want to do it, but be careful what you do. Don't do anything crazy.

Don't worry, I'll just think about what I'm going to do, in the future, with my life. Go have lunch and have fun.

Just Beginning

Worried, she left and I stood there, looking at the restaurant.

– How could he do this to you, Sueli? – Julia, agape, asked.

– He did it because I allowed him to. I believed everything he said without caring if it was true or not and I surrendered myself.

– What did you do? Did you go to the restaurant?

– My wish was to go there and expose him, Julia, but I thought of the woman and the child who had nothing to do with that or his bad behavior. I looked around and saw a bench where I could sit and look at the door of the restaurant where Nilson had got in. I knew that when he left he wouldn't be able to see me. I waited, for a long time, until they finally left. As soon as he showed up at the entrance, I noticed that he was looking everywhere, probably looking for me.

When he thought I wasn't nearby, he put one arm around the woman's shoulders and with the other hand he held the boy and they walked towards the car, which only then I saw was parked in front of where I was. They got into the car and I stood there not knowing what to do with my life.

All I wanted was to die.

– Wow! I imagine what you felt, Sueli! I can imagine because it's the same I feel for Anselmo...

– No, Julia, you can't imagine it, because Anselmo never lied to you like Nilson did.

– You always knew he was married, You had the option to accept it or not. You decided to accept. I didn't have that option.

Julia was silent. Sueli continued: – I sat on that bench for a long time. Desperate and unhappy, I couldn't believe or accept that he had done this to me. I started to rave: No, he didn't do that.

That woman is not his wife. It must be his sister or friend.

Just Beginning

So, with that thought, I went to our house hoping that he would come so we could talk. I cried the whole time.

I would've done anything not to lose him, Julia. I was there for what remained of that day, until it was time to go to work.

I didn't feel like going, but since it was Sunday I knew there would be a lot of clients for dinner.

Despite everything, I was and am a good professional. I went to the restaurant and, as I had expected, there were a lot of clients.

Deborah realized that I was not well, but she was silent, she only helped me. That was good for me, because with so much work, I didn't have time to think. A few minutes that I was waiting for a table to be cleared out, I thought:

"This is all a big mistake, a misunderstanding. When I leave, I know that he will be there waiting for me like he did at the beginning. "

When I left, I looked at the place where he used to wait for me, but he was not there. Crying, I took the taxi with Débora and went home. Before entering the house, I wiped my eyes so that my mother would not realize that I had cried, but it was in vain. She noticed it and worried, asked: – Were you crying, Sueli?

Yes, but don't worry. I'm fine, it's just a problem at work. You know how much I fight with the chef for taking so long to prepare my orders.

I don't understand why you keep working with this man. You don't have to work, your father and brothers earn enough for you to stay home.

I like my job.

I did not want to continue that conversation, so I said: – I'm not going to have tea, I'm very tired.

Just Beginning

I'm going to shower and go to bed. Go to bed too, mom. How many times have I told you not to wait for me?

It isn't necessary. I take a taxi here, there is no danger.

She was not surprised, because sometimes when I was very tired, I would not drink tea. I went to the bathroom and while I was taking a bath, I let my tears mix with the water and run down my face.

After the shower I went to bed and cried until I fell asleep.

– Did you sleep, Sueli?

– Yes Julia. Although I don't understand how, I fell asleep. I woke up, looked at the cracks in the window and saw that it was dawn.

I continued lying down, thinking about everything that had happened. When I remembered, I started crying again.

Excited as I was, I couldn't believe or see the truth before me, I thought: That woman can't be his wife!

She is sick and cannot be pregnant! He said he has a sister; it must be her. I will call him. I know he must have an explanation.

I got up and told my mother that I was going to study at a friend's house. I left, went to the corner and from a public phone I called his company. A girl answered and after a few seconds said that he was not there.

I believed what he said, I took a bus and went to our house, waiting for him to show up.

While waiting, I cleaned everything, changed, and washed sheets and towels. I wanted, when he arrived, to find everything in order. However, I waited in vain. He didn't come. I stayed there until it was time to go to work.

Every day I called and he never answered me because he was in a meeting.

Just Beginning

Still, I refused to believe that it was all over. The weekend arrived.

I knew I couldn't see him, but I still went to the house and waited.

– Even after a week had passed, were you still waiting?

– I kept on going. I couldn't imagine my life without him, Julia. On Monday I didn't go out in the morning so that my mother didn't suspect. In the afternoon, when I was supposed to go to school, I went home, still expecting him to come at any time.

When I got to the front of the house, I stopped. There was a big sale sign. The door was open. I opened it and went through.

I tried to open the living room door with the keys, but it didn't open. I looked out the window and saw that it was empty.

I went to the back and tried to open the kitchen door, but it didn't open either. I looked into the garage and saw many cardboard boxes. I went there and, incredulous, saw my name written in large letters. I opened one and to my desperation, inside were the sheets that I had bought so expensively. I opened the others and therein were the towels, toothbrush, combs and all my personal things. Only then did I understand and accepted what had happened, that everything was over.

That he had really lied to me all that time...

Sueli finished speaking, crying. Julia was moved: – I'm sorry, Sueli. It really couldn't have been easy.

Sueli wiped her eyes with her hands and continued: – I sat on the garage floor and cried like I had never cried in my life. More than when I saw Nilson with his wife.

After a lot of crying, an uncontrollable anger invaded me: He will pay for everything he did to me!

Just Beginning

I didn't know where he lived or where his company was, I just had the phone number, but I'd find both addresses and I'd expose him.

I'd tell his wife everything he did to me! My life is destroyed, but I will destroy his too!

I knew there was no way to find out his address because it was Sunday. I just sat there until it was time to go to the restaurant.

That day, I thanked God for having a job. At the restaurant, I focused on work and served clients in the best way possible. When I left, I didn't look at the place where he always waited for me. I knew he wouldn't be there.

Very angry and without crying anymore, I went home.

I went in, had tea with my mother, and went to my room. I have never regretted so much not having a phone at home.

It didn't mean that I would call from there, but I could check the phone book. I didn't sleep that night, Julia.

I had so much anger that as much as I wanted the night to pass quickly, it didn't.

I was all the time thinking about how to take revenge. In the morning, I had a plan and was going to set it in motion.

I lied to my mother again, telling her that I needed to study at my friend's house. She had no suspicions and I left, knowing what I was going to do.

– What did you do, Sueli?

– As I couldn't sleep, I got up, took a notebook and wrote a long letter addressed to Nilson's wife.

– I told her everything he had done to me and her. To verify that what I said was true, I wrote the address of the house that would be ours. I took an envelope, put it in my bag, left the house and went to the restaurant.

Just Beginning

When I got there the door was still closed. I knew it would be. I entered through the back door and whoever passed by outside would not have imagined the movement inside. Some people were cleaning and fixing the tables.

Others, in the kitchen, were preparing the meal that would be served at lunch. Since I always worked nights, I didn't know any employee other than the manager, because he only left when my manager of the night shift arrived.

As soon as I saw him, I walked over to him. After shaking his hand, I asked him to lend me the phone book.

He didn't know why and for what purpose I wanted a list, but he didn't ask. He went to the counter where the phone was and from below, he took the list and handed it to me.

With the list in my hands, I sat down at one of the tables and started looking up the alphabet. I looked for the letter "N" and found it.

I ran my fingers through the pages, until I came to what would probably be his name and phone number of his house.

Soon his name appeared. With a pen, I wrote it on paper. I thanked the manager and left.

On the street, I knew where there was a payphone. I walked over to it, took some coins out of my bag, and dialed the number I'd written down.

On the other side, a woman's voice answered. From the sound, I could tell it was someone young.

I asked her: – Are you from Mr. Nilson's house?

Yes ma'am.

I realized that she was a housekeeper. I wasn't sure, but I took a risk.

Is his wife at home?

Just Beginning

No ma'am. She is expecting a baby and went to the doctor to make an appointment, but she is not sick, no.

She just went to see if everything is okay with the baby.

Perfect! "I thought happily." That's exactly what I wanted to talk to her about. I am a manager of a baby clothing store and I wanted to send her some pieces to evaluate our work.

Will you give them away?

That's right, – I answered, laughing inside and continued: – But for that I need her full name and address, can you give it to me?

Yes, I can! She will be happy!

I guess she will. You can be sure.

She spelled the name and gave me the address and I wrote it on the same paper where I had written the phone number.

I thanked her and hung up.

Happily, I thought. Okay, now I have the address, just cross the street, go to the post office, fill in the address and send it.

Nervous, I thought. When she receives it and reads it, she will find out who she is married to.

The way I wrote it, I doubt she can tell it's a lie! He will see that in the same way that I liked him, now I hate him and I want him to be destroyed, to suffer!

Julia got up and went to the stove to get more tea.

Cup in hand, she sat down again. She asked: – Didn't you care that she was pregnant, that she could lose the baby, Sueli?

– Yes, but I also thought: I know she may lose the baby, but after everything he did to me, whatever his wife might feel, it is his fault, therefore his problem, not mine!

I crossed the street and went into the post office. I waited in line to be served.

Just Beginning

When it was almost my turn, I thought: it will take a long time for it to arrive in the mail and I won't know if she received it.

If Nilson finds out? If he finds the letter, he will destroy it. No, I will not send it this way, I will do it in person.

I know his wife is not at home. I go there and give it to the maid. Only then I'll be sure that everything went well. I can't risk leaving it safe!

– Did you think about it, Sueli? Did you think about going in person? Wasn't it too risky? His wife could be home by that time.

– If she saw you, what would she do?

– I didn't even think about the possibility of finding her, but if that happened, it would be good, because I would give her the letter and leave. That way, she would know that I really existed.

– You were very brave, Sueli...

– It wasn't just anger, Julia, it was anger, hatred. Before continuing, I need to have some tea, I talked non–stop and my throat is dry.

Sueli put tea in the cup, sweetened it, and took a sip. Then she continued speaking: – I went to the sidewalk, I waited a while and a taxi appeared. I waved my hand and it stopped. I got in and showed the driver the address. He set the car in motion.

Some time later, we came to the street where the house was. I shuddered and said: –Please stop. I'm going this way.

He said the price, I paid and got out. I looked at the number that was written on the paper, then the house number.

I needed to walk a few meters. I started walking, looking at the numbers. I was almost there when a taxi passed me and stopped in front of the house. The driver got out and opened the door. A woman got out.

Just Beginning

The driver handed her some bags and packages. As soon as I saw her, I recognized her. It was Nilson's wife.

She smiled, paid the driver, and entered the house. All this time, I stood up, nervous, unable to walk and thinking: I can't do what I'm trying to do. From the size of her belly, it seems that the child is about to be born.

She seemed very happy. I can't involve an innocent woman in what happened to me.

It was Nilson's fault, not hers. Like me, she is his victim.

I don't want to be responsible for her life or the child's life. I can't. Nilson got me involved, fool me, and I'm sure he'll be exposed one day, but not now, not even for me. I can't risk two lives.

Looking down and taking slow steps, I turned and started walking.

I can't explain what was happening to me, Julia, but it was fine. I felt a great weight lift off me. I walked to the corner and waited for another taxi to pass. I made a signal, a taxi stopped.

I got in and went home.

6.- The rebeginning

Sueli took a sip of tea. Julia did the same.

The entity that accompanied Júlia smiled and looked at another entity that had arrived just before Sueli stopped talking: – How is she, Alzira?

– Good now, Ciro. She arrived feeling devastated, but while listening to Sueli's story, she forgot about her problems for a while.

– That was very good, you encouraged Sueli to tell her story.

– Julia, from now on, will have a lot to think about.

– Ciro looked at Julia, smiled and said:

– You're right. Curiosity accompanies us forever, even after death. Julia was really curious to know what had happened.

Julia sat down again and looked incredulously into Sueli's eyes, and asked:

– Did you give up, Sueli?

– I gave up, Julia. As the taxi headed home, I didn't cry, I just remembered everything that had taken place.

– The many times these signs appeared, how I liked to be lied to and how I accepted an illusion.

– I understood that Nilson lied to me because I let him. In the end I was certain of one thing only, I needed to get that man out of my head and, especially, out of my life. I couldn't stay there. I needed to go far and try to rebuild my life.

– Just like it happened to me. I was also carried away by the illusion that, one day, Anselmo would leave his wife to stay with me.

Although he never lied to me and said several times that he would never abandon his son.

– I'm glad you understood that, Julia. From my own experience, I can say that romance with a married man, most of the time or almost always, never works. The woman is always the one who suffers the most.

– I know about it. Right now I am suffering a lot...

– This suffering will pass and later you will realize how good it was.

– Now you are free to go your own way. You are no longer trapped in an illusion.

– I don't know how I can live without him...

– You're going to manage. Everybody does.

– How did you manage?

Sueli laughed.

– It wasn't me, Julia. It was life, some guardian angel or God himself who took care of changing everything.

– I'm not understanding...

– When I got out of the taxi, I saw that my mother was at the door. She was surprised to see me coming: – Have you come back Sueli?

I thought you were going do the same as before.

Do what, mom?

Just Beginning

When you go to study at your friend's house, you don't come home. You go to school and then to the restaurant.

It's true, but she's not doing well. She has a severe headache. That's why we couldn't study.

I will do it alone.

Okay, lunch is almost ready.

What are you doing out here?

— Today is the day the mail comes in the morning every time, I wonder why it hasn't come yet.

Why are you waiting here?

Today is the day we receive the light bill. I want to see how much we spend. It's stupid!

We spend more every month. I don't know what else to do to spend less.

I started to laugh: — Don't worry about it, mom. We will have money to pay the bill. Will we come in?

No, I'll wait a little longer. It should be here any time.

It's okay. I'm going to my room to study.

Laughing, I entered and went to my room. I sat in front of a dresser, looked at my face and thought how stupid was to believe everything he said. Everything I did to stay with him and how much I was willing to do. I didn't cry.

I just stood there looking at myself for a long time. Then I took a notebook and went to bed.

I had stopped studying, I needed to make up for lost time. I also thought of a way to leave, but I knew it would be difficult, because for that I would've needed to have money, which I did not have. During the time I was with Nilson, I spent all the money I had on buying clothes and shoes to look better for him and things to

Just Beginning

make the house nice. My mother came to tell me that lunch was ready and that my father had arrived.

I got up and went to the kitchen. My father, as he did every day, was sitting at the table. I sat next to him and, even without feeling hungry, I ate something. My mother was still nervous about the late bill.

Something must have happened that caused it to be late, Mom, it will be here soon.

I know, but did it have to be late today? That has never happened. It's always on time!

I looked at my father who was laughing at my mother's nervousness and went back to my room.

I was lying down trying to study when my mother came in. She had an envelope in her hand: – It's for you.

Do you know what it is about?

I was scared, I had no idea. I took the letter, opened it, and started running around the house and screaming. My mother was surprised: – Stop running and screaming, Sueli! What is written in that letter?

I was accepted, mother!

Accepted by whom?

This letter, it states that I won a scholarship to that school I wanted to go to.

Won?

I won mom! Now I can study and become a prestigious chef!

Well, my daughter! You deserve it and I guarantee that this school will not regret it and they will be very proud of you, just like me!

– Our Sueli! Did you really succeed? – Julia asked, laughing.

Just Beginning

– Yes, I did, Julia. A few hours prior, I was desperate, thinking that my life was over and not knowing how to continue and suddenly my problems were over. Everything had changed for the better.

– Weren't you afraid to leave home and go to a place you didn't know?

– Didn't you also say that you didn't have a lot of money? How did you do it?

– I was not afraid, Julia, because all I wanted, at that moment, was to be as far away from Nilson as possible.

– As for money, I took what little money I had left. My family had also saved some money and gave it to me.

– The most important thing was that I had a profession and there is always a restaurant anywhere in the world, so I wouldn't be without a job.

– How wonderful, Sueli! What do you think happened to the school that they gave you a scholarship?

– I didn't know at the time. When I sent the letter to the school asking for a scholarship, I did so without much hope of being responded.

– After all the time I spent with Nilson, I completely forgot about the letter and the school.

– Anyway, what happened didn't matter to me. What mattered was that I could go and fulfill the dream of my life. This is how I came here and to school.

– You said you didn't know then. Do you know today? How do you know today what you didn't know at that time?

– I don't understand, Sueli.

Just Beginning

– Yes, I know, Julia. Since I didn't know where I was going to stay, I took a bus at night. It would arrive in the morning, very early.

– I went directly to the school to do my enrollment. When I was there, I asked how I would find a place to live.

The girl who helped me said: – There, on that wall, there are ads for houses and apartments for rent.

Some students share housing and rent.

I looked at the wall and, from a distance, I saw several papers stuck together. I couldn't read from where I was.

After the enrollment, I went over to the wall. There were actually several announcements. I knew I couldn't rent one on my own, as I still didn't have a job. The money I brought would only last a month or two.

Among all the ads, one caught my eye. A girl wanted to share the apartment.

I looked around and saw a payphone. I called and a girl answered. After explaining what she wanted, she gave me the address and said it was very close to the school. There was a place in the school where to leave the suitcases, until the students could settle. I left there the two suitcases I was carrying and, address in hand, went to look for the place. Quickly, asking for directions, I got to the street where the apartment was. When I got to the number I was looking for, I was surprised. The building was beautiful and it seemed to be very expensive too. I almost left because I knew I didn't have the money to pay a very high rent. However, my curiosity to get to see such a department made me go in and take the elevator. The apartment was on the sixth floor. As soon as I got out of the elevator, I walked to the door, where the number sixty–one was.

Just Beginning

I rang the bell. The door opened and a young and very beautiful girl appeared who, smiling, asked:

Are you Sueli?

Yes, I am! – I answered in a low and very nervous voice.

My name is Rosana, you can come in.

Curious, I went in and, seeing the room, I was delighted, Julia. It was beautiful, decorated, with very cheerful furniture and colors.

I couldn't help it: – The room is beautiful!

I decorated it myself. Do you really like it?

A lot! It's nice!

I'm glad you liked it! Then you will feel good living here. Shall we sit?

I sat on one of the sofas that she pointed to me. Before she said anything, I said: – I'm sorry, Rosana.

I would love to live here, but I know I can't.

Why can't you, Sueli?

I told you that I was from another city, from a humble family and that I was only there, after having won a scholarship.

I also said that I was happy, because my biggest dream was to be a chef. I thought it would the best not to talk about Nilson.

She listened to me attentively, without moving a muscle on her face. I ended up saying: – As you can see, I am here by a miracle.

She very seriously said: – It is still very early. Did you drink coffee already?

Not yet. I came straight from the bus station to the school and then here.

Let's go to the kitchen. I want you to see it and we'll have coffee.

Just Beginning

We went into the kitchen, which was also beautiful. With the same youthful and fun decoration.

I was delighted: – It's beautiful, Rosana! I had never seen anything like this!

I also think it is beautiful and, like the rest of the apartment, I decorated it myself.

She put a kettle on the fire and said; – Come on, let's see the rooms.

Delighted with what I was seeing, I followed her. She opened another door and, in front of me, a room appeared that, like the rest of the apartment, was beautiful, following the same pattern.

This is my room. I decided to buy a double bed for more comfort. The crochet bedspread was made by my grandmother and I chose the pink lining.

I was almost speechless.

Really wonderful, Rosana! It must be great to sleep in a room like this and in a bed like this.

– I can guarantee that is true! – Julia said laughing and continued:

– Now come, I'll show you the other room.

I followed her hoping to see another wonder. She opened the door and, to my surprise, the room was empty, without decoration or furniture.

She noticed my surprise and, still laughing, said: – I left this room empty, so that the person who lives in it can choose the furniture and decoration they want. So, you can start thinking about the decoration and furniture you want to buy.

Surprised, I tried to say: – I can't pay the rent, Rosana.

Just Beginning

She didn't seem to hear me, she took my hand and pulled me into the kitchen – the water must already be boiling, Sueli, let's have coffee.

Although perplexed, I just had to follow her. The water was really boiling. As she put the coffee powder in the strainer to strain it, she said: – There in the refrigerator, there's milk, cake and jam. There's no bread, because I am too lazy to go to the bakery, there is toast in the cupboard, but don't worry if you want to eat bread in the morning, the bakery is just around the corner.

I can't live here, Rosana. I would love to, but I can't pay half the rent, which must be very high.

She, who still didn't seem to listen to me, just smiled: – Take a seat,, Sueli and, while we have coffee, let's talk about it.

She put the milk, cake and jam that she had taken from the refrigerator on the table.

She took a packet of toast from the cupboard, placed it on the table, and sat on one side and I sat on the other.

As she was spreading jam to the toast, she said: – I know you're worried about rent, Sueli, but you don't have to.

Why not? Renting this apartment must be very expensive!

I know I'm going to get a job, but I also know that what I earn from it will only pay a very low rent and my food. It's a shame, Rosana, but I can't...

You are right, the rent must be very high, but since I am not paying it, you shouldn't worry.

You don't pay the rent? How?

My father is a very rich man. He has a cattle ranch and he doesn't even know how many heads of cattle he has.

I like the ranch and animals, but I never wanted to live there. I'm more from the city, I like talking to people.

Just Beginning

Now, my brother loves living in the ranch. My father wanted me to be a veterinarian to take care of the cattle and other animals, but I refused. In fact, I didn't study at all. I was worried about other things.

I came to spend a few days on vacation here in this city. I already knew the city. Many times, as children, my parents brought us here. Now, recently when I came back here I fell in love with the city. After a while, my father came to visit me.

Since he has an enterprising spirit, he realized that the city had a lot of potential. In addition to its natural beauty, it had two schools, a catering school and restaurants.

He thought for a moment, then he called me and asked me: – Would you like to live in this city, Rosana?

I was scared, Sueli, and I asked him: – Live here? Of course I would, Dad! The city is beautiful!

But why are you asking me that?

I have been looking at the city and I realized that it does not have a high–class hotel. So, I decided to build one, here in the center, a inn within walking distance, and then maybe a good restaurant. What do you think?

I started to laugh: – Only you, Dad, could have such an idea.

I didn't understand why he asked me if I wanted to live here.

You know I can't leave the ranch. There is a lot to do there. I need someone here to monitor the construction.

Nobody better than you for that, but you would need to live here, until the hotel and inn were ready. Then if you want to continue living here, you can either stay here to manage everything or go back to the ranch.

Just Beginning

I was euphoric, because I could live alone, out of sight of my parents. I needed to get away from them to think a lot about how my life had been up to now. I spoke to my father and he said: – Okay.

I will buy an apartment so that you feel comfortable.

I trust you, I know you will manage the construction.

– I was surprised, Julia, because whoever saw her would never imagine that she was a rich person.

Smiling, she continued: – So, Sueli, this apartment belongs to my father, I don't pay rent and you don't have to pay either. You can live here, with me, as long as you need. The construction of the hotel and the inn has not yet started and will take a long time to complete.

– I just don't understand one thing, Sueli. If the apartment was hers, why did she place in the ad that she wanted to share the room?

– That's what I asked. She laughed and replied: – After decorating the apartment, I stayed a few days living alone.

Yesterday afternoon, I was right here, having coffee, when, without knowing why, I thought: I hate living alone.

I need to find a girl to live here. I went to schools and universities. Since I had studied in another city, I knew that there were many students from other cities who needed to rent a place to live.

Last night, I put the ad in all three places, and you called this morning.

As soon as I saw you, I liked you and, after telling me about your immense desire to work and study, I knew that you needed my help and that you would be a great company. Also, you said

Just Beginning

that being here is a miracle, since I believe that a miracle must be complete, I am helping you, she said, laughing.

I'm thinking, Rosana! I'm not believing all the good that is happening to me! I am really lucky!

I don't believe in luck, Sueli. I believe in merit. You must have done something very good to have so much protection and so many spiritual friends who help you.

Spiritual friends? Who are they?

I am studying a Doctrine in which I learned that, when things seem to be going well, it is first a matter of merit, then it is because we are on the right path.

I do not quite understand.

It is very simple. It teaches us that before we are born, we choose the life we want to live and that when we are on the right path, the doors open so that we can walk smoothly and everything begins to work.

Another reason is that when we get through a difficult time without causing harm to anyone, the reward comes. You must have done something very good. For that to happen, we also always have spiritual friends by our side who hope to find the way.

Who are these friends?

Looking into my eyes, Julia, she laughed again: – For now, Sueli, let's say they are guardian angels.

You must have many angels. I just want to know what you did so well to deserve all that help.

I don't remember doing anything good, Rosana. I have a common life like everyone else.

It does not matter now. We'll talk about it another day, Sueli. Now, we have to go out and buy the furniture four your room. Are you ready?

Just Beginning

– Of course I am! I still don't believe what's happening, Rosana. After settling in, I'll go out to explore the restaurants in town. Who knows, as lucky as I am, I'll get a job today.

You will get it. You're going to get it...

We went out and she let me choose the furniture and everything I wanted for my room.

It felt like I was living a dream.

I got a job in one of the restaurants in town, which weren't many. The restaurant was frequented by students who went there because the food was good and the cheapest in town. I met many young men, some of them wanted to go out with me, but I didn't want to. My only goal was to finish school and go to a big city. Rosana treated me like a sister.

In the early days when I moved into the apartment, she hired a maid who was already working there, only now, she took care of my things too. She never allowed me to pay the rent or the food, the only thing she asked me to do, and I thanked her for that, was to cook at home, so that we could eat, all the food that I learned at school , which I did with great pleasure, because in addition to trying the food, she always praised my seasoning.

When she said that, I laughed: – Isn't that funny? They all use onion and garlic, but the taste of food is totally different from person to person.

– Cooking is a gift, Sueli. Not everyone has this gift. I can assure you have it. Your food is delicious.

– Did you see how lucky I was to let you come to live here? I am a terrible cook.

– She was a lot of fun, Sueli!

– No, she wasn't, Julia! She still is! She is alive! Very much so!

Just Beginning

– I'd like to meet her!

– You will. She and her husband will be maid of honor and best man!

– Did she get married?

– Yes, and they are very happy!

– You haven't told me how you met Eduardo. You said after Nilson, you weren't interested in any man.

– That's another story. It's almost time for me to go to work. I'm going to take a shower and when I get out of the bathroom, I'll tell you.

– Okay, I'll be waiting for you.

Sueli went into the bathroom. Julia was anxious, waiting for her to come back and tell the rest of the story. Alzira and Ciro, the entities that were there the whole time, smiled and watched Sueli walk away.

7.- The recipe for unhappiness

While Sueli took a bath, Júlia washed the cups, the sugar bowl and the kettle that they had used and thought: Sueli's story is very beautiful. She managed to escape and forget Nilson. Today she is happy and has her wedding scheduled with Eduardo, a boy who loves her very much and does everything possible to make her happy. She did it, but am I going to do it too? I don't think so. I know that I will spend the rest of my life thinking about Anselmo and how we could have been happy.

Why did it take me so long to find him?

Why wasn't I the one he married? Why is life so unfair? I know he never promised anything, but I was very hopeful...

Sueli came out of the bathroom with a towel around her hair.

She came to her room and was followed by Julia, who, curious, wanted her to continue telling her story.

As Sueli opened the closet door to get the clothes she was going to wear, Julia sat on the bed and looked at her, who smiled: It's almost time to go to the restaurant. You know it's my job and when it comes down to it, there is no negotiation.

– My job is my life. Without it, I wouldn't be here and this good. If it weren't because of it, at the time of what happened with Nilson, perhaps, I wouldn't have been able to survive.

Just Beginning

– I know what you think about work, Sueli. So, I don't care if you talk too fast.

– I just want to know what happened next and how you managed to recover and have your own restaurant today. Sueli smiled and continued speaking: – Rosana and I, with each passing day, we became more friends.

– She spent most of the day watching the buildings. In order to study in the mornings, she worked every night at the restaurant.

– She used to sleep early, so we only met at lunch.

– In the early days, I still remembered Nilson and, when that happened, I always cried.

– Rosana and I never talk about our emotional life.

– Why not?

I was very ashamed of what had happened to me and how I humiliated myself, even thinking about accepting Nilson even if he was married, even after lying so much. She never asked about my emotional life and I never asked about hers.

– You never asked? Weren't you curious? You said she was young.

– Never Julia, because I knew that if I asked her about her life, I would risk her asking about mine and I didn't want to tell her about it.

– I understand the shame you felt Sueli, it is the same I feel today. I also accepted Anselmo, even though I knew he was married and would never leave his wife.

Hearing that, Sueli smiled: – I already told you that you weren't the first and you won't be the last, Julia.

– Then there is no point in suffering or feeling shame. Leave that part of your life behind and walk without pain, without

Just Beginning

sadness and especially without hatred. In life, everything that happens to us always has a reason.

– What is the reason I was so stupid, Sueli?

– I don't know now, but one day you will laugh at all the suffering, at all the tears you shed.

– Do you think that can happen?

– No, Julia! I don't think! It will happen!

– Talking is easy, the hard part is getting there.

– You can do it, Julia. Like me, one day you will understand why I met Nilson and had that affair with him.

– Do you know why? What is the reason? How did you find out?

– That's another story, Julia. One day I'll tell you.

– It's okay. I'll wait. Now tell me, did you manage not to know about her life or even tell her yours?

– Nothing is hidden forever, Julia. One night when I left the restaurant, I remembered the day Nilson was waiting for me.

– At the same time I began to remember everything that had happened. As I walked home, I couldn't help the tears that kept running down my face. I went into the house and, to my surprise, Rosana was in the living room, sitting on the sofa and reading a book. As soon as I entered, she looked over her shoulder and asked:
– Are you already here, Sueli?

– How so already, Rosana? I always get here at this time.

Whoa! I was so immersed reading this book that I didn't even notice the hours go by.

What book are you reading? I asked as I went to the kitchen.

A very nice novel.

Romance is only beautiful in books, in real life it sucks.

Just Beginning

She got up and went to the kitchen. I, to avoid showing my red eyes, turned to the stove, where a kettle was boiling. I wanted to make some tea.

Why do you say that, Sueli? Romance and love also exist in real life. Have you never had a romance?

Have you never had a love?

I couldn't take it anymore, Julia and I cried again. She, desperate, came to my side.

Why are you crying, Sueli? What happened?

I'm crying because romance and especially love do n't exist! Lies and betrayals exist...

Why are you saying that?

I don't know why, Julia, but in that moment, I wanted to tell Rosana my whole story.

I told her everything that had happened since I met Nilson. She listened to me carefully, as soon as I finished, to my surprise, she started laughing.

She laughed, why, Sueli?

I didn't understand that reaction either and I asked: – Why are you laughing like that, Rosana?

She continued laughing for a long while, so much that she couldn't stop. It was stressing me, until she stopped and still laughing, but, calmer, she replied: – I'm laughing because you used the recipe!

What is this recipe, Rosana?

The recipe for unhappiness!

Perplexed and without understanding, I asked again: – Unhappiness? I'm not understanding.

Just Beginning

It's very simple, Sueli. I will give you this recipe and you will see that you have already used it.

Me?

Yes, you and many other women and men too.

I still don't understand. What recipe are you talking about?

Take a pen, paper and write it down.

Are you kidding, Rosana?

No, I mean it, Sueli.

Do you want me to write it as a cake recipe?

That's right, never forget it and move on. I know one day; you'll have to pass it on to someone.

She looked at a bookshelf, where there were books, notebooks, and some pens. Not understanding, but curious, I went to the bookshelf, took a pen and a notebook. I sat down again and watched.

Now write down everything I'm going to say. Sueli?

Yes, you can start to speak.

Well. This is the recipe:

If a woman wants to be alone all the time, if she wants to spend weekends and holidays waiting, if she doesn't want to dream about the future or plan it and if she wants to see time go by, lose her youth and old age and only get there to realize that she lost her whole life waiting for something that would never happen; If you want to stay home without going for a walk, going to the cinema or the theater because you are waiting for that person who does not always show up; if you want to live for someone else, forget about yourself; if you want to be emotionally dependent; if you want to travel, vacation or even go to the cinema, always alone; if you want to see time go by, without getting anything.

Just Beginning

Anyway, if you want to be unhappy, just date a married man and be satisfied with being the other one. Before I forget, Sueli. – This recipe is for men and women.

She finished talking and looked at me, Julia and I looked at her.

I couldn't avoid it:

– Is that your recipe for unhappiness, Rosana?

Yes, and many other disadvantages that, for now, I can't remember.

Do you have any questions about it, Sueli? Wasn't that everything that happened with Nilson?

I was thinking for a while, Julia, and I just had to say: – You're right, Rosana, I went through all this while I was with him. I waited for him many times and he didn't show up.

I spent every weekend alone. It was worse when I found out he was married and waited too long for us to talk and he just ignored me, pretended I didn't exist. You're right, Rosana...

She was silent, Julia, she just smiled. I asked her: – Where did you get that idea from, Rosana?

I used this recipe myself.

Were you in a relationship with a married man?

I was. That is the real reason why I am here, in this city, so far from home. I came here trying to forget everything I went through.

Didn't you come to help your father build the hotel and restaurant?

That is a long story.

Are you going to tell me? I confess that I am curious now, Rosana.

Just Beginning

I don't have much to tell you, Sueli. You know exactly how this story begins and ends.

Were you also lied to?

No, Sueli. My story was different from yours. I was different from you, but the result was the same. Suffering

Tell me, Rosana!

Well, I'll tell you, but first, let's have a tea that, after all this time, must already be cold.

Just Beginning

8.– The power of money

Rosana put the tea in a cup and, while she drank, began to tell her story: – My family, as people know, always had a lot of money, Sueli. My parents tell us that we are descendants of aristocrats of the French court. I don't know if it's true, but I like to imagine that it is.

Why, Rosana?

I don't know, I think it's a luxury! – she said laughing and continued speaking: – I only have one brother who is older.

Ever since I was little, I have always been very spoiled. My parents fulfilled all my wishes.

I never received no for an answer. I grew up like this, thinking I could do everything. I became a mean and selfish person.

I only thought of myself. I mistreated all the housekeepers. Always making it very clear that I was in charge.

I always organized big parties, so I had a lot of friends who frequented my house almost every day. – They were my friends, because they knew that I didn't wear a dress or a shoe more than once, and that I would give it to them.

All the boys who knew me, came up to try a courtship and preferably a wedding.

Just Beginning

I never knew if they really liked me or if it was just because I was a rich heiress.

I didn't care for any of them. I just wanted to have fun. I never wanted to study, because I knew that the money my parents had would never run out. Studying was a lot of work and I didn't need to do it, I wanted to live my life.

– When I heard what she said, I couldn't help it, Julia. I couldn't believe it and said almost screaming.

You can't be talking about yourself, Rosana? You are not that person!

She began to laugh: – You don't know me, Sueli. You don't know how I was or how I am.

I haven't known you for a long time, but what little I know has nothing to do with this Rosana that you are describing.

The Rosana I know was the one who, even without knowing me, gave me refuge. She let me live here, with all the accommodations for me to study! You're good, Rosana!

– She continued laughing, Julia, and said: – This one here, is really the way you described me, but I will never forget who I was.

It can't be! It can't be, Rosana! – I almost shouted, Julia.

I'll keep telling you how I saw myself, and then you'll see if I'm telling the truth.

Like I said before, in my entire life, Sueli, I hadn't ever received a no for an answer. I didn't wear a dress or a shoe more than once and I didn't study or work, I spent my time shopping, always accompanied by an opportunistic friend.

One afternoon, I went with my friend, Joana, to a shoe store. That night there would be another party at my house and I, as always, had to be elegant and more beautiful than anyone else.

Just Beginning

We walked into a store I'd never been to. As soon as we entered, a young man approached us. When I saw him, my heart was beating. He was beautiful! Tall, with green eyes. I've never seen such a handsome boy.

He, smiling, asked: – Can I help these two beautiful girls?

I couldn't answer for a while, delighted with his smile. After a while, I pointed to the shopfront and said: – Please, I want to see that shoe.

He smiled and, showing with his hand a sofa that was there, said: – Take a seat, I'll get it. What size number?

Thirty–six.

He walked away and I was so moved by his beauty, I said: – He's handsome, Joana!

– That's right, Rosana.

– I want this man for me, Joana!

If you want it, it will be so, Rosana! You always have what you want!

I was a little envious, Sueli, but I didn't care, I was used to it.

The only thing I wanted and knew I would get was this man. We left there and returned to my house.

There I was thinking of a way to get closer to him and seduce him. I soon realized that it wouldn't be difficult, it was enough for me to go back to the store and buy shoes. That's what I did, the next morning, very early, I was there.

When he saw me there again, he was amazed and, smiling, asked: – So early here? Did you come to change any of the pairs of shoes you bought?

No. I came to buy one of those over there. – I answered pointing a finger at the shopfront.

Just Beginning

That's great! Come, sit down, I'll get it.

As he walked away, I thought: I definitely want this man for myself!

He returned with a few pairs of shoes. I don't even know if I liked it, but I chose one and bought it.

For a month I went to the store two or three times a week and bought shoes. I have no idea how many pairs of shoes I bought. Every time he arrived, he greeted me with a smile. Of course, it was because of the commission he received.

He always treated me like a customer, but in my sick mind I believed it was because he was in love.

Since he never tried to win me over, I thought it was because of his shyness. So I decided that I needed to take the initiative.

My parents were in the ranch and my brother was studying in São Paulo. I was almost always home alone, alone with the employees. I always did what I wanted and no one dared to bother me, not even my parents.

So, without asking for permission, I organized another party for the next week, on Saturday.

I knew that with him in my house, drinking and eating, it would be easier to get closer to him and show my feelings for him.

After all, I went back to the store.

As always, he welcomed me with that wonderful smile: – Did you come to buy another pair of shoes?

Not today. I came to invite you to a party at my house, it will be next Saturday.

He, surprised, said: – I would like very much, but I can't go. I need to work.

The party will start at nine at night and you will only work until six, you will have plenty of time.

Just Beginning

I can't take a no for an answer. I will be waiting

Excuse me, miss, but I need to work.

I already said that I will not accept excuses.

He looked at me, Sueli, and after a while he said: – I don't know, I'll try, but it will be difficult.

I already said that I will not accept excuses. Here is my address. I will be waiting

He was silent, I left happy. I was sure he wouldn't refuse.

After all, parties at my house were popular. I knew that some people would do anything to be invited.

With him, it would be no different. Like what happened to everyone else, no one could resist even if it was just for curiosity.

And did he go, Rosana?

Take it easy. I'll tell you everything, Sueli. I spent the rest of the week getting ready for the party. As the party had been planned at the last minute, I had a lot to do. That same day, I hired several people who were already used to organizing parties at home. They knew everything I liked. I kept going to the shoe store to reinforce the invitation, but he always said he couldn't go. I thought he was playing hard to get. I bought a new dress and shoes, of course. – How many pairs of shoes do you have, Rosana?

Rosana laughed: – Today I don't have many, but at that time I had a lot, I don't even know how many.

Some of the shoes, I only wore them in the store, when I tried them before buying. For me, money was worth nothing.

It was easy and I knew that with it, I could buy whatever I wanted.

How I wish I had all that money, Rosana. It was always different for me. Although I never lived badly or lacked any food, I never had many clothes or shoes.

Just Beginning

Money is good, yes, Sueli, but it should not be turned into a murder weapon. It should only serve to bring us happiness, to have what we want, not to try to buy people.

Buy people?

Yes. Buy people. Money makes everything easier, and people are fooled into trying their best to get more.

They all have a price.

I can't imagine what you're talking about. I never had the money to buy some things that I wanted, imagine buying a person. But keep going. What happened after? Did he go to your party?

On Saturday, before the scheduled time, everything was ready. I walked around the house looking at the decorations, tasting the sweets, the salty snacks and seeing if the amount of drink was right. When the guests began to arrive, I greeted them with a smile, hugs, and kisses, but I couldn't take my eyes off the front door. I really wanted to see him arrive.

The interesting thing is that I didn't even know his name. I never asked and he never told me. People were coming.

Some I knew, some I didn't, but I didn't care who was there, I just wanted him, who didn't come.

He didn't go?

No, Sueli. I waited until the last guest left. As soon as everyone left, I looked around the great room. You can imagine what it was like. Glasses, bottles and plates with food scraps, scattered everywhere.

I looked at everything and very nervous, I went to my room. There, I cried with hatred for his bravery in not responding to an invitation from me. How dare he do that? How?

I stayed in the room all Sunday. Luzia, who, although she was our maid, took care of me since I was little, she was more than

Just Beginning

a mother, seeing that I didn't leave the room, she went there and knocked, gently knocked on the door and entered, carrying a tray with some sandwiches, which she knew I really liked, a glass and a jug of grape juice.

What's wrong, Rosana? Why don't you want to leave the room or even eat?

Nothing is wrong, Luzia! I'm tired.

I never saw you like this, especially after a party. Something is wrong. What is it Rosana?

I told you I'm fine! Please leave me alone! I need to think!

Seeing that she had never seen me like this, she put the tray on a small table and left.

I was very upset. I couldn't admit what he did to me. How dare anyone ignore me?

After thinking a lot, I decided: Now, it's a matter of honor, I'm going to have that man anyway!

I spent the rest of the day thinking about what I would do on Monday. I thought a lot. At night, after deciding what to do, I fell asleep.

As soon as the store opened on Monday, I was already there.

When he saw me, he, smiling, as always approached: – Good morning, miss!

It's not a good day! Why didn't you come to my party?

– Did you do that, Rosana?

– It seems incredible, Sueli, but I did. I was possessed.

– What did he say?

– Nothing, Sueli.

– What? nothing?

Just Beginning

– He just showed me his left hand and on it, I saw a huge ring.

– Was he married?

– Yes. There was no rock there, but I didn't need one.

– I knew I was white as a ghost, because I felt that all my blood stopped.

– What did you do?

After taking a deep breath, I asked: – Why didn't you tell me you were married?

There was no reason for that. I'm just a shoe salesman.

Now, I think it's time to clear up a few things.

I am married, I have two small children, and I am also very happy with my marriage.

I didn't know what to say or do. I just tried to smile and, humiliated, I left.

I walked through the square until I reached my car.

I got in, sat down and started crying without being able to stop. I couldn't accept that situation.

I didn't know if I really liked him, I just felt that a wish of mine was not coming true.

I couldn't accept that a mere shoe salesman had humiliated me like this.

I went home and cried the rest of the day. I didn't want to talk to anyone or eat. I just wanted to think.

Luzia tried to talk to me, but I refused.

– I imagine how you felt, Rosana...

– I think, no matter how much you imagine, you won't be able to get close, Sueli. It was a very difficult day.

Just Beginning

– Today I know that I wasted a lot of time suffering and wondering what to do next. I suffered a lot for nothing.

– How, Rosana? You were in love with him...

– No, Sueli. Today I know that I wasn't in love. I was humiliated for having always fulfilled my wishes, for believing that power was with those who have money, I could not accept that denial.

I really couldn't, so I needed to do something.

– What did you do?

– In the afternoon I left the house. I decided that I would go to the city. My plans were to walk, see shopfronts to distract myself.

– I needed to clear my mind.

– I walked down a street where there were many shops. I looked through the shopfronts, but nothing caught my attention.

– I had everything, I didn't need anything. As I passed a watch store, I stopped and looked. I saw a man's watch.

– I looked at it for a while. It was really beautiful.

– It must have been expensive, but that didn't matter. I went in and asked the seller to show me.

– By holding it in my hands, I discovered that it was really beautiful. I asked the price. The seller told me the price.

– For some people it might be expensive, but for me, the price meant nothing.

– I bought it. With it in my hands, I went back to the shoe store. As soon as he saw me, he came to meet me.

This time he wasn't smiling. He came over and, before saying anything, I took the box with the watch, opened it, and showed it to him. I was thrilled when I saw the sparkle in his eyes. I knew he had never seen a watch like this.

Just Beginning

He, surprised, asked: – The watch is beautiful, but I don't understand, why are you showing it to me? – What does it mean?

It means it can be yours.

What? What are you saying?

That's what you heard. It can be yours. When you get out of here, go with me to a restaurant, and while we have dinner, I'll give you the watch.

– He looked at me with wide eyes, Sueli. He didn't seem to know what to say.

I was waiting for an answer, but the owner of the store, where he was, called him: – Joel. I need you to come here.

It's only for a minute.

He, who seemed to be returning from a long distance, said: – Excuse me, miss, but I need to see my boss.

Quickly, he left and went to talk to the owner of the store. I smiled and left, Sueli, with the certainty that he wouldn't be able to refuse.

– How was that certainty, Rosana?

– This is called power. I knew the power of money and the power of human greed.

– We are never satisfied with what we have. We can achieve everything we dream of, but we always want more.

– The best, the best car and the best clothes, without worrying about whether all this is necessary or not.

– We just want others to know how powerful we are.

– You're being very radical, Rosana! Dreaming is good and achieving even better. What would happen to as human beings if we had no dreams?

Just Beginning

– You are right about this, Sueli, if human beings didn't dream, we would still be in the stone age, but that is not what I am talking about. I'm talking about greed, and especially power.

– I'm not understanding...

– Dreaming is very good. Chasing a dream is even better, but we can never forget that everything we achieve here on Earth will stay here. Therefore, we can't harm or hurt another person in order to achieve a dream.

– And power too. It is everywhere. Not just with the so-called powerful people.

Power is in the hands of that official who mistreats someone who needs his services.

Power is in the hands of a bank employee, in the hands of the housekeeper, when it comes to an employee.

Power is everywhere. It is enough for one person to have little power over other to know how to use it.

Corrupt power and money. They make some feel like gods.

Julia, who heard Sueli tell Rosana's story, interrupted her: – Wow, Sueli, how bitter she was!

– I thought so too, Julia and I asked her: – Why do you say that, Rosana? You seem very bitter and sad!

To my surprise, Rosana laughed and replied: – No, Sueli. I am not sad nor bitter today.

Today I know that money helps us help others and that power can be used for good.

I learned this after a lot of suffering.

I don't think you were bad, Rosana. You liked it and used the weapons you had. What happened after?

Did he accept the watch?

Just Beginning

I stayed in front of the store until after six o'clock, when the store was closed and he left.

As soon as he saw me standing there, he came over and asked: – Are you still here?

Yes, I am waiting for your answer.

I already gave my answer. I am married and very happy. I don't want to get involved with you or any other girl.

Who said I want to marry you? I just want to have dinner and give you a gift.

Thank you, but I cannot accept your watch, much less your invitation. Now I'm sorry but I have to go home, my wife is waiting for me.

– Did he say that, Rosana?

– He did and it was very hateful. I couldn't accept that he was ignoring me.

– After all, nothing similar had ever happened in my life.

– I wonder what you felt. It must have been frustrating...

– You're right, Sueli. I was frustrated and angry, but he didn't care. He walked past me and walked away.

– Outraged, I followed him with my eyes. I saw that he stopped in front of a bus stop.

I went to my car and waited. After almost half an hour, he got on a bus that left immediately and I followed him. The bus stopped at every point where people got on and off.

As the bus drove away from the city, places that I had never seen or imagined could exist began to appear. The poverty was evident, wood houses, streets without lighting.

Dirty water dripped down the sidewalk. The stench invaded the car, causing me to close the windows.

Just Beginning

I was watching if he got off. After almost an hour, he finally got off and walked onto a street, also without lighting. He walked for more than fifteen minutes and I followed him from a distance so he wouldn't see me. After he got inside a house, I waited for a moment and walked through it. At the front, there was a large plot and at the back of that plot, a small house, really small, Sueli. It was dark, but still, I could see that there shouldn't have been more than one room. That surprised me, because at home there were four rooms and they were ten times bigger than that house. I passed the house and left, thinking: how could he, living in a place like this, refuse a watch like the one I offered him? And reject my love?

– I saw a shadow pass through her eyes, Julia, as if she, when she remembered what happened, would suffer again.

– Then I asked: – What did you do next, Rosana? Did you understand that he didn't want to know about you? Did you move off from him?

I should have done that, but I didn't. I was humiliated and couldn't accept that someone annoyed me, especially a person like him, poor and ignorant. From that day on, I started chasing him.

Every day, I stayed in front of the store until he arrived at work, at lunchtime and when he left work, always with some expensive gift, but he ignored me and didn't accept the gift. I didn't give up and I became more and more irritated. I knew that what I was doing was not right, but even so, I continued for more than a month, until one afternoon, when he left the store, I was surprised, because I saw that he was walking towards me, something that he had never done. When he approached, with a serene face, smiling, he said: – Okay, you won. Let's go to that bench, there in the square.

We need to talk.

Not believing what was happening, I went to one of the benches in the square.

Just Beginning

As soon as we arrived, I sat down and then he sat down too and said: – You know that I am married and that I am very happy with my marriage and that I have no intention of having another woman, whatever happens. You are a beautiful girl, it seems that with a lot of money, any man would be happy to get your attention. You need to get away from me.

Your presence is embarrassing me in front of people who know me. Please come back to your life.

Get another toy.

– Whoa! Did he say that, Rosana?

– He said so down to every letter, Sueli.

– What did you do? Did you get up and leave?

– To my surprise, Julia, Rosana began to laugh: Then she replied: – No, Sueli, that had become a disease.

– For a long time I lived for him and did not know how I would live without him.

– I started to cry and, between sobs, I said: – I don't want to ruin your life or your marriage, I just want and need you to pay attention to me.

– Let me Love You.

He smiled and, putting his arm around my shoulders, said: – You know there is no future for us both.

I love my wife and I will never leave her.

When I felt his arms on my shoulders, I shuddered.

I hugged him and, still crying, said: – I know and I don't care. I just want to spend a few hours with you, nothing more.

He walked away, held my face with both hands and, looking into my eyes, said:

Just Beginning

It's okay. I know you don't really like me, you just want to achieve something that is being difficult.

Let's meet in an intimate place and then we'll see what happens.

Although until then, I hadn't had a man in my life, I didn't care that he was the first or what it would be like. I was happy, because I loved that man and he would be mine. That was all that mattered to me.

Still, tears streaming down my face, he said: – I'll do whatever you want.

– I kept looking at her, Julia, not believing what I was hearing and, although I knew that when we are in love, we do things that are difficult to explain. I myself had done unmistakable things to be with Nilson.

I lost all my scruples, I humiliated myself, and only gave up when he abandoned me. When we can judge, it is easy to forget our own mistakes. At that moment, unable to believe it, forgetting what I had done, I asked: – How can you humiliate yourself so much, Rosana?

– She looked me in the eye, Julia, and smiling, she replied: – I don't know, Sueli. All I thought was that I could stay with him for even a few hours. He, passing his hand over my face, said: – Today, I'm all yours.

Where are we going?

What?

Why this reaction? Didn't you say you would do anything to be with me?

I did...

– So, the first thing we are going to do is be together for a few hours. Shall we go?

Just Beginning

Where do we go?

– We can go to a hotel, but as you know, I have no money, so you have to choose the hotel and pay. Since you are the owner of the money, you decide.

– I thought for a while, Sueli. Internally, I felt humiliated by the proposal and the way he spoke, but my passion was greater and I said: – Okay, let's go to a hotel.

We went to a hotel. Everything happened very fast. It seemed like he was in a hurry. There was no affection or attention. When it was over, I felt really bad. Since it was the first time, something I never told him, I thought it would be different, but it wasn't. He got up, put on his clothes and, as if showing hatred, said: – Now that you have your toy, it's time for a decisive conversation.

What conversation?

You finally got what you wanted. We are here and we can see each other once or twice a week.

Are you talking seriously?

Yes, as long as you do something for me.

What?

– You always knew that I am married and that I am happy in my marriage. Still, since you had a lot of money, you thought you could buy anyone and anything. You are right about that. It took me a while, but now I must admit that you are right. I have a price.

What price?

You know I live far away and I waste a lot of time on the bus. My house is small and now that another child is coming, I need a bigger one.

I'm not understanding...

Just Beginning

Yes, you are! You're smart. So if you want to continue meeting with me, here or somewhere else you prefer, you will buy me a car, so it takes me less time to get home and money so I can move in with my wife and wait for our child.

What?

What you heard and I will not repeat it. I don't want an answer right now. You have up to four days to decide. If you agree, go to the store and I will know that you have accepted. Then we will make an appointment any day of the week. If you don't agree, never go back to the store again. I want to live in peace!

Whoa! Did he say that, Rosana?

He did. When he finished speaking, he left without saying goodbye.

What did you do?

I sat on the bed, staring at the door, where he had gone. Feeling ashamed, humiliated, and not knowing what to do, I stayed there for a long time. I couldn't think, I just cried, unable to stop myself, unable to forget what he had said. Then I got out and went home. In silence, I entered the house and, without speaking to anyone, I went to my room. Leaning against my bed, I cried not only because of what he had said, but because I understood that he was right.

Because my family has a lot of money, I grew up with everything, spoiled and proud. Really, I always thought that money could buy anyone and everything. I stayed there crying nonstop, until I fell asleep.

It must have been very difficult, Rosana.

Yes, it was, Sueli, but it also served to open my eyes. The next day when I woke up, I remembered everything that had happened. Like he said, I had gotten my toy, but was it worth it?

Just Beginning

After thinking a lot, I needed to decide what to do.

Did you accept his terms?

In the morning, I still didn't know what to do.

I didn't even leave the room for coffee or lunch, something I always did. As always, my parents were not at home. They were traveling through Europe. Therefore, there would be no charge. I wasn't hungry, I could only cry, think about what he said and what my life had been like. In the middle of the afternoon, the door to my room opened and Luzia entered through it. She had the clothes she had ironed in her hands.

When she saw me in the room, she stopped at the door and said: – Excuse me, Rosana, I didn't know you were home. Can I come in to put these clothes in?

Of course, Luzia. Enter.

She entered and, while putting the clothes in the drawers, she asked: – Are you crying, Rosana?

I am.

Why? You are beautiful and you can have whatever you want! What happened?

It took me a while to respond, then I told her everything that had happened and ended by saying: – It's over, Luzia. My life has been a lie.

I don't know what to do. I wanted to die...

She dropped the clothes on a stool and sat next to me on the bed.

She looked me in the eye and said: – Nothing is what it seems, Rosana. Most of the time, when we think it's over, it's actually just beginning.

With everything that happened, you have the opportunity to review your life, start over.

Just Beginning

How to start over? There is no new start. I don't know how to live in a different way than I have always lived.

You can and should! When we are born, we come with a path to follow, a mission to fulfill.

When we get lost, life takes care of putting everything in its place.

When I heard that, I couldn't help but laugh.

Where did you get that idea, Luzia?

She answered seriously: – I follow a Doctrine that teaches this.

What Doctrine? Please don't bring a religion into this!

I'm not talking about a religion, but about a Doctrine of life that teaches us to live well here and after we die.

I couldn't believe I was hearing that, Sueli, so I asked her: – What are you talking about, Luzia?

A Doctrine that teaches that we all have free will and that, therefore, we are responsible for our actions.

That everything we do right and wrong always has a return in the same proportion. It teaches that we must value life in all its dimensions.

What does this have to do with what is happening to me?

That's what it's about, Rosana. You were born rich and beautiful. Conditions that many people would like to have. With these qualities, you could help many people.

Are you saying that I need to give all the money I have to the poor?

Not! I didn't say that! I'm saying that you could help, yes, with some money, but you also could help with words and comfort. On the contrary, however, you used this money to humiliate and use people.

Just Beginning

Sadly, I have followed everything you did.

What did I do?

You know. Throughout your life you thought that money could buy everything and everyone.

Today, you see that it's not so. That there are people who, although they want and fight for money, have their own principles. This guy showed you that.

He is married and loves his wife. You didn't respect that and you thought that with money you could make him change his mind and what happened.

Are you criticizing me, Luzia?

I am. I've known you since you were a child and I knew that day would come.

Do you think I deserved what happened to me?

No. I can't judge you. I'm not the owner of the truth and, like all people, I have my mistakes and successes.

I'm just saying that, since you have been on a dangerous path for your spirit, life has undertaken to making you stop and think about everything you've done so far.

– You're right about that. Since yesterday, I have thought a lot about my life.

Did you come to any conclusion?

No. I don't know what to do...

During our life, we always have two paths to follow.

So, you have two paths. Accept what he said and continue to be humiliated and pay for a happiness that doesn't exist or continue your life in a different way. Use your time for something productive and wait until happiness comes through sincere and selfless love. It is time to choose what you want for your life.

Just Beginning

How am I going to make that decision, Luzia?

For that we all have free will. Whichever path you choose, it will be your path and I will be here to support you. Now, I'm going to finish putting these clothes in order. If you need me, I'll be in your parents' room. I'll tidy up the closet.

– Having said that, she left Sueli and left me alone without knowing what to do.

I leaned back on the pillow and, lying on my back, I looked at the ceiling remembering everything I had said and how my life had been until then. I remembered how spoiled and selfish I was and how happy I was to give a dress or shoes to a friend who didn't have one. I was happy not giving, but feeling superior.

I remembered how I treated employees at home and in other places I went to.

To me, they were worthless and were there to serve me, that's all.

After much thought, I came to the conclusion that everything Joel and Luzia had said was right.

I cried, I cried a lot. I stayed there, in the same position for a long time. It was very difficult for me to make a decision because, in my entire life, I never had to make a decision on any subject. Everything I ever wanted, I had.

In the end, not really knowing what I was going to do, I got up and went to find Luzia. I went to my parents' room.

I opened the door and the room was in order, but empty. She wasn't there. I smiled, because while I was thinking, I didn't see time go by. – I left the room and went to look for Luzia throughout the house. I found her in the garden, watering the plants.

I approached her: – Luzia, I need to talk to you.

Just Beginning

She turned, looked at me, smiled and said: – You will have to wait until I finish watering the plants, or if you prefer, you can help me by watering that side. There is another hose.

I was indignant, Sueli, but I knew Luzia and I knew that she knew me and wanted me to understand that she wasn't different from me.

She was a maid, but also a human being. If she had done it another time, I don't even know what I would have done. But that day, I had thought a lot about what my life had been like and she knew it too.

I walked to the other side and grabbed the hose. I turned on the tap and began to water the plants, something that only Luzia did.

She loved that garden. Even though she wasn't looking at me, I felt like she was looking at me and smiling.

When we finished watering all the plants, she sat on a small bench that was there and, as she approached me, she asked me: – What do you want to talk to me about, Rosana?

– I also sat down, Sueli: – Regarding everything you said. You're right, I'm a very bad person, Luzia.

I thought I was superior to everyone, but I understood that it wasn't true.

I didn't say you were bad, did I?

No, you spoke clearly, but you hinted at it.

That was not what I said. I said you were out of your path and that when that happens, life takes care of putting everything in its place. I said you always had everything you wanted, so it never crossed your mind that you might get frustrated.

I've been thinking a lot. I tried to find excuses for my actions. I tried to blame my parents for never saying no and for

Just Beginning

letting me grow selfish and smug, but I couldn't. My parents gave me everything, I was the one who didn't know how to enjoy it. They raised me and Edu in the same way and my brother is completely different from me.

He isn't arrogant, he doesn't care about expensive clothes, on the contrary, he hates shopping.

He doesn't like to attend society or parties.

He has many friends of a different class than ours, who I have always criticized. Why is this happening, Luzia?

Because we are free spirits and with free will. Of course, family education is important.

It is in the family where we learn, in childhood, the principles of society, what is right and what is wrong, but as we grow up, we will strengthen these principles or modify them. We make our decisions, because everyone can and should choose the life they want to live. Edu is really different from you. He has other principles, but that doesn't mean he is better or worse. Most people go through difficult times of choice.

Many times, we get out of our path, but it's always time to go back.

Since it's up to us to choose the life we want to live here on Earth, that choice takes place before we are born.

We write our story.

What are you talking about, Luzia? Do we choose how to live? What madness is this?

She laughed and I looked at her without understanding.

She continued: – You, as you grew up, got involved with money and the power it provides.

By doing that, you strayed away from the path you chose before you were born. I know it's very difficult to understand what

Just Beginning

I am saying, but that is what happened. You never wanted to know about religion or God. You never cared about other people who didn't have as much money as you. Being rich was also your choice.

This always happens because after death, when we know what we did wrong, here on Earth, in the last incarnation, we almost always blame the life we had and ask for a new opportunity and a new incarnation with a life different from the previous one. I don't know what you did in the last incarnation, but I do know that you asked to be rich and to be able to use that money for your spiritual growth.

However, here on Earth with a human body, you forgot what you had promised and used that money to humiliate and buy people, straying out of your path. Every time you stray out of your path, friendly spirits take care of getting us back on path. This guy got in your way so you can think about everything you did and choose the path you want to follow. We are never alone, Rosana and we always have a new opportunity.

– The more she said, the less I understood. Sueli, it seemed like she was speaking a different language than me.

– It seemed that she understood what I was thinking and continued: – I know you don't understand what I'm saying, don't worry, because everything has its time. Now, the important thing is that you say what, after thinking so much, you decided.

I decided that I want to change. I want to see people as they are, regardless of skin color, profession or amount of money they have. I won't look for Joel anymore. I want to know more about this Doctrine that you spoke about. I really want to change!

I am happy with your decision and I thank God and the friendly spirits who helped you change your attitude.

Just Beginning

No matter how much I want to change, I know it won't be easy. I will need your help, Luzia. I don't even know where to begin.

– You can begin, using your money to go to the city that you like so much. Stay alone for a while and think about what you can do with your money. Regarding the Doctrine, no matter how much I talk, it will be very difficult to understand.

Then I'm going to give you some books to read. With them you will learn much more.

Start reading. However, if you don't want to or don't like it, you don't need to continue reading. You can give it back to me. I won't get mad.

I think it's a great idea, Luzia. I'm going to take a few days off and think a lot about my life and how I can change it. I will read too!

She smiled. We got up and went into the house, went to my room and started packing.

This is how I came here. I brought some books that she gave me and I read a lot. Through these books, I learned things that I had never thought of before. When I finished reading the books, I bought others. I felt that my soul needed knowledge.

I looked for a Spiritist House and began to attend and understood a lot of what had happened in my life.

So, I convinced my father to invest here in this cozy city. He accepted and began to build the hotel and the inn. – I came here with the intention of staying only a few days, but I am still here and I don't intend to return to my home, to that life. When you showed up that day, I saw you as a fighting girl with an immense desire to study and learn. I knew you needed help and that I could help. I don't regret that, Sueli.

– After all, I'm eating really well. You are a great chef.

Just Beginning

– Sueli stopped talking for a moment, then continued: – We continued living together for another six months, Julia.

Rosana told me about the Doctrine she followed and gave me some books to read.

When I finished reading, I understood a few things I had been through. I didn't know why Nilson appeared in my life, but I knew that during the time we were together, I learned a lot about love, trust, and disappointment, but I also learned that my life was just beginning and that I still had a lot to do. Live and learn.

I learned that some things can be changed, but others cannot. When what happens to us cannot be changed, we must believe in God and move on. I learned that our lives are made up of good and bad moments, but that they are only moments. The most important thing I learned is that we are never alone.

That we have friendly spirits on our side. I learned that they are ready to help us with whatever is allowed.

After that day, my friendship with Rosana increased a lot. We continued to live together.

She met Paulo, the son of a wealthy landowner, started dating, and in a short time they were married and are now very happy.

Of course, they invited me to their wedding and it was there where I met Eduardo.

– What, Sueli? Eduardo, brother of Rosana?

Sueli laughed and replied: – Yes, Julia. We met at the wedding and we're still together today, and, as you know, we're getting married soon. At Rosana's request, her father built the restaurant and left me in charge of the cooking and management. After getting married, Rosana went to the capital with Paulo. She has business there and Eduardo came here to take care of the hotel

Just Beginning

and the inn. As you can see, despite everything I went through, in the end, everything turned out fine.

– Now I remember something Rosana said when she found out that Eduardo and I were dating:

– Did you see how much you had to go through to find my brother and me in Paulo?

– Isn't God really wonderful?

– I could only smile and agree, Julia. She was right. She had come to this city, sad, desperate and thinking that it was all over, but she didn't know that she was actually only beginning.

– It's true, Sueli. After everything you've told me, I can only agree.

– As for work, are you still worried about going back, Julia?

– After everything that happened, do you think I can go back to work?

– Why not? You like what you do and the salary is very good. You will hardly find another job like that.

– Didn't you hear what I said Sueli?

– Of course, I did, but I still don't understand why you can't go back to work.

– Everything I told you happened during lunch and right at the restaurant, where almost all my co-workers were having lunch and who, until now, didn't know.

Everyone is laughing at me! How can I go back?

– By returning as if nothing had happened. After everything I've told you, do you still think you're the only woman who has stupidly dated a married man? I assure you that you're not the only one. Many have already done so and many others will.

– I can't face them...

Just Beginning

– Of course, you can. Tomorrow, go to work and when you arrive, say hello to everyone, smile like nothing happened. I assure you that even if they are thinking about something, they won't be able to talk to you.

– Even if they don't talk to me, they will surely think.

– So what? There, you are just an employee, no one has anything to do with your private life. Now I have to leave.

– I have a lot of work. Stay calm, try to stay calm. Surrender your life to the hands of God.

I learned that, at the time of despair, this is the only thing we can do. See you, Julia.

Júlia smiled and responded to the hand of Sueli, who, smiling, left the door. Julia saw her leaving, then went to her room, lay down, and thought about everything Sueli had told her.

Just Beginning

9.– Life begins again

Sueli waited and got into the elevator. When she reached the ground floor and the door opened, she found Anselmo waiting for the elevator.

As soon as she saw him, she said: – Anselmo, are you here?

– Hello Sueli. I need to speak to Julia, is she at home?

– Yes, she is. I just left her.

– Is she fine?

Sueli smiled: – It seems that way, but go there and confirm it.

– That is why I came here. I need to speak to her urgently.

He got into the elevator. On the street, Sueli thought: "Our life is really strange. What does he want here?"

Julia was in bed when she heard the doorbell. She thought: Who could it be? It can't be Sueli, she has keys.

She got up, went into the living room, opened the door, and when she saw Anselmo, she was surprised: – Anselmo! What are you doing here?

– We need to talk.

– We have nothing to talk about! After the embarrassment I went through today, there is no conversation that makes me forget

Just Beginning

everything you have done to me. You always said that you loved me, that you wanted me to stay by your side, even if you weren't going to marry me, but when your wife showed up, you just stood there and didn't defend me!

– I know you're annoyed and you're right, but I'm here to talk and I can't be in the hall. Let me in

– I want to apologize and make a very serious proposal.

Julia looked and only then realized that she was speaking loudly and that a neighbor could hear.

– She walked in and let him in.

– He entered and she showed him the sofa to sit on. Before sitting down, he tried to hug her, but she moved away, saying: – I don't want any hug. What happened today, I will never forget in my life!

– You're right, Julia. I confess that when Suzana appeared, I didn't know what to do.

– You know that, although I no longer love my wife, I never thought of leaving her because of my son.

However, things have changed. Today, after everything that happened, I came to the conclusion that it is you who I love and want to be with.

She looked suspiciously and asked: – What are you saying, Anselmo?

– What you heard. I have come to the conclusion that you are the woman I want to stay with for the rest of my life.

– When did you come to that conclusion?

– When I saw you after Suzana humiliated you among all those people.

– Suzana doesn't love me, she just thinks about her work and her promotion. She spends all the time humiliating me.

Just Beginning

– I can't take this anymore. I love my son and wanted to be by his side until he became a man, but, unfortunately, that won't be possible. I want to be happy and that happiness, I will only find it by your side, Julia.

– Are you telling the truth, Anselmo?

– Of course I am! I want to be with you, Julia! I'll settle my divorce, then we'll get married!

– She, not believing what she was hearing, began to cry.

He, who was sitting next to her, hugged her: – I don't know why you're crying, I hope you're happy.

– Of course, I'm happy, Anselmo! I thought I had lost you forever.

– You didn't lose me, Julia. There is one more thing. I received a proposal for a promotion and salary increase.

– What?

– It's true, but for that, I need to go to Recife and I want you to come with me. I know that the job won't be easy, but I also know that, with you by my side, everything will be fine. Will you go with me?

– I don't know if I can believe what's happening. It's wonderful! When we started dating, you always said that you would never leave your wife and son. Because you liked me so much, I accepted and resigned myself.

– I never imagined that one day I would be listening to what you are saying to me now.

– Are you sure you're telling the truth, Anselmo? For real, do you want to marry me?

– That's what I want the most! I know we will be very happy!

Just Beginning

– Have you talked to your wife after what happened at the restaurant?

– No, I'll do it tonight when I get home.

– What if she doesn't accept the divorce?

– She will accept. She knows our marriage ended a long time ago, Julia!

They kissed with affection and a lot of love.

Julia, although happy, was also worried.

– To accompany you, Anselmo, I will have to quit my job. I'll have no work!

– Don't worry about it. My salary will be enough to have a good life. You never have to go back to work.

– I didn't want to go back to the office anymore. I'm very embarrassed of what happened.

– You don't have to be embarrassed. You go back just to quit.

– Pack your things next week, we'll leave.

– Are you sure about that, Anselmo? I cannot be unemployed.

I am alone and I need to support myself.

– Of course, I am. Do as I say. Don't think of anything else, except that I chose you –. Julia, euphoric, said: – I'm going to resign right now.

– Not now! Today I want to stay, the rest of the afternoon, with you to love us like never before.

Go early tomorrow morning. Hugging each other, they went to the room.

It was almost eight when Anselmo left Julia's apartment. She went with him to the elevator.

Just Beginning

Before entering, he said: – Tomorrow, very early, go to the office, resign and wait until I return.

– I may not be able to come for four or five days. I need to prepare for the move.

– I will certainly have to attend many meetings to get to the northeast with everything well planned.

– Never forget that I love you and that we begin a new life with happiness.

– Well, I'll do what you said.

The elevator came, they kissed and he entered.

Julia entered the apartment happily and went to her room. She went to bed and remembered everything that had happened that afternoon.

Hours passed, but she couldn't sleep. She waited for Sueli to arrive so she could tell her about everything that had taken place.

When Sueli arrived it was past midnight and she was surprised to see the light on in Julia's room. She thought: she must have slept without turning off the light. I'll turn it off.

She was heading into the bedroom when Julia appeared in the doorway.

– Sueli, I'm glad you arrived!

– What happened, Julia? Why are you awake until this time?

– I couldn't sleep, I need to tell you everything that happened today after you left for work. Sueli smiled: – I think it all has to do with Anselmo. I found him when I was leaving the elevator.

– That's right, Sueli. He was here! I'll tell you everything that happened.

– I'm curious to know, but if you don't mind, I'd like to take a shower.

Just Beginning

You know the smell I have after spending a lot of time by the restaurant stove.

– Of course, I don't mind, but don't take too long.

Sueli went to the bedroom, then to the bathroom. Meanwhile, Julia went to make tea for them to drink together. At Julia's request, Sueli took a quick shower and, still wrapped in the towel, sat down and, while Julia served tea, said:

– Okay, Julia, you can start speaking.

Julia explained in detail everything that had happened and ended by saying:

– Can you believe that all this happened?

– That I am going to get married and move to Recife?

– I believe it and I hope, Julia, you are very happy. Didn't I say that everything that happens to us has a reason?

– And that in the end it is always right?

– You said that, but at that time, I confess that I didn't believe much. Now I am sure of that.

10.– Life begins again

– I need to ask only one question: will his wife accept the divorce?

– He said she will, because their marriage ended a long time ago.

– I hope it's true, Julia, and that you are really very happy. Now, shall we sleep?

– Tomorrow you must go and quit your job. Are you sure you want to do this?

– I'm sure, Sueli, it seems you don't believe everything Anselmo said.

– I swear I want to believe it, but you know how it is: the scalded cat escapes from the cold water, right? I don't want you to suffer.

– This time, you shouldn't worry. I won't suffer!

Anselmo told the truth, I saw it in his eyes.

– It's okay. Now I need to sleep. I'm very tired. Today, at the restaurant, it wasn't easy. Good night!

– Good night, Sueli!

Sueli smiled and went to her room. Already lying on her bed, she thought: My God! I know how much I suffered by believing a man. Please don't let Julia suffer in the same way...

Just Beginning
***

Anselmo was near his house and he thought: I need to get ready. Suzana must be very angry.

She will never forgive me. I knew it was going to happen one day, but even if it didn't, our marriage broke down a long time ago.

We haven't talked in a few years without fighting. It was partially good that it happened that way.

I was at a dilemma. I really want to grow professionally and this proposal shortens the way.

However, if Suzana didn't agree to go with me and I know it won't happen or it will happen, perhaps I wouldn't have the strength to abandon my son. I would probably decline the offer and go on with my life, just as it is, unhappy and frustrated. With the end of my marriage, I will take care of Julia. She is a good girl and she really likes me.

I feel like my life is changing, I need to keep up.

He looked at the clock on the dashboard of the car: it's almost nine, Suzana hasn't arrived yet. She doesn't arrive until ten. She always arrives tired and nervous. Since she's not going to dinner and, as I always do, I'll be watching TV.

Maybe she will ask me to leave today. I will go to a hotel until my transfer is complete. When everything is ready, Júlia and I will begin a new life, I hope with great happiness.

He went into the garage and was surprised: is Suzana's car here? Has she already arrived? She must be very angry. I need to prepare to face the beast.

He smiled, got out of the car, and went to the elevator.

Just Beginning

Fearful but prepared, he put the key in the door and opened it. As soon as the door opened, he stepped inside and looked around. It seemed like it was at peace. He walked into the dining room. As soon as he got to the room, he stopped and was puzzled. Every night, it was only when he arrived that the maid would prepare the table for him to have dinner.

She used to do that because, since he always had dinner alone, sometimes he didn't sit at the table. He used to take a plate and go sit in front of the television and while he had dinner he watched his favorite show.

But that night, something was happening. The table was not only prepared, but with flowers and lighted candles. What's going on? Why did Edit prepare the table and in this way?

He was standing, watching, when Suzana entered the room.

She walked up to him, hugged him and said: – It took you a long time to get here, Anselmo. He, perplexed by this reception, asked: – What is happening here, Suzana?

– Is it too much? I just told you that I prepared the food you like best. Do we have dinner together?

He, without understanding what was happening and without knowing what to do, broke away from the hug and went to the room. She, following him with her eyes, said: – While you shower, I will ask Edit to prepare dinner.

– When you come back, everything will be ready.

He entered the room. He took off his jacket and tossed it on the bed. He went into the bathroom and, while he was moistening his face, which was feeling very hot, he thought: What is happening here? Why is Suzana acting like this?

What is this reaction?

He turned on the shower and began to shower.

Just Beginning

He was there when Suzana entered the bathroom and asked him: – Can I shower with you?

He opened the shower door, poked his head suspiciously and asked: – What did you say?

– I want to shower with you. I don't understand the surprise, at the beginning of our marriage, we did it a lot.

– That was long ago, Suzana. We haven't seen each other in a long time, we're more distant, and we behave as if we were just friends. I don't understand why, just today, you are behaving like this.

– Because today I realized that I may lose you forever and I don't want that.

11. Unexpected Situation

Before he said anything, she undressed and got into the shower.

She showered in the same way as before. Anselmo didn't understand, but he didn't think much about it. He liked that and now he understood that he liked Suzana a lot.

They finished bathing, dressed in silence, and went to the dining room.

While eating dinner, Anselmo, still confused, asked: – What's going on here, Suzana?

– Why are you, after everything that happened, having this reaction? I confess that it is very strange.

– You're right to be confused. Today, when I saw you with that girl, I was very angry and did that crazy thing.

– That scene, but after I left there and, as I returned home, I thought a lot.

– I understood that if you looked for and found another woman, it was my fault.

– During all this time, I was only worried about my work and I put you aside.

– I just wanted more money and promotions. So I didn't think about you and what you were feeling.

Just Beginning

– Today, I remembered the moments when I humiliated you, not only here at home, but sometimes in front of our friends.

– I understood that without you none of this has a value. We are married, we have a son and I don't want my home destroyed or my son growing up without a father. Therefore, I want to apologize. We will forget everything that happened so far and begin our life again. I promise to be the wife you've always wanted.

Anselmo, amazed by what he was hearing, remained silent. As soon as she finished speaking, he got up and started to walk around the table,

She approached him and kissed him warmly.

As soon as she left, he said: – It can't be like this, Suzana. A lot has happened and we have to talk.

– It doesn't matter what happened. I know you think about that girl, but I'll make sure you forget about her.

– I love you, Anselmo.

– It's not about her, Suzana. We can't begin over again or continue because I'm moving. I'm going to Recife.

– What are you saying, Anselmo?

– I received a very good offer and I can't miss this opportunity.

I have the opportunity to make a lot of progress. Everything is fine and in a few days I will go to Recife.

– I'm going with you!

He got up and almost shouting, asked: – What? Will you quit your job to go with me?

– I will, Anselmo! I already said that I like you, that I don't want to destroy my home or our son to grow up without a father.

– For all of these reasons, I'll go wherever you go.

Just Beginning

– I can't believe what you're saying, Suzana. Today you managed to get to the place you always dreamed of.

– Still, are you willing to drop everything to follow me? Suzana was going to tell him that she had been fired, but decided to skip it.

She replied: – I said I'll go wherever you go. I'm serious.

Anselmo, I let my work be more important than our life. I don't want to do that anymore.

– Today, after what happened in the restaurant and now that you are telling me that you should go to Recife, tomorrow morning I will go to the company and resign.

– Wait, you can't do that, Suzana! I will have a salary increase, but even then, it won't be possible to keep the lifestyle that we have. I won't be able to pay for this apartment or your car!

– I don't care anymore, Anselmo. We will return the apartment and the car.

– In Recife, I can find a new job that won't take me so long. We can live in a smaller place and have a less expensive car. What I don't want or will not accept is being away from you. We'll live well. I'm sure of that.

– It can't be like that, Suzana! You are not thinking!

– Wait for me to go and see if it will work. Then when everything stabilizes, we can get back to this matter.

– There is nothing to think about. I have already decided. Whatever happens, we will continue together.

– At the beginning of our marriage, we had nothing and together we managed to get here.

– I know that if we stay together, we will be successful again. Anselmo was a bit dizzy with all that. It seemed to him that he was dreaming.

Just Beginning

He saw again the Suzana he had met and fallen in love with. During the married years everything had changed. She had become cold and selfish. She began to think only of herself.

With a haunting gaze, he thought: – What happened to make her change so much? Is it true that you are afraid of losing me? I don't know, but I can't believe it.

Suzana, without knowing what he was thinking, said: – Now let's go to bed. Tomorrow will be another day. They went to the room and, after loving each other, Suzana fell asleep.

Anselmo was thinking: I'm still dizzy with everything that happened. I never imagined that Suzana would have a reaction like that. What am I going to tell Julia?

My God, Julia! She's going to quit her job early tomorrow!

She can't do that, but I can't talk to her today! I can't call from home!

I need to get up very early and call her before I go to work. I need to tell her what happened.

I know she will suffer, but there is no other way. Suzana is right, we have a family, a son and, in fact, despite everything, I still like her very much.

He got up and went to the bathroom, moistened his face, looked at himself in the mirror and thought again: I never saw myself in a situation like this...

He went back to bed and, after a while, fell asleep.

Just Beginning

12.– Taking note

Julia woke up and looked at the clock on her nightstand.

It's still very early. I am so anxious that I couldn't sleep well and woke up several times.

Now, I feel like I won't be able to sleep again. I'm so happy! My life will change and something will happen that I never imagined would happen.

I like Anselmo very much, but he always made it clear that he would never leave his home and his son. Now everything has changed. She got up and went to the bathroom.

She turned on the shower, looked at her watch, and kept thinking: I need to get there early, pack my things, and tidy up my work. I will resign and prepare for the trip.

I feel that I will be happy with Anselmo, although I'll go to a distant place and with different customs from mine, but I will adapt. The important thing is that I will be by his side!

She showered, went back to her room, and looked at her watch again.

It's still very early. Why doesn't the hour pass? I can't stay here at home making noise. Sueli is sleeping. I think I'll go to the bakery for a coffee, go to the square and walk a bit. I plan to walk, I will relax.

Just Beginning

Then I'll come back and, if necessary, I'll take another shower. What happened at Anselmo's house?

What did his wife do? Did she kick him out of the house? Is he sleeping in a hotel? He knows he can't call here at night, because Sueli arrives late and needs to sleep. Well, it doesn't make sense wanting to guess what happened. He will tell me.

She put on comfortable clothes and went out. She got to the square and saw some people walking. Every time I went to work, I saw them walking, but I never had time to walk.

Many times, she felt jealous and, that day, she was able to fulfill her wish without worrying about the time. As people did, she began to walk and think about everything that was happening.

People walking greeted her and she greeted them too. She smiled and received smiles. After walking for more than half an hour, she decided to return home.

She entered in silence. She looked at the door to Sueli's room, which was still closed. She went into her room, took another shower, and dressed in work clothes. When she was ready, she took her bag and left.

Before leaving, she looked in the mirror in the room, smiled and thought; after what happened at the restaurant yesterday, I thought I wouldn't have the courage to go back to work, but today I'm going to go back and face everyone without worrying about what they're thinking. After all, it will be the last day that I go there and see those people. From now on, it will be just happiness.

She got off the bus that took her to work. She stopped right in front. She looked at the place where Anselmo was always waiting for her. He wasn't there. She didn't care.

He said that for a few days we wouldn't meet. After I quit, I'll go home and wait for him to call or show up.

Just Beginning

She walked into the office. Smiling, he greeted everyone. She didn't want to pay attention to the stares. She knew what they were thinking, but that didn't bother her now.

She looked at the door to her boss's office. It was open, which meant he was already there. She walked over and knocked lightly. He was sitting, looking at some papers, he looked up.

– Good morning. I need to talk with you.

– Good morning, Julia. Come in.

She came in and sat down. He looked at her and, in a strong voice, asked:

– What do you want to talk about, Julia?

– I'm here to resign.

He surprised: – What are you saying, Julia? resign, why? Don't say it's because of what happened at the restaurant!

– Did you hear about it?

– I was there, Julia. I'm not saying that I approve of that, but it's not reason for you to resign. Your private life has nothing to do with your job. You are a great employee.

– That's not the reason. I'm moving to Recife.

– To Recife? What are you going to do there?

– I'll begin my life over. I can no longer live here –. She said smiling.

– Why not? What do you know about Recife?

– Very little. In fact, what most people know. I have never been there

So, I think it will be a good opportunity to get to know its people and their customs.

– You must not be thinking straight, Julia. Don't act hastily.

Just Beginning

– You know that, although I really like your work, it is company policy not to rehire employees.

– So, if what you're looking for doesn't work, even if you come back, I won't be able to hire you again.

– I know, sir, but don't worry. It will work and I won't be back. My life is changing and I feel alive again.

– He smiled again.

– You have to give me some time so that I can put someone in your place.

– It isn't necessary. My work is up to date. Also, I have been working with Jorge for a long time and he will be able to handle all the work until you hire someone else. I can't wait. I need to move in a few days.

– In that case, I can only accept your request and wish you luck. I hope everything goes well in your life.

– Thanks, it will! I'm sure.

– When do you plan to leave the company?

– Now

– Now?

– Yes! I need to prepare my trip. Don't worry about my work, everything is in order.

– The person who will replace me will have no problem. Jorge, who has worked with me for a long time, knows everything. I promise, you won't have a problem.

He stood up and extended his hand and, smiling, said: – Good luck.

She shook the hand he extended to her and, also smiling, left the room, went to her desk, and began to put in order her personal things.

Just Beginning

Jorge, his coworker, was surprised: – What are you doing, Julia?

– Packing my things. I quit my job and I'm leaving.

– Leaving, why, where?

– I'm moving to Recife.

– You never said you were moving or that you had the intention of moving by the way.

She smiled: – I didn't even know it, but it's true, I'm leaving. My life has completely changed in a second.

– Does your decision have something to do with what happened yesterday at the restaurant?

– No! I can't deny that right after what happened, I wanted to disappear.

– Nobody knows what happened, but since you are my friend and know everything about my life, I will tell you what happened. She told him everything that had happened and what Anselmo had told her.

She ended by saying: – As you can see, I am changing my life for the better. In the end, it was good that I went through that embarrassment at the restaurant. I'll be fine, Jorge, and I'll be happy.

– According to everything you told me, he said all this before talking to his wife.

– What if she doesn't want him to leave and doesn't accept the separation? I am a man and, as a man, I know that many times, our feelings are left behind and we don't like conflict. I think you should wait for him to talk to his wife and then make such a extreme decision.

She began to laugh: – Don't worry. Anselmo is different; he knows very well what he wants out of life.

Just Beginning

It won't happen, but even if she doesn't want to separate, they won't get back together, no. He loves me!

He said it several times. He couldn't be lying, and I assure you that he was honest.

Also, even if that happens, it's too late. I quit and there is no turning back.

– All right, Julia. I know it's too late now. I sincerely hope you are right to do this and that you are happy. Have you already said goodbye to people here?

– You know that I am a bit shy and therefore I have a hard time making friends.

– Even so, I spoke with some people, but after everyone found out about my relationship with Anselmo, they ignored me. I didn't worry about that, because, in my own way, I was happy with him.

You were the only one who didn't change his attitude towards me.

People are extremely easy to judge. It's easier to criticize what others are doing than to look at their own belly button. And that's old, Julia. Jesus already spoke about that. Prejudices, as well as pride and power, are feelings that delay the spirit's journey.

– Spirit's journey. What are you talking about, Jorge?

– I follow a Doctrine that teaches us that each one of us is unique and is on a long journey towards perfection with its successes and defects. It also teaches that each of us has their own free will and is responsible for it.

– Yesterday I spoke with Sueli and she told me something about this Doctrine, but I didn't pay much attention to it.

Jorge smiled again: – It is always like that, Julia. People take time to believe in something.

Just Beginning

– I'm not one of those people. I never felt the need to follow any religion.

– I'm not talking about religion, Julia. I'm talking about a stronger force. The one we call God.

– I didn't understand. This force, this God isn't in the religions?

No, Julia. He is in each one of us. Religions serve to help us find that force, but even if we don't have religion, it will be there and by our side when it's time to find it or need it. God is the creator of all of us and it doesn't matter if we follow any religion or none.

He doesn't judge his children. He hopes that each one will find the way forward. That is why he gave us free will.

We all learned as children what is right and what is wrong.

We just have to try to live our lives the way we think is right.

– That depends, Jorge.

– Depends on what, Julia?

– Time goes by very fast and everything changes too, Jorge.

– Many things that were wrong yesterday, are no longer so today and others that were right are no longer so.

– You're right about that, time passes and things change.

– However, Julia, what changes are the laws of customs, but the morality of ethics, they never change no matter how much time passes and modernizes and, no matter how much people insist on ignoring them. From the beginning of humanity, killing and stealing, betraying and cheating, not to mention others, are unforgivable mistakes and will remain so. Despite the progress, material and scientific, there are minor forces that still dominate the human being. You said that when people heard that you were with Anselmo, they judged you and condemned you. Prejudice is not just about people's color or race. It is everywhere.

Just Beginning

It's present in the president of this company for feeling better than us, his employees. It's present in us too, for feeling better than those who work in a job below ours, such as janitors or cooks.

And It's present in them too for feeling better than those who don't have a job.

As you can see, in one way or another, we all have prejudices. The same is also true for power.

– Power exists, but it is in the hands of those who have a lot of money.

– You're wrong, Julia. Power is not only in the hands of those who have money.

– Any of us, at the first opportunity to use it, will do it very calmly.

– Power is in the hands of the car driver when he doesn't respect the pedestrian. It's in an employee, when he is behind the counter and he doesn't serve well someone who needs his help. It's with the head of a team department, when he doesn't respect his subordinates. It's with us when we don't treat people who work as domestic workers and who are in less condition than ours. And finally, among many others, it's in the hands of that politician who forgets that he was elected to create laws to help the population and only thinks of himself.

As you can see, the spirit has a long way to go to perfection. I haven't talked about pride yet, but that will be for next time.

– Now that I think about it, I think you're right, Jorge. I myself have been in power several times.

– I think that's part of being human, actually.

– I'll try to change my attitude. Now I understand people's prejudices against me.

Just Beginning

I am happy and as they say: half the world speaks ill of the other half. Julia said laughing.

Jorge also laughed: – Although I don't criticize you, don't forget that I always told you that getting involved with a married man could end badly. Didn't I?

– Actually. You got tired of telling me, but I was in love and I never paid attention. However, you were wrong, Jorge.

– My relationship with Anselmo worked. We are happy.

– I'm happy for you, Julia. I see that you are happy, and I hope it continues for a long time.

However, if something changes, never lose faith in a God who is a loving Father and who will always be ready to give us new opportunities. When you need the force I spoke of, I know you will find it.

Julia hugged her friend and said: – You are very serious today, Jorge. In my case, I don't think I need to look for that force anywhere. I'm happy and I intend to continue like this.

Jorge, responding to the hug, said: – Be happy, Julia. Remember that if you need me, I will always be here –. Releasing herself from the hug, she happily said: – Thank you, my friend. Even from afar I will send news.

– Thank you for helping me throughout the time we worked together. Now I need to go to the staff department.

– Then I'll buy some clothes for the trip.

– Godspeed, Julia.

Julia, smiling, went out the door.

While this was happening to Julia, Anselmo opened his eyes and looked at the clock on the nightstand.

He jumped: My God! It's almost ten o'clock! How did I sleep like this? Where is Suzana that didn't wake me up? He went to the

Just Beginning

bathroom to take a shower. Soon after, he got out of the bathroom, and to his surprise, there was a breakfast tray on the bed. Next to the bed, standing, was Suzana, who smiling said: – Good morning, my love.

– I was waiting for you to shower and come to have a coffee with me.

He almost shouted: – Why didn't you wake me up, Suzana? You know I need to get to the office early!

– No, you don't! After the night we spend, which can even be considered the first night of our honeymoon, you have the right to go later and have a romantic coffee with your little wife.

– I'm so happy for us and our change!

– I don't understand you, Suzana. What's going on?

– Nothing! I'm the one who doesn't understand your reaction. I know you think that I should be very angry and that I should want to get out of the house, but that's not what happened. I understood that it was my fault that you found another woman. I got away from you, I let my work take over my life and I don't want it to continue to happen. I love you; we have a son and a marriage that we must defend. Let's begin over, my love, and I promise that this time everything will be different. I am willing to do anything to maintain our marriage.

Anselmo, silent, returned to the bathroom. He looked at himself in the mirror and thought: Oh my God!

By this time, Julia must have resigned! What am I going to do? She can't be unemployed. No one in the world. I need to go now and try to stop her.

He came out of the bathroom and said: – I can't have coffee, Suzana. I'm late, I have to go now.

Just Beginning

– Of course, you can! Don't you go to the company just to prepare for the trip? I also need to prepare.

– We will reach an agreement and try to return the apartment and my car.

– What? Will you return the apartment and your car? You can't do that; you're going to lose a lot of money!

– That's what you heard. We only paid a few fees.

We still have a long time to finish the payments. I know I will lose a lot of money, but I will lose a lot more if I try to keep something that I can't afford. If we are going to live on your salary, we won't be able to afford these unnecessary luxuries.

– Unnecessary? These are the most important things to you, Suzana. You worked hard for them!

– True, but it was because of them that I almost lost you and my marriage. I said I would do it and I will, Anselmo.

– I will do everything possible so that us and our marriage don't end.

– This apartment and the car are just things, as long as we are alive.

– You're not thinking, Suzana. You're acting hastily.

– There is no need to do anything. I'm going to Recife next week. For the first few days I will stay in a hotel. – Then when I get settled, you will come. For now, stay in the apartment and with your car.

– While I'm gone, you can think well about what it means to change your life so radically.

– With my salary we can live well, but never as you always wanted. We will have a modest life.

– But we'll be together and that's all I want. Neither the car nor the apartment are ours, Anselmo!

Just Beginning

– We are paying, but by now they belong to the bank. Today, after going to work, I'll go to the bank to talk to the manager and see what needs to be done to return these products. As for you going alone, you won't!

– I will go with you and we will stay at the hotel, while you work, I will find a small apartment so that we can move. It has to be this way, Anselmo. Working like you do, you won't have time to search for an apartment with a rent that we can pay.

– I will do that. Don't worry, everything will be fine in the end.

He, without arguing and used to doing what Suzana wanted, sat down to drink coffee and thought: It seems that she really changed. Did she really find out that she loves me and wants to save our marriage?

It's hard to believe, but let's try. What am I going to do with Julia? She won't understand. I have no other way out, I can't see her, especially after I said I'd take her with me and that, probably by now, she must have already resigned.

I have no other way out. I told her I was going to leave for a few days. It will be long enough for me to go with Suzana and begin my life over again. Julia will have to stay here. I know she will suffer for some time, but she is a strong woman, a good professional. Soon she will forget me, find a job, and get on with her life.

Alzira who was there, next to Ciro, looked at him and said: – Again, Anselmo? Same mistake again... Ciro, sorry too, touched his arm and they both disappeared.

Anselmo left and Suzana returned to the room and went back to bed.

Just Beginning

13.– The story of Julia

When Júlia left the company, after going by the staff department, it was already time for lunch. She looked around to see if she could see Anselmo, but he wasn't there. She thought: – It's time for lunch. He must be having lunch. I'm going to the restaurant to see.

She walked into the restaurant, noticed some people were looking at her. But she didn't care.

She looked around the room: he's not here. He must be taking care of our trip. Before moving, he must have everything in order. I'm going home and I'm getting ready too.

She took the bus and went home. She entered slowly, trying to make as little noise as possible, since she knew that at that time, Sueli was sleeping.

She went directly to her room. She got in and closed the door, then lay down on the bed.

She didn't imagine it, but next to her, and also on the bed, Alzira sat on one side, and on the other, Ciro, who, at the same time, illuminated her with bright white lights. After a few minutes, Julia thought: Jorge said so much that it confused me.

I always knew that God existed, although I never took this matter very seriously. However, the way he said it makes me think more about it.

Just Beginning

She was thinking when she heard a light knock on the door.

– Come in, Sueli –. She said laughing. Sueli opened the door.

– Did I wake you up? I tried not to make noise.

– No, Julia. I was awake when you arrived. I was eager to know what you decided. Being here at this time, I can only deduce that you quit your job.

– Yes, I did. I am very excited about my trip and my new life. I'll finally be happy, Sueli!

– I wish for that to happen. I'm hungry and curious to know what happened. Did you have lunch?

– No.

– Then let's go to the kitchen. I'll make something to eat and we can talk.

When she got up, Julia said: I'm hungry, but even if I wasn't, I wouldn't miss a meal made by you for nothing in this world. Let's go.

In the kitchen, Sueli started cooking. Julia sat down and looked at her friend.

– How was everything, Julia?

– I really quit. I'll tell you how it went.

– Great, I'm curious how you acted.

Júlia told her all the conversation she had with her boss and ended by saying: – After talking with him and, before going to the personnel department, I said goodbye to my co-worker, Jorge. I was surprised to learn that he follows the same Doctrine as you.

– Really, Julia?

– Yes. I worked with him for so long and we never talked about religion. Today, I don't know why, he spoke about this Doctrine that he follows. Weird...

Just Beginning

– What's weird, Julia?

– You told me yesterday and today he did too. The two practically on the same day. Is it a coincidence?

– It isn't, Julia. Everything has its time and its hour.

– The time must have come for you to learn about this Doctrine.

– Now that I'm doing so well and I don't want to think about anything other than my happiness with Anselmo.

– Let's leave that for another day.

– Oh, it's fine. Tell me everything.

– I think I'm a special person, Sueli. Even though I grew up in an orphanage and didn't know my parents, I was always very happy. I was adopted by a family that, for a long time, gave me education and a lot of love.

– I didn't know you were adopted, Julia. You never talked about it.

– I never talk about it, because I try to forget about it myself. Unlike many children, I was fortunate to have been adopted by a family that gave me a lot of love.

– How was your adoption and what happened? If you want to tell me, I would like to know how your life has been so far.

Julia looked away, thinking. Then she said: – When I found myself among others, I realized that I lived next to children who, like me, had no parents. However, it only started to bother me when I saw that my friends were leaving with a family. For each one who left, I suffered a lot, because they were the only family I had.

– When I asked where they were going, someone replied that they had been adopted.

Just Beginning

– Later, I understood what it was like to be adopted. I learned that they went to live with parents and brothers and that they would never be separated again. I liked that idea, having a father and a mother and, who knows, brothers and sisters.

– It seemed to be a very good thing. Every time a couple came to the orphanage, I would do anything to be seen, but they never chose me.

– This separation from your friends must have been very sad.

– It was, but I was always sure that, one day, I would be chosen too. I never despaired, I just hoped.

– I used to think that I had a guardian angel by my side who helped me. Alzira looked at Ciro and they both smiled.

Julia continued: – Today I know that, since then, I have been very lucky. The orphanage was very good.

– The children had what they needed to grow up healthy: food, school and social education.

We just didn't have that hug, that motherly affection. It didn't bother us either, because we didn't know what it was like, we just imagined it.

– When did you leave that place?

– I was eleven years old and I was still waiting for the family that would take me, but, little by little, I had lost hope, because all the couples only wanted small children, preferably newborns.

– One Sunday, a couple entered the patio, where I and other girls played.

– The girls who played with me went to this couple. On other occasions, I would have gone to meet them so that they would notice me, but this time I preferred to continue playing, because I knew they wouldn't choose me.

Just Beginning

– The couple walked through the yard. I kept pretending to cook with plastic pots.

– The lady stopped in front of me: – Why are you playing alone, girl?

I was with some other girls, but they preferred to be next to you. They want to be adopted.

– You, don't you want that?

– I do, but I know it won't happen.

– Why are you saying that?

– All the people who come here, they only want small children. They don't want children of my age, no...

– Why do you think that happens?

– I don't know, but it's always like this.

– Well, I want the opposite. My husband and I want a child in our home, but we no longer have the patience to care for a small child. They demand a lot of work.

– I, who had my head down, looked up and looked into the eyes of that woman who seemed honest.

– She continued: – You look perfect to me. Do you want to try? You can go with us and if you want you can live with us forever.

– I couldn't believe it happened, Sueli.

– Just at the time I had already lost hope.

– Life is like this, Júlia, we are surprised every moment and most of the time, when we think that everything is lost, really, it is just beginning. What happened next, did you move in with them?

– Very shyly, I looked at her and replied: – I don't know. You are the one who knows.

Just Beginning

– So, I'm going to talk to Neide, the director of the orphanage and see what I need to do for you to live with me and my husband. Is it okay?

– I didn't answer Sueli. I just nodded saying yes. She went to meet her husband, who was surrounded by some children and they must have talked about me, because then he looked in my direction and smiled.

– The two of them hugged and left and I followed them with my eyes when they entered the office of the director of the orphanage.

– My heart was beating hard. Gloria, one of the girls who was my best friend, came over: – What did the lady say, Julia?

– I didn't quite understand it, but I think she wants to take me home.

– Are you leaving. Julia? – She asked almost crying. Also crying, I replied: – I don't know Gloria, but I really wanted to go home, have a father and a mother. It should be very good...

– Days passed, Sueli, and I spent most of the time looking at the front door to see if they would return, but for a long time they didn't return. I had already lost hope when one morning the director called me.

– I was in the classroom and without knowing what was happening, I accompanied the secretary.

– Upon entering the room, I was surprised and stopped at the door with no courage to enter. The couple was there.

– The director, seeing that I was standing there, said: – Come in, Julia. We need to talk.

– Shy and shaking a lot, I went in. The director pointed to a chair, I sat down.

Just Beginning

– Then, smiling, he said: – This couple wants to take you to live with them. Do you want that?

– I lowered my head, I didn't know what to say, Sueli. I really wanted to live in a house, but now that it was happening, I was very scared. I always lived in the orphanage, I didn't know what was going on outside. I didn't answer.

– He asked again: – Do you want to move in with them, Julia?

– I took courage: – I want to do it, but I'm afraid...

– The lady got up, took me by the hands and, looking into my eyes, asked: – Afraid of what, Julia?

– With my head down, I replied: – I don't know, I'm just afraid...

She held my chin and made me lift my head and still looking me in the eye, said: – Never lower your head or eyes when talking to someone. It's important that people can see your eyes, because it is through them that anyone can know when the truth is being told and what you really feel.

– I understand that you are afraid. The fear of the unknown affects us all. You have always lived here and are afraid of change. Let's do something, let's get out of here together, you, Altair , who is my husband, and I.

– You will stay in our house as long as you want. At any time, if you're not feeling well, just ask us to bring you back. We want to take you to our house so that you are happy and make us happy and that will only be possible if you are well.

– I looked at the director who, smiling, said: – As you can see Julia, you are not obliged to do what you don't want.

– I think that with Teca and Altair you have the opportunity to have a very good life, but you can come back at any time.

Just Beginning

– I will always be here, supporting you, the doors will be open. Will we try?

– I looked at her and her husband. They both smiled, they also smiled and nodded saying yes.

– Smiling, the lady extended the hand that I took.

– She, holding my hand tightly, said: – You still don't know my name, do you?

– I nodded, Sueli.

– My name is Tereza, but everyone calls me Teca.

– How do you want me to call you?

– However you wish, you must understand that you won't be forced to do what you don't want to do. Of course, this agreement doesn't apply to studying. There is no other way, you will have to study.

She said smiling and looking at her husband, she continued: – You, in addition to studying, will study a profession so that you can take care of your life. Do you want to try?

I nodded, accepting. Holding my hand, we left.

The director hugged me: – You will be happy, Julia. I'm sure of that.

I also smiled and we left.

– They seemed to be very nice people, Julia. Did your life work with them?

– You're right, Sueli. She and her husband surrounded me with great affection and were very important in my life.

When we got to the street, I saw a huge black car stopped in front of the door.

As soon as he saw us, a man in a uniform and a cap opened one of the doors of the car, where we entered.

Just Beginning

Teca made me sit by the window so I could see the landscape. For me, who only knew the orphanage, everything was wonderful. During the entire trip, I was silent, just watching myself and having fun.

I saw tall buildings that I had never seen. Cars of different colors passed us.

– It all seemed like a dream. After a while, the car entered a large street with trees on both sides and big and very beautiful houses. I watched, and I was ever more delighted.

A large door opened, the car drove through it and down a lane and stopped in front of a very wide and tall wooden door. The man in the cap got out and opened the door where he was standing. I got out and Teca and Altair got out after me.

Holding my hand, they made me enter the house. As soon as I walked in, I was excited with the size of the room. I've definitely never seen anything like it. A girl, dressed in white, approached and, smiling, extended her hand. Teca, also smiling, said: – This is Margarida, Julia. She will take care of you when I'm not at home.

I, a little dizzy and lost, Sueli, extended my hand.

– Welcome, Julia! You will be very happy here at home!

I was going to lower my head, as always, but when I remembered what Teca had said the day she met me, I raised my head, looked, and smiled. Teca noticed and smiled too. Then she said; – Let's go, Julia! Let's see the room I prepared for you!

We climbed the steps of a very high staircase. In the upper part, there was a free space with a sofa, an armchair and a beautiful image on one of the walls. Everything, for me, continued as if it were a dream.

I could never imagine there was a house like this.

We entered a corridor and stopped in front of a white door.

Just Beginning

Teca opened the door. I walked in and, as soon as I saw the room, I stopped without being able to breathe or say anything.

– Come in, Julia! This is your room.

– I saw it, but I didn't believe her, Sueli. The room was huge. In the center, there was a bed with a pink bedspread, the color I liked best. Two windows with curtains also pink, only in a darker shade. A white closet.

In one corner, a small chest with many toys and some dolls scattered on the bed.

– Did you like the room, Julia?

I didn't know how to answer. My mouth went dry and my heart raced.

Teca smiled and asked again: – Did you like your room, Julia?

– Am I going to sleep here alone?

She laughed and Margarida, too : – Yes, Julia. I prepared this room for you.

– It is very large! I've never slept alone, especially in such a large room. At the orphanage, we all sleep together.

– I don't know if I'll be able to sleep, here, alone. I think I will be afraid.

– Teca hugged me: – Get used to it, Julia. Besides, you will not be alone.

– All these dolls will be here to accompany you.

– Julia! What a good woman, right?

– It's true, Sueli. She was wonderful! The first few nights, before I fell asleep, she and Altair would come to my room, tell a story, kiss me, and leave. The first nights that I was scared, I cried and they came back to comfort me. Little by little, I got used to it. Fifteen days later, they invited the whole family to a party, where

Just Beginning

they introduced me as a daughter. I was really living a dream life. I started attending a school, totally different from the orphanage. Jonás, the driver of the house, would take me in that black car and pick me up.

I had some difficulty to adapt, but soon I was playing with the other girls.

Although I had already thought about what a mother, a family would be like, I never got close to what I was experiencing.

I was happy.

– They were very rich, weren't they, Julia?

– Yes, very rich, Sueli. At the time I didn't know and wasn't interested in it.

Later, I learned that he owned a bank. He traveled a lot, but Teca was always by my side.

We went to the stores, where she bought me clothes and shoes. There were so many dresses in my closet that I couldn't even wear them.

– I don't understand anything, Julia.

– What? Sueli

– Having been raised this way and attending a good school, how are you alone today and always say that you have no family? I can't understand...

Júlia, with a sad smile, replied: – Today, as an adult, I learned to respect that old saying: there is no good that always lasts, nor bad that doesn't end.

– What happened, Julia?

– Time passed, Sueli. Little by little, I forgot my life in the orphanage and the friends I left there.

– They treated me like a princess.

Just Beginning

– Both Teca and Altair have always treated me like a daughter, but their family didn't think the same.

– At that time, I thought that everything was fine and that everyone loved me, but the reality was different.

– Why do you say that, Julia?

Julia didn't reply. She kept her eyes on the horizon. Sueli insisted: – Keep telling me, Julia!

– Excuse me, Sueli. I was remembering how it all happened.

– I'm going to continue! That year, we vacationed in Rome. I visited the Vatican, the Colosseum and many places that I didn't even know existed.

We went to the catacombs from the time of Christ. One night, before I went to sleep, as always, Teca came to my room.

She sat down in bed and said: – Julia, people are very bad, so I don't want you to talk to anyone about your childhood. No one needs to know that you were raised in an orphanage. Always remember that you are our daughter and that we love you very much.

I smiled; I didn't quite understand what she meant. After her kiss, I fell asleep. As always, time passed.

I was with them for a little over a year and I was still happy.

I studied a lot because I wanted my parents to be proud of me. One day, I was at school, when two girls approached. From their faces and smiles, I could tell they were up to something.

One of them asked: – Are you an orphan?

At that moment, I remembered that Teca had talked about it. I replied: – No! Why do you ask that?

– You are an orphan, yes!

– She spoke aloud, with a smile that made me feel very bad, Sueli.

Just Beginning

I looked around and realized that all the other girls were looking at me and laughing.

I tried to get out of there, but they wouldn't let me.

– The girl continued speaking aloud: – You're an orphan, yes! I heard my mother talking to your Aunt Rosa!

– Aunt Rosa? – I asked in amazement.

– Yes, she was at home talking to my mother and I listened.

– Aunt Rosa, Sueli, was the wife of Altair's brother who was a partner in the bank.

– Without noticing my surprise, the girl continued: – You are poor and you never had a mother or father! It's a shame that if it weren't for Mrs. Teca, you would still be living in the orphanage today!

– You live a life full of lies! I heard my mom say that!

– When I saw that everyone was laughing, I left there and ran to the classroom. I wanted to leave, but Jonas would only come to pick me up when school was over and I didn't know how to leave school on my own. For the rest of the class, I noticed that they were still talking, looking at me, and laughing. Finally, when the classes ended , I took my things, got up and, with my head down, as I hadn't done since that day at the orphanage, when Teca forced me to lift my head, I left as soon as possible. As I was walking, the girls chased me and said many things to me.

They said that I was poor, poor and that even my mother hadn't loved me. That I was worth nothing.

That those who adopted me didn't know who I was. I walked out of the school gate and looked at the place where Jonas always waited for me.

I ran to the car door that he opened. I got in and, still with my head down, sat on the corner of the seat.

Just Beginning

He was surprised, but quiet, he got in the car, started the engine and got out. For a moment, he drove in silence.

I didn't know why my head was down, but I could feel him looking at me in the rear view mirror.

– Some time later, he asked: – What happened, Julia?

– Nothing!

– Nothing? You look weird.

– I'm the same as always. Nothing happened.

– I don't think so? Every time you get in the car, you don't stop talking for a minute. You talk so much that sometimes I had to ask you to shut up.

I never saw you like this, only in the early days when I brought you to school. What happened, Julia?

You know that I am your friend and that you can therefore trust me.

– I couldn't take it anymore, Sueli and, crying, I told him everything that had happened. When I finished speaking, he, looking through the rear–view mirror, said: – None of this is a reason for you to cry, and not even stay as you are.

Still with my head down, I said: – How not, Jonas? That girl is right. I am nobody!

– I have no family or anyone! Although I live this life of wealth, I have nothing... nothing...

– Stop it, Julia! You have everything to be happy! Your parents love you!

– But the girl said many things and they all began to laugh at me...

– It doesn't matter what that girl said or that everyone laughed, you are a wonderful girl and much love by your parents and all the employees of the house.

Just Beginning

– I don't want to go back to school...

– Why?

– I am ashamed...

– Don't be ashamed of anything! You will go back to school, raise your head and face them all. Let them talk, Julia.

– Don't listen to bad people. Talk to your mother.

– No! I won't talk to Teca! She will argue with me!

– Argue, why, Julia? She loves you!

– He was right, Julia.

– Now I know, Sueli, but we must not forget that at that time, I was just over ten years old.

– I was a teenager and we know that at that age anything becomes a great drama.

Sueli started to laugh: – It's true, Julia! This age is really difficult. I remember crying about something and thinking the world would end. But what happened next? Did you talk to your mother?

– No. We got home. He left. I went straight to my room and there I cried a lot as I had never cried.

Just that day I thought of my real mother. Why had she abandoned me? I don't think she really liked me. – That girl was definitely right, I was worthless. I stayed there for a long time, unable to stop crying. – I was like that, when the door to my room opened and Teca entered through it. Silently, she came over and sat next to me on my bed. She was silent for a moment, then she said: – Why are you crying, Julia?

– For nothing...

– There must be a reason. What happened at school?

Just Beginning

I was silent, Sueli. She started running a hand over my hair. I couldn't resist and told her everything that had happened.

She listened carefully. When I stopped talking, she, smiling, raised my chin and looked me in the eye.

– Didn't I tell you never to lower your head and eyes?

– But that girl talked and the others laughed...

– Then I'll talk to Rosa. Now, I need to tell you a story. Do you want to hear it?

– I do.

– All right, come here.

– I leaned against her chest and she began to say: – There was a girl who was very happy.

She had no brother or sisters, but still, she played, ran and always had someone by her side to prevent her from getting hurt. Her parents were very wealthy, so she never missed anything. She grew up to be a beautiful girl.

One night, with her family, she went to a party. She met a boy who was the son of a one of her father' friends.

That night they danced, talked and became friends.

From that day on, they never stayed apart and ended up getting married. That girl who had always had everything in life, now, was completely happy. That girl, Julia, was me. I married Altair, whom I loved.

There was a beautiful house and a greenhouse where there were many orchids that I took very loving care of.

For some time, I didn't worry about anything other than living that wonderful life.

Altair's father died, so he and Roberto, his only brother, needed to be prepared to take care of their business.

Just Beginning

So, he worked hard and was hardly ever home. Little by little I began to feel very lonely.

I began to feel that my house was beautiful and too big for me. During the day, while Altair was working, I wandered around the house, through the garden. I took care of the plants, especially the orchids, which I loved, but still, I felt alone. I decided that I would talk to Altair. I thought it was time to have a child.

I thought that with a child at home, I would have a lot to do and wouldn't have time to feel alone.

At first, he didn't agree, because he wanted to participate in the growth of the child and, at that moment, that would be impossible. However, at my insistence, he agreed. He likes me very much and would do anything to make me happy. After a while, I was expecting a child. You can't imagine how happy I and the whole family were. However, it was short–lived. Soon after, I lost the baby. I consulted a doctor and he said that after seeing the tests, I could hardly get pregnant again. That news made that girl who had always had everything and had always been happy, become a sad person. I was always crying

Although Altair did his best to make me go back to the way I was before, nothing made me smile again.

Over time, it got worse. Altair was desperate.

I didn't know what else to do. Neide, who was my friend for a long time, not knowing what was happening and not knowing how to explain the reason, felt an immense desire to see me again. We haven't seen each other in a long time.

One night, accompanied by her husband, she decided to visit us. She called to see if we were home.

Although Altair didn't want to see anyone, he was happy and said that he was expecting them.

Just Beginning

Even without feeling like it, I managed to wait for my friend. When I looked in the mirror, I noticed that my eyes were deep, red and with dark circles. I didn't look like the same girl he had met.

As soon as they arrived, Neide noticed my change, but didn't comment on anything. Altair led them into the living room. I, quietly, just accompanied them. They sat down and Altair asked them if they wanted something to drink, they said no, just coffee. The atmosphere was heavy. Altair asked the maid to bring coffee for everyone.

For a while, there was only silence. Nobody knew what to say.

Unable to imagine, Alzira and Ciro were there, listening to Teca tell her story. They smiled

I was listening to Teca, Sueli, and I didn't understand why she was telling me that story.

I was unhappy and didn't want to know anything about a girl who had everything and who, as an adult, was unhappy.

It seems that she noticed it, smiled and continued speaking.

Neide, not knowing what to say, looked at me and asked: – Are you sick, Teca?

I started crying without being able to stop. The shame was total.

Altair hugged me, saying: – I'm sorry. She has been like this since she lost the baby.

– Neide stood up: – Did you lose a baby, Teca? I didn't know...

– I did and the worst thing is that the doctor said I can't have another one.

Just Beginning

– It was everything I wanted. I'm desperate. It was all over for me...

– Over? What is she saying? You have it all. A beautiful home, money to buy whatever you want, and a husband who loves you! How can you say it's over?

– It's true. I've always had everything; I just can't have a child. I would trade everything I have to have a child here at home.

– To be able to give my child all my love and affection.

– Why don't you do that?

– Do what?

– Have a child here at your house. Give a child all the care, love and everything a child needs to grow up healthy?

– Didn't you hear me say that I won't be able to have children, Neide?

– You can't have yours, but you can adopt as many as you want.

– Adopt?

– Why not, Teca? I have been working in an orphanage for a long time, we have children of all ages who need everything you have to give. Why don't you go there and pick one? Then later, who knows, you can choose other children. You can fill this house with smiles and mess!

– I can't do that, Neide!

– Why? Would you rather continue as you are now? Looking horrible and fatal?

– The child will never be my real daughter!

– Of course she will! After some time, you will forget that she has been adopted. Like I said, I've been working on this for a long time and I've seen a lot happen. If you wish, I can show you many letters from parents and children who they have adopted and they are happy.

– Altair was excited: – Teca! We can try! I can't bear to see you like this anymore.

– How to try, Altair? If we take a child home and we don't get used to her or we don't like her, we can never send her back.

– Neide interfered: – Who told you that? This is not how it works. The child you choose will come here.

She will stay for a while and she will only be adopted when she want it and all the paperwork will be done and will take some time.

If, for some reason, you don't want to keep her, you can talk to the judge and he will understand.

The child will return to the orphanage and wait for another family.

That is cruel to the child...

Neide began to laugh at Julia, and said: – It would be cruel if it happened, but it's very difficult for it to happen.

No couple returns children. At least, at the orphanage where I work, it has never happened.

In general, children are very young when adopted and all their first experiences are followed by parents who, over time, fall in love and forget that they're not their real children.

– I don't know.

Altair almost shouted and said excitedly, of course you know, Teca! Neide, when can we visit your orphanage to meet the children?

Neide looked at me and said: – I didn't know why I was thinking about you all day, Teca.

Just Beginning

I was surprised because even though we have been friends for so long, knowing that you were married and well, I never cared about your situation.

Today, curiously, you haven't left my mind.

If I believed in these things, I'd say I was sent here.

– Is that what happened? Did God send you to help me?

– I don't know, but what is important is that you need to get out of this apathy, this depression.

– Do you really think it will work, Neide?

– Of course it will, Teca! Like I said, there are children of all ages there. You can choose a newborn.

I wasn't sure, Julia, but seeing Altair's animation, I said, Okay. Let's do that.

– The child we are going to choose must have our features. I don't want people to comment.

– You shouldn't worry about that, Teca. We have children of all ages and races there. You can choose the one you want.

– I know that any child you choose will be very happy in this house.

– Okay. Let's choose a baby. I want to raise her with great affection.

– We scheduled for the next day, Julia. I confess I was a little scared, but still, to please Altair, I went.

When we arrived, Neide took us to the nursery. Wonderful babies were there.

I looked one by one, but was attracted to none. I really didn't want to adopt a child, I wanted one that was mine.

When I couldn't make up my mind, Neide said: – These are the babies we have, it seems that none of them interested you, Teca.

Just Beginning

That's not all, Neide, I just wanted to have a little more time to think about it.

These babies are so beautiful, Teca! Let's choose one of them!

I know that, in time, we will love her as if she were ours...

When I heard what Altair said, I felt a tightness in my heart. He was excited and wanted a son very much.

Before saying anything, he kept talking.

If we adopt a baby, we can monitor her growth.

We will see when she starts walking and say the first words.

Let's choose one, Teca...

Neide, realizing that I wasn't making up my mind, said, It doesn't have to be today, Altair. She can think calmly.

The children who are here will stay for a long time, and almost every day more children will come. Let's go to the yard.

There are older children.

– We don't want older children. We want to raise and educate the child in our own way.

– Okay, I won't interfere with your will, Teca. We can save it for another day.

– I confess that, intimately, I was happy, Julia. I didn't want a child that wasn't mine.

– Neide was going to accompany us to the exit, but first, she opened a door that led to the courtyard. I saw children playing, running.

They seemed happy. As soon as we entered the courtyard, many of them came over. Some took us by the hands.

I looked at all of them, but I wasn't interested in any of them. We were leaving when I saw a girl who didn't come to greet us. I

Just Beginning

walked over to her and as soon as I got closer and looked into her eyes, I felt an inexplicable happiness, it seemed like I had known that girl for a long time.

– Did you feel that when you saw me?

– Yeah. So, I decided to try spending time with you to see if we could get used to each other.

– Altair and Neide found my choice strange but respected my will. The rest you already know.

– You came here and since then I have been the happiest woman in the world.

– But didn't you want a baby?

– I did, but I was wrong. A baby would be a lot of work and you, on the contrary, became my companion.

– We walk and go out to buy clothes.

– You will grow up, you will study and on your wedding day I will be very happy. When you give me a grandson, my happiness will be complete. – Thank you, Julia, for agreeing to be my daughter.

– Are you really happy?

– Yes Julia. Therefore, when someone says that you're not our daughter, that you are worthless, raise your head and say with a strong voice.

– I wasn't adopted, my mother didn't adopt me! She chose me and I saved her life!

– She hugged and kissed me several times, Sueli. Hugging each other, we left the room, and when Altair arrived, we had dinner and went to watch a program that was playing on television. From that day on, I never worried about being adopted again. I was happy and knew that Altair and Teca were too. They were my parents and I loved them very much.

Just Beginning

– After everything you just told me, Julia, I don't understand how you can say that you are alone in the world, that you have no one. These people seemed wonderful to me.

– They were the best people I ever met.

– But, what happened, did they die?

– A tear formed in Julia's eyes. Her gaze was lost, and Sueli could see the great suffering her friend was going through. Then she was silent. After a while, Julia replied: – Yes, Sueli. They died...

– How, Julia?

– From that day on, I went back to school and met the same girls. They tried to humiliate me again.

– I did what Teca said and they never said those horrible things again.

– Over time, they even became my friends. A month after that day, when I returned from school, I realized that Teca was different.

– As soon as I arrived, she hugged me and said: – Julia, my mother is very ill. I need to visit her

Since she lives in another city that is four hours from here and you are at school, you won't be able to accompany us.

Altair and I will go there, stay for a few days, and then come back. You'll be fine with Margarida.

It will be only a few days, but I promise you that as soon as we return, we will take you for a walk and, at the end of the year, we will make an unforgettable trip.

– After saying that, Sueli, she hugged me and I was calm. The next day, in the morning, before going to school, she came back to my room and said: – It will only be for a few days, Julia. I know I don't have to say it, but be nice.

– I will be good.

Just Beginning

– When I came back from school, they weren't home anymore. They called me every night to say good night.

– The third night, she called again and said: – Julia, unfortunately my mother passed away.

– I'm alone in the world, like you. I'm suffering for the loss of my mother. But she was suffering a lot.

It was the better for her. Despite my suffering, I need to do what my mother taught me.

– She always said that, whatever happens, life must go on and that death is only one for a long time.

– I can only pray for her. We will be back early tomorrow. When you get home from school, we'll be home and talk better.

– I was sad because my grandmother died, but happy because they would return, Sueli. Well, even though I was fine with Margarida, I missed them. The next morning, I woke up excited and went to school.

When Jonas came looking for me, I realized that he was strange. He didn't joke as usual and he only spoke a little, he only answered what was asked.

When we got closer to our house, I saw that there were many cars. I was surprised, because that wasn't normal.

Altair and Teca rarely received many visitors. As soon as I entered, Aunt Rosa ran to me and, crying, hugged me:

– Poor thing, what will become of you now?

– I didn't understand what she meant, Sueli and I asked her: – What happened? Where are Teca and Altair?

– She, not caring that I was just a girl, said: – They died in a car accident when they returned. A truck lost its steering and hit their car and they didn't survive.

Just Beginning

– Whoa! How sad, Julia! They were such good people that they shouldn't have died that way.

– I think so too, but it happened, Sueli. Desperate, I ran to my room and cried for hours without being able to stop.

– It was the people who, in such a short time, gave me the love I never had. I was happy and so were they.

– Why did that happen? Why did God allow that to happen? I got tired of asking these questions, but there was no answer.

– I wonder how you must have felt. It must have been a very painful time.

– The worst thing in my life, Sueli. I felt like my world had collapsed and that it was over for me.

– I also wanted to die. Later they took me to the place where they were.

– There were two coffins that I will never forget. inside them were Teca and Altair.

– I looked at them and it seemed like they were sleeping. They were beautiful, surrounded by flowers. I was there for a while, until Jonás took me home. On the way, I said – Jonás, why did they die?

– I don't know. We all have a day and a suitable time to die, Julia. Their time had come!

– It's not okay, Jonas ! They were wonderful. I've never met people as good as them...

– Maybe that's why they died. They say this world is not for the good ones.

– Now, you need to continue your life.

– Study, graduate and, one day, have your own family.

– I don't know if I want a family. Will they die too?

Just Beginning

He smiled and said, No, Julia, I don't think so. Life is not just about sadness. There are very good moments, you'll see.

– That man was also very good, right, Julia?

– Yes, he was, Sueli. I don't know what would have happened to me that day if I hadn't had him and Margarida by my side.

– I think they were angels that God put in my life to help me.

– What happened next, Julia?

– A few days passed and Aunt Rosa came to the house. Her face was different. With a serious face, she said, Julia! Pack a suitcase!

– I looked at Margarida who, by her expression, I realized that just as me she didn't understand what was happening. Aunt Rosa, still with the same expression, said: – What are you waiting for, girl? I don't have all day!

– Why do I need to pack a suitcase?

– Because you're leaving this house.

– Margarida stood in front of me.

– What are you saying? She can't leave, she was adopted!

– She wasn't adopted yet! The papers are not ready yet.

– She has no right. You are going back to that place that you should never have left. With the death of both, my husband is the only heir. I will move to this house, which I always wanted and I want this girl away from here!

– It's not this girl! She has a name! Julia is her name!

– I know her name, but I don't care. She's still nobody to me! Enough arguing, pack your suitcase.

– Jonas is out there waiting to take you!

Just Beginning

– You can't do that! Mrs. Teca and Mr. Altair adored her! She was everything to them!

– They would never accept that!

– She, with a malicious smile, Sueli, said: – She was everything for them, but for me she is worthless!

– She is just a girl that I don't want in my house, much less in my family! For the last time, pack her suitcase or she will go with what she came. Nothing!

– You can't do that!

– I can! So, I am here ordering you to prepare a suitcase with few things, because, at the place where she goes and that she should never have left, she won't need much.

– As for you, girl, if you want, you can stay here taking care of my daughter. She is the same age as that girl.

– Margarida, unable to hide the hatred she felt, Sueli, she almost shouts: – I would never work for someone like you! Come on Julia, pack your suitcase and God have mercy on this woman!

– Accompanied by Aunt Rosa, Margarida and I went to my room. There, Aunt Rosa gave her a small suitcase and didn't allow me to choose anything. With the same sarcasm, she said: take only a few dresses and underwear.

– It's a pity that Teca has thrown away the clothes you came here with, because if she hadn't, you would have left only with them.

– What a horrible woman, Julia!

– It's true, Sueli, but I try not to remember it.

– Did you hear anything else about her?

– No. She must have moved into Teca's house, who she always envied, and should be happy.

Just Beginning

– You do well not to remember her, Julia. She, one way or another, will pay for the evil she did.

– I never worried about that. I hardly ever think about it, and when that happens, I try to stop thinking.

– She is proud, selfish and envious, therefore unhappy.

– Aren't you really mad, Julia?

– No, Sueli. Not even on that day when I had to go back to the orphanage. I was sad for the loss of Teca and Altair, but I wasn't mad at her.

– It can't be true! Anyone would be very angry, Julia! At least that day!

– After all, she took you out of that beautiful house and a life of wealth and brought you back to a life of poverty!

– That day and, even today, when I remember that, the only feeling I had and still have is sadness for having lost the two people who really loved me.

– I'm sorry, Julia.

– I was sorry too, Sueli, but as Teca said the day her mother died, life needs to go on and, because of that, it's always beginning.

– You're very good, Julia. I would hate her to this day.

Julia smiled and was silent. Sueli asked: – How was your return to the orphanage?

– Accompanied by Margarida, I went to the car where Jonás was waiting for us. I was dejected and sad. Crying, I got in the car.

Margarida sat next to me. During the trip, we were silent for a while.

Then Jonas said, I'm sorry about what happened, Julia. They were wonderful people, I also feel like you have to go back to the orphanage.

Just Beginning

If I could I would take you to my house, but I can't.

Mrs. Rosa notified the judge that you would return and, if I don't take you, I will be considered a kidnapper.

If I had money, I could try to adopt you, but I don't. I have a big family, I have three children and my salary isn't very high. I'm thinking of changing jobs. I won't be able to work for that woman.

Therefore, no judge would allow me to adopt you.

– Margarida said almost the same thing, Sueli. I knew they were being honest, but they were simple people living off their wages.

– Besides, I didn't want to hear anything. I just wanted to think about Teca and Altair, how good they were and how much they liked me. When we arrived at the orphanage, Mrs. Neide, the director, met us at the door.

– She had a bad expression. After hugging us, she said: – Welcome, Julia. We will come in.

– We went into a room, Sueli, and after sitting down, she looked at Jonás and Margarida: – I heard that you always treated Julia very well. I can only thank you. Now you can go. She will be alright.

– Margarida, crying, asked: – Can we visit her?

– Of course. Whenever you want. She will be here and, God willing, it will be for a little while.

– I'll find another family for her to be adopted.

– When I heard that, I yelled: – I don't want to go to another house! I want to stay here forever!

– Mrs. Neide also got up and hugged me and said; – You are very nervous, Julia. You are not thinking clearly.

Just Beginning

– Say goodbye to Jonás and Margarida and enter. Your friends are waiting for you.

– Still crying, I hugged them both and went inside. In the yard, several children ran up to me and hugged me too.

– I was stunned, I felt like I was in another world. I hugged them all, but what I really wanted was to be alone.

– I went to the room where I used to sleep before, lay down on the bed and cried. I cried a lot until I fell asleep.

– That night I had a strange dream that made me accept the loss of Teca and Altair more easily...

– What dream?

– I don't remember very well. It was a long time ago. I just remember that I was in a beautiful place.

It had many flowers and a lake with crystal clear water. I was sitting on the grass by the lake with a woman and a man. – They smiled at me. The lady said: We are and will always be by your side. Today, you went through another stage of your rescue. We are proud.

Others will come, but never lose faith. God is our Father and never abandons us. In the morning, you will not remember this dream. – You'll only remember it when it's important for you to have courage and continue your journey and end with praise.

We will support you. You will get up and go on with your life. You still have a lot to do.

– The next day, did you remember the dream, Julia?

– No! I'm just remembering now! Why? Why just now, Sueli?

– I don't know! It must be because you are remembering everything that happened.

– It must be, really.

Just Beginning

– Well, let that dream go. How was your life at the orphanage?

– The next day, when I woke up, I was fine. That immense pain that I felt was gone.

I could only remember Altair and Teca in the good times we had.

And she told me: – Life needs to go on. Death is only one, bye, Julia.

– Do you remember that?

– Yes, Sueli, and that thought made me feel good. I knew that someday, somewhere I would find them.

So, thinking, after breakfast, I went to the principal's office.

As soon as I entered, Mrs. Neide, with a smile, asked: – Julia. How are you?

I'm fine, Mrs. Neide.

– Sit down, Julia.

After I sat down, she said: – Teca and Altair were my friends and I'm sorry for what happened.

– I know the love they felt for you. Unfortunately, her family didn't consider this feeling.

But don't worry, I'll find another family, another home so you can get on with your life.

– I've been thinking too, Mrs. Neide. I don't want to go to another house or another family.

I grew up here, I got used to it and it always felt great. I don't want to get attached to anyone else.

I want to stay here forever.

Mrs. Neide smiled: – You can't stay here forever, Julia. By law, you can only stay until you are eighteen.

Just Beginning

– It's okay. When the time comes, I will go, but for now I want to stay here. So, I don't want you to worry about finding another house for me.

– Meanwhile, we should wait for time to pass. It is the best medicine that can exist.

– While we wait, I will enroll you in that nearby public school that you attended and in a typing school so that, when the time comes to leave, you will have a way to survive.

– Thank you, Mrs. Neide.

She smiled and I left the room.

– Did you stay until you were eighteen, Julia?

– When I was eighteen, she called me into her office.

As soon as I walked in, she said, well, Julia, next month, you'll be eighteen, so you can't stay here as an intern. I've been thinking of a way to keep you here so you can finish your secretarial course.

– The only way is that you start working here as my secretary. What do you think?

I couldn't help it, Sueli. I got up, walked around the table and hugged her.

– Thank you, Mrs. Neide!

– I'm curious, Julia...

– About what Sueli?

– You never wanted to know who your real parents were?

– Before meeting Teca and Altair, I knew there was a family, a father and a mother, but I wasn't sure who they were.

After them, I wanted to meet my parents to know why they abandoned me.

Just Beginning

All I knew was that my mother's name was Jandira dos Santos and that my father was unknown.

That bothered me. I didn't understand why they abandoned me. One day, I asked Mrs. Neide, since she was the only person who could help me. As soon as I asked her, she replied: – You were already here, when I started working, Julia.

– So, I don't know how or when you came here.

– So, you can't help me?

– I can...

– Can you?

– In another situation I wouldn't involve myself, but in the face of your suffering, I think it's better for you to know.

– There must be a folder informing of your arrival here. Since I don't know what year it was, I'll have to look it up.

– As soon as I find it, I'll call you. When I arrived, you were four years old. So it won't be too difficult.

– Thank you, Mrs. Neide.

– I left anxious for the answer, Sueli. A few days passed and she called me to her office.

– When I went there, my heart was beating fast. I was finally going to find out who my parents were and maybe find them.

– As soon as I walked in, she asked me to sit down and started talking.

– I managed to find your file, Julia. Here says that you were born in the municipal hospital and that you came here a few days old.

– Few days? – I asked intrigued.

– Yes, that's what your file says. Your mother's name was Jandira dos Santos.

Just Beginning

– She died?

– Unfortunately, yes, Julia. Here in her file, there is nothing written, so I went to the municipal hospital. I have a friend there.

– I told her about your situation and how important it's for you to know what happened to your mother.

– She offered to help me and she did. This is a copy of your mother's file the day you were born.

– She opened a folder and handed me, Sueli: – I must warn you that what is written there is very sad, Julia...

With that folder in my hands I started to shake, Sueli.

She, noticing my nervousness, asked: – Do you want to read what is written there or do you prefer that I read it?

Still shaking a lot, I returned the folder: – Read, Mrs. Neide. I don't feel prepared.

She took the folder, smiled, and began to read.

– From what is written here, some policemen found your mother. She was lying in the middle of the street.

She was very weak and could only say: – My name is Jandira dos Santos. Save my daughter, please...

The police officers realized that she was bleeding and in labor. They quickly took her to the hospital.

When the doctor was examining her, she died.

– Died? Before I was born?

– Yes. They did a cesarean section and managed to save you...

When imagining the situation of that girl who gave birth to me and showed so much love, without worrying about her life, only about mine, I began to cry without being able to stop. Mrs.

Just Beginning

Neide let me cry for a while, then got up from her table, came over to me, and hugged me.

– She was very brave, Julia, and she didn't abandon you. From what is written here, she was very young and malnourished.

– Who is my father?

– There is no reference to it. She didn't have time to tell what had happened.

– I tried, but I couldn't stop crying, Sueli, while I was sad, I was relieved to know that I hadn't been abandoned and that my mother, even without knowing me, had loved me very much. Mrs. Neide continued.

– After a few days, when you were safe, they brought you here.

The judge ordered that you shouldn't be registered under your mother's name. Your name was chosen here at the orphanage.

You were put up for adoption, but inexplicably you were never adopted. I confess that I don't understand why this happened. You were always beautiful. I imagine you must have been a wonderful baby.

I smiled and thanked her, Sueli, and I said : – I would like to know more about her, Mrs. Neide.

You said she was malnourished. What happened to her to be in that situation?

– I don't have answers to your questions, Julia.

Perhaps, through her name, I can find the rest of my family.

– When you get out of here you can try, but I think it's almost impossible, Julia. Santos is a very common last name.

Since we have no other reference, the best thing you can do is go on with your life.

Just Beginning

Study and manage to live without depending on anyone. You owe it to your mother. She fought for you to be born.

I understood that she was right, Sueli. I went to my room and, that day, I didn't participate in the orphanage activities.

I remember that I cried a lot. I thought of my mother with great affection. I mixed Teca's face with one of a stranger.

At the end of the afternoon, I decided that I would go on with my life to honor her and that if I ever had a child, I would give her all my affection. Every day I thought of her and felt that she was by my side.

I decided that I would not try to find my family or my father. That is why I agreed to work at the orphanage until I finished my studies. The whole time I went to high school and college, I stayed there, working as a secretary.

The next day, after I graduated from college, Mrs. Neide called me at her office.

– As soon as I walked in, she said: – Now you're graduated, Julia. The salary you receive here is very small.

– With your diploma you can have a better job. I spoke with a friend of mine and he offered you a place to work at his company. The salary is very good.

– Thank you, Mrs. Neide. I don't know how to thank you for everything you have done for me. You are a good angel that God put in my life.

– I'm not an angel, Julia. You are a wonderful girl, who knew how to overcome all difficulties.

– I'm glad you're like that. Life is full of worries. One day we are fine and the next everything changes.

Just Beginning

– The important thing is to always trust that there will be better days and that is what you have always done. God bless you for that.

– When and where should I apply for that job?

– There is a problem...

– Which one?

– You're a recent graduate, so it was hard for me to find a job.

– The one I have is in a rural town. You will have to move there. Do you have a problem?

A little scared, I replied: – I don't know. I never lived outside, Mrs. Neide. Will I be able to live alone?

– Of course, you will, Julia! You are well educated and by nature you are a very good person and you know what you want out of life.

– I don't know. I'm scared.

She smiled: – Let's do this. Tomorrow morning, you go there to know the city and if you can find a place to stay, it will solve half the problem.

– Half of all the problems? – Is there another problem?

– The other problem is if you will be able to do the job and I know that you will take the letter.

– All right, Mrs. Neide. I'm going there tomorrow and God help me find a place to stay.

– This is how I came here, Sueli, and I'm here today.

– Now that you're talking about it, I remember that day, Julia. Strange things happened.

– What things, Sueli?

Just Beginning

– At that time, I was working alone in the morning. After Rosana moved, I was alone in the apartment.

I confess that I didn't like it, but I was afraid of living with someone unknown.

That night, I went to bed and woke up some time later, feeling very bad. My stomach hurt.

I went to the bathroom and threw up for a while. Then I wanted to go back to the room, but I couldn't.

My head weighed down and I gradually fell.

I couldn't hold my body. Scared, I wanted to go to the living room or kitchen to call or talk on the intercom, but I couldn't. I stood there, desperate, thinking that I was going to die alone. I don't know if I passed out or fell asleep.

When I woke up, I was still in the bathroom, but I felt fine. I got up, went to the room and decided that I no longer wanted to be alone. That I needed someone by my side, in case it happened again.

I went to the restaurant and as soon as I arrived, I told them what had happened to me and that I needed someone.

My employees said they were going to look for someone.

It was on that day that I arrived, Sueli.

– As soon as the bus entered the city, I liked it. It was small, but much bigger than the orphanage.

I felt that I would like to live here. I looked at the address of the company and, asking questions, I went there.

It was big and, on the street,, there were other companies.

I spoke with the manager and gave him a letter that Mrs. Neide had written.

Just Beginning

After reading the letter, he smiled and said, Neide is a great friend of our family. I couldn't stop responding to your request. Besides, I also liked you. Can you start tomorrow?

– I went back to the center and, as I was hungry, I went into your restaurant. A girl introduced herself and handed me the menu. I looked, ordered the cheapest and ate. The food was very good, I remember thinking:

"I already have a job and a good place to eat. Now all that is missing is a place to live."

When I finished eating, the girl returned to my table.

– Do you need anything else?

– I do, but I don't know if you can help me. I'm moving to this city and I need a place to live.

– Wait a moment. My boss is looking for someone to live with. I'll talk to her.

– I was happy, Sueli, and anxiously awaited the return of the girl. Shortly after, she returned: – I spoke with my boss, she said that she can't talk to you now, since it's time for lunch. She asked if you could come back at three o'clock.

– Excitedly I got up and said: – Okay. Tell her I'm going for a walk, I'll see the city, and I'll be back later.

I left there and went to that square in front of the restaurant.

– I sat on one of the benches and wondered what my life would have been like. I remembered Teca, Altair, Mrs. Neide and my mother whom I hadn't met. I asked everyone, wherever they were, to help me.

– It seems they helped you, didn't they, Julia?

– Yes, they did, Sueli. I walked through the city and, just before three o'clock, I returned to the restaurant.

Just Beginning

– I was getting ready. I asked you to wait a little longer. As soon as I saw you, I felt like I had known you for a long time.

– The same happened to me.

– After talking for a while, I felt that you were being honest. I remembered what Rosana had done for me and decided to do the same. I invited you to come to my apartment.

– When we got to the front of the building, I realized that, like it had happened to me, you were also scared:

– It's true, Sueli, but you said: – Don't worry about anything, Julia. We'll go to the apartment and then we'll talk.

– As soon as I entered, I fell in love with the apartment and my room. You let me live here, paying a miserable rent.

– I don't know how to thank you.

– There is nothing to be thankful for. I liked you and I don't regret it.

– You have been a great company. After hearing your story, I feel like I did the right thing.

– Everything went so well that it seemed that everything was planned.

– Maybe it was? According to the Doctrine that I am following, everything that happens in our life, good or bad, always has a reason, Julia. They sent me because I was in a position to help.

– I had the opportunity to give back what Rosana had done for me. You suffered a lot, Julia.

– Besides being a very good person, you needed to be helped. The spirits that accompany you must be very happy.

– You're right, I suffered a lot. Shortly after, Mrs. Neide passed away. She was my guardian angel. However, now, everything will change.

Just Beginning

– I feel that, with Anselmo, I will finally be happy. I don't regret having forgiven everyone who hurt me. I'm happy today. I don't know if there are any spirits by my side. However, if there are, I can only thank them.

– You really should be grateful, Julia. I will take advantage of this moment that you are happy to talk about another topic.

– By the expression on Sueli's face, Julia realized that the matter was important.

– What topic, Sueli?

– About this department.

– What's wrong with it?

– As you know, I'm going to get married and Rosana, as soon as I move out, intends to sell it.

– Ah! Is that it, Sueli? I was very concerned about the expression on your face. I thought I had done something wrong.

– When Rosana spoke to me, I was worried about your situation, since you would have to move.

– You don't need to worry, Sueli. I'm moving out now, long before your wedding.

– Better that way, Julia. I'm glad your life has taken a turn to the right. I hope you are very happy with Anselmo.

– Whoa! We talked so much that we didn't even see the time go by. It's time for me to get ready and go to work.

– Will we have lunch?

They had lunch and then Sueli went to work. Julia lay down and wondered what her life would be like with Anselmo.

Just Beginning

14.– Taking action

That morning, after Anselmo left, Suzana remained lying on bed and thinking.

How long has it been since we had a night like this? I think it only happened at the beginning of our marriage. At that time, we only thought about our happiness, the children we would have and the house we would buy.

When did that change? We had many dreams. Anselmo has always been more modest than me, even in his dreams. For him, having a small apartment, a used car was enough to make us happy, but not for me. I always wanted so much more. I wanted a career, a huge apartment and the most expensive and beautiful car that could exist. I got everything I ever dreamed of, but how much did I have to pay?

Today, after everything that happened, having lost my job and almost my husband, I'm forced to review my life.

Maybe I took for granted things that I didn't really have. This apartment is big and luxurious, but what do I do in it? I work so hard that when I arrive, I am so tired that I walk through the living room and into the bedroom, use the bathroom, and otherwise hardly see it myself.

Just Beginning

Would it be different if I lived in a two–bedroom apartment, as Anselmo always wanted? Why do I need a newer luxury car? With a smaller car, I can go to the same places.

She got up, went to the bathroom, turned on the shower, and looked at herself in the mirror. Her eyes were shining. She smiled: love is really good for the skin.

She showered and, as she got dressed, she kept thinking: – I know I told Anselmo I'm going with him, but is that what I really want? During the night and today I felt and feel very good, having met my husband again, but will it continue like this? Will I still be happy like I am today? I was desperate when they fired me. However, I can't imagine what my life will be like living in a state that I don't know, with another culture and, mainly, living without my own money. No matter how much Anselmo earns, it will never be like what I always earned. My life is going to change dramatically.

Will I be able to live this way? Although I don't enjoy everything I have achieved, I do like to have achieved it.

I like it when I have visitors and I see the look in their eyes when they see my apartment. I feel like everyone would like to have the same. That look makes me feel very good. I can't accept losing everything I worked so hard for. Today I understood the points I lost, the exaggerations I put on. I know that from now on it will be different. I will give more valued to Anselmo and my son.

I want to work, but without forgetting them. I need to find a new job. If I can, I will speak to Anselmo again. Today I'm going to look for some employment agencies and see what the possibilities are.

She did it. She dressed carefully. She needed to give a good impression.

Just Beginning

She left Rodrigo at school and visited three agencies and received the same response from all of them: – The country is going through a very difficult time and due to her salary range, there aren't many vacancies. We will keep your data and, if any vacancies appear, we will call you.

She knew it well. She knew that when that happened, most of the time there would be no answer or call. I may be able to get another job, but how long will it take? Car and apartment fees are due each month. Without working, it will be impossible. I know that with what I will receive as termination of employment, I will be able to pay some benefits, but if I don't get a job, what will it be like? I need to make a decision, but which one? If I go with Anselmo, without trying, I may never be satisfied, but if I don't get a new job, how am I going to do it?

She returned to the car and, as she drove, kept thinking: – The problem is that I don't have much time.

I need to decide immediately what to do. Anselmo needs to go to Recife and it has to be soon. Why does everything have to happen at the same time? Why did my life change that way?

If my mother were alive, I know she would say: – Life is like that, my daughter, but don't despair, everything always ends well. Be patient, this bad time will pass.

It ends well, how, mom? When will that happen? I don't understand how you can always think like this...

She thought for a while, then decided: I don't have time to think, much less to wait for something to happen. Anselmo is in a hurry. For him, it is an opportunity to grow in his profession. I need to organize everything so that we can move. As my mom always said, let's see what happens.

Just Beginning

She came home. She entered and went to the office. From a drawer she took out two folders. Inside there were papers from the apartment and the car.

She calculated how many fees she still had to pay. Then she took her bag and went to a real estate company specialized in buying and selling high–end properties. The same one through which she had bought the apartment.

She offered the apartment for a price much lower than it was worth, which excited the broker.

– For that price, I'll sell your apartment in a few days.

– I hope you do it soon, because with that money I will be able to pay the debt and I will still have some money left. She left and went to a car agency. She talked and sold her car for what was left to pay.

Before leaving, she looked at it lovingly and left. Out on the street, she thought: – I have no money, but on the other hand, I will no longer have to pay the fees. This is a relief.

A taxi was approaching, she called it with her arm. It stopped and she got in.

As the taxi drove, she thought, Well, I made the necessary decisions. From now on, it's to face what comes next. I'm sad. My life has changed and for the worse. After so much study and work, I see the things that I managed escaping from my hands. What will my life be like in the future? If I stayed here, getting a job would be easier, but in Recife I don't know...

Her throat clenched and a tear formed in her eyes. With the tip of her finger, she didn't let it fall. Meanwhile, Anselmo arrived at the company.

He was confused by everything that had happened that night: so far, I don't understand what happened.

Just Beginning

"I never thought that Suzana would give up everything she achieved to accompany me. Much less now, after discovering I was involved with another woman. We didn't talk about her work and the promotion she would have today. Did something happen that made her change so radically? Wasn't she promoted and therefore she decided to drop everything? No... she wouldn't do that. Unless she understood that it was her fault for leaving me.

That doesn't matter either. The important thing is that we are going to begin a new stage of our lives."

He entered the company and went directly to Alfredo's office. He communicated his decision to accept the offer and that he would go with his family. When he finished speaking, Alfredo was euphoric: – This is very good, Anselmo. I know that if you go with your family, you will be calmer and you will be able to earn much more.

That is my intention. My intention is, within a short time, four our products to be accepted and sold a lot.

– I'm sure it will happen, Anselmo. The situation there is serious. I need you to leave no later than two days.

– Two days? It's very soon. I have a lot to figure out before I move. You know that such a change is not easy. I am changing my whole life.

– I see. That's why you will be financially rewarded. Talk to your wife. She can stay here and simplify everything to make the change smooth. You will stay in a hotel. I'm going to talk to the girl who will be your secretary and ask her to find a house so you can move in. Don't worry about paying the rent, we know your competition, so the company will pay.

– Your salary will also increase and you will have a car at your disposal.

Just Beginning

Anselmo listened to everything Alfredo said. His head was confused.

I knew the change would benefit me, but I never imagined it would be so much.

After doing everything right, he left Alfredo's office and went to his. As soon as he entered, he sat down and began to think.

Everything is going so well that I'm afraid. That job offer, and Suzana's consent to accompany me.

It feels like I'm living a life that isn't mine.

Alzira and Ciro were there. They spread their hands over his head. Immediately, white lights appeared and covered Anselmo completely. Alzira asked: – And Julia, Anselmo. What about her?

As soon as the lights covered Anselmo, he felt a chill through his entire body and, without knowing why, he thought of Julia:

What am I going to do with her? How am I going to tell her that she can't come with me? She said she was going to quit her job, if she did, she will be in a difficult situation. I did what I had never done before. She always knew that I would not abandon my family and now she said she would stay with me. I need to talk to her, but what am I going to say?

Alzira looked at Ciro and said: – You are in a moment of decision again, Anselmo. You have failed so many times. You have another chance. Enjoy this moment.

Anselmo continued thinking: – I feel that I am in a moment of decision.

If I look for Julia and tell her what happened to Suzana, maybe she, as she always did, will understand me and forgive me, but if she doesn't? She can find a way to talk to Suzana and tell her everything I promised her.

Just Beginning

Someone knocked on the door that opened. Marta entered:
– Your wife is on the phone, Anselmo.

– I'll answer. Thanks, Marta.

She smiled and left the room. He picked up the phone. Suzana told him everything she had done with the apartment and the car.

– Did you sell your car, Suzana?

– Yes, I took a taxi home.

– I can't understand how you changed so much!

– I told you. I realized that I was losing my marriage and especially you. Today in the morning after you left, I was remembering the beginning of our marriage and how we were different.

– I was remembering the dreams we had and I realized that everything began to change when I let myself be carried away by greed, by the desire for power. – I came to the conclusion that I wasted precious time.

– I don't understand what happened, but I can only say that I am very happy for your change.

He told her what Alfredo said and the benefits he was going to receive. He ended by saying: – You won't regret the actions you are taking, Suzana. We are going to be happy. You will see.

She smiled: – I hope you don't regret it, Anselmo. I hope we'll be happy too. Now go back to work, you have a lot to do and little time.

– That's true. See you tonight.

Suzana hung up the phone and thought: You can't believe that with my resignation, I was forced to make that decision. Now, I'm going to call Judit and see when I can go back to complete the resignation process.

Just Beginning

Two days later, as soon as they woke up, Anselmo said: – I have to go. As soon as everything is settled here, you and Rodrigo will meet me. Everything is fine. When I arrive, after calling you, I will take my job.

– I'm anxious.

– I also want to see how our lives will go on.

– Don't worry about it. I already said that we will be happy.

Anselmo looked at the clock on the bedside table: – I'm late. In half an hour, a company car will pick me up and take me to the airport.

– If I hadn't sold my car, I could take you. He kissed her lips lightly.

– Don't think about that. Soon you will have your car. It will not be a luxury like the one you had, but one that will take you wherever you want.

She smiled. She got up and went to get ready to leave.

Alzira looked at Ciro: – Nothing else can be done here, Ciro. Let's go now to Julia's side.

Just Beginning

15.– Fatal decision

Almost fifteen days passed. That morning, Julia woke up worried: Anselmo didn't call or show up. Did something happen? He said he would go away for a while without coming here or calling, but it's been a long time. What happened? I will call again.

She tried to dial Anselmo's work phone number, but his phone was dead. Broken again? I need to complain to the company.

She looked at her watch, and even if the phone worked, she couldn't talk to Anselmo. He hasn't come to work yet. If I hurry, there is still time to meet him, before coming in.

Since she moved there, she made coffee and the table for Sueli every day as she was late and therefore slept later.

I won't have time to make coffee today. I need to find Anselmo.

She quickly dressed and ran out. She went to the cafeteria, where she knew that Anselmo, before going to work, drank coffee.

It was there that they met every day.

She arrived at the cafeteria, fifteen minutes before the time he used to arrive. She sat down and ordered a latte, bread, and butter. As soon as the waiter brought it, she began to eat without taking her eyes off the entrance.

Just Beginning

Fifteen minutes passed, another fifteen and another fifteen: did you arrive early? Haven't you come to work? Is he sick? Did he have an accident and was unable to notify me?

Not knowing what to do, she paid, left the cafeteria and started walking down the street. She passed the company where Anselmo worked.

She stopped. A few seconds later she continued walking. Without imagining it, Alzira and Ciro, one on each side, accompanied her. I can't go inside and ask to speak to him.

Without knowing why, she looked aside and saw a payphone: I know what to do. I'm going to call Marta.

She, as Anselmo's secretary, is discreet and knows about our love. She will tell me what happened to him.

She walked over to the phone. She looked and remembered that she had no chips. There was a bar in front. She went there, bought chips and got back on the phone. She dialed a number.

On the other end of the line, Marta replied: – Hello!

– Good morning Marta. It's me, Julia, can I speak to Anselmo?

– He's not here, Julia. He went to Recife over a week ago. He went to work there. Didn't he tell you?

– He said he was leaving, but I didn't know he was gone.

– Yes, he is. He had to hurry.

– Was he alone?

– Yes, but his wife is preparing everything to meet him. She is leaving this afternoon.

– I bought the tickets for her and the child. Didn't he tell you?

– No, he didn't tell me. I knew he was leaving, but I didn't think he was with her...

Just Beginning

– Yes, she is going with him and he is very happy about it. Sorry Julia. I thought he had told you –. Julia swallowed hard. With her throat closed, she could hardly say: – Thanks Marta. I need to hang up...

– All right, Julia. You can be sure I'm sorry...

Julia hung up the phone, but amazed, she continued with it in hand. She heard a voice: – I need to use the phone, girl. She looked up and saw the woman who had said that. She hung up the phone and, staggering, began to walk. She felt her mouth and eyes go dry and her body began to shake. Immediately, Alzira and Ciro began to throw white lights on her. Little by little, she calmed down. She continued walking without really knowing where.

She couldn't and didn't want to think or cry. She continued walking aimlessly.

Alzira and Ciro continued by her side, throwing the lights. Alzira, worried, said: – Right now, we have to help her, Ciro.

– I know, but we must not forget that we can't interfere with her free will.

– She needs to pass this test.

– So far, she's done very well.

– Everything you said is true. We really can't interfere.

– Until now, everything she's done has always been right. Although we cannot interfere with her free will, we must try everything we can. She needs to feel that she is not alone.

Julia kept walking. She thought of Anselmo's last words: – Don't forget that I love you and that we are going to start a life full of happiness.

An immense revolt seized her. Furious, she thought: how could he do this to me?

Just Beginning

How could you lie to me like this? I'm so hateful that I can't even breathe. I don't know what to do.

I lost my job, how will I survive? Also, survive for what? For this life full of suffering and disappointment? I don't want to live anymore! I want to die, I just don't know how to do it. I need to think.

Upon hearing Júlia's idea, Ciro and Alzira tried to approach her, but failed, they were violently pushed aside and some figures that passed, approached and completely enveloped her.

As she walked, they turned and they all said at the same time.

– You can jump in front of a car! You can drink poison! You can hang yourself from a tree!

Julia, without imagining that those thoughts weren't hers, kept walking.

She was thinking of all the ways she could kill herself: – no, I can't do any of that. I want to die, but I don't want to suffer anymore. I am tired of suffering. I need to think a little more. I'm sure of one thing, I don't know how, but I will find a way to leave this life.

She kept walking. Ciro and Alzira, in vain, tried to keep those figures away, but they couldn't.

The only thing they managed to do was keep walking by her side and, now, so did the figures. Desperate, Alzira asked: – What are we going to do Ciro? We couldn't get close or move these figures!

– You know there is nothing we can do, Alzira. She is in a moment of decision, to use her free will.

– We have to wait and see what she will decide.

– We can't wait! We need to act and do something, Ciro!

Just Beginning

– We can't do anything Alzira. She is firmly thinking about suicide and therefore attracting our brothers, who are also suicidal.

– If human beings knew the strength of their thoughts, they would avoid having destructive thoughts and would only think of good things.

– I won't give up, Ciro. I will find a way to push these brothers away and make her think better.

– She can't go back to do what she has done for several incarnations. This time, she needs to overcome it.

– Well, if she doesn't overcome it, her next incarnation will be much worse than this one.

– Let's try, but you know the moment is serious, Alzira.

– Yes, I know. Although I know a lot about the spirit world, there are things that, even if I know them, I don't fully understand.

– What things, Alzira?

– We know that Julia, in this incarnation, is having the opportunity to redeem herself for the several times she committed suicide, right?

–Yes.

– So why did she come with so much trouble, with so much suffering?

With all that happened, I'm not surprised to see that she is tired and won't hold out.

She will fail again, Ciro.

The only way for her to win would have been if she had been reborn with the plan of a calmer life, without great suffering, as it happens to many.

– It would be easier, Alzira, but she wouldn't have overcome this deficiency. She needs to get over it to move on.

Just Beginning

– I know you're right, but I'm desperate to see that she's about to lose another incarnation.

– She hasn't decided yet, Alzira. Furthermore, we can't forget that it was she who chose the life she was going to have for the evolution of her spirit.

– I know that when we are in the spiritual realm, Ciro, surrounded by friendly spirits and feeling protected, knowing our qualities and defects, it is easy to choose the life that would be best for our evolution, but when we are there, in the physical body, we often want to give up.

– Unfortunately, Alzira, despite all the fighting and strength that friendly spirits manage to give, it's not always possible to help.

We must not forget that each one is responsible for their actions and evolution.

No test, however bad it may seem, is greater than the strength of the spirit to endure. We will wait and do everything in our power so that she can get rid of that thought.

– How, Ciro? We can't get close! They, attracted by her destructive thoughts, don't allow it, they keep us away...

– We will stand next to her and, at the first opportunity, we will get close. That is the only thing we can do Alzira.

Sad, Alzira nodded.

Julia kept walking. Her steps were short, but heavy. Her gaze was lost on the horizon.

Influenced by the thoughts the figures sent, she thought, there are a thousand ways to kill myself. I just need to pick one that won't make me suffer. I'm tired of this life of suffering.

I think that when I was born, I was already marked by suffering and by this day. I can't take it anymore, I'll give up...

Just Beginning

She looked at the watch on her wrist: Sueli already left for work this time. I'm going home and I already know how I'm going to kill myself without suffering.

She stopped, looked around and thought: – I walked so much that I don't even know where I am.

She kept looking, trying to locate herself. She passed a bus stop. She went there. She saw a bus passing that would take her downtown and to her apartment. She waited for it to arrive.

Until the bus arrived, surrounded by figures, she continued thinking: – That was the best decision I made.

I'm in no shape nor do I want to continue living. I have suffered too much. I was abandoned at birth, I had a happy moment with Teca and Altair, but they were taken away from me. Now, without a job and a place to live, I have nothing left.

Due to the way I'm going to kill myself, I won't have pain. They say suicide is a sin, but for me, sin is having a life like mine. It's enough! Enough!

Alzira and Ciro, although they couldn't get close, were still there.

Worried, she said: to try to stop her from continuing and doing what she's thinking, we'll need help, Ciro. We need to find a way to reject those brothers of ours who are lost and suffering.

– Alzira you're right. But you know that despite all we can do, the decision is still hers.

– I know, but we need to try everything in our power. We will ask for help. They held hands and prayed. At the same moment, two entities appeared. Showing concern, one of them asked: – What is happening to her?

– Check it out, Jandira. She is in a very difficult time and has allowed these figures to come closer.

Just Beginning

– We couldn't get any closer.

Jandira looked and held her arms out to Julia. Strong white lights shot out of her hands. Still, with all their might, they couldn't reach Julia.

Sadly, she said: – My child, I know you are in a difficult time, but you must pass this test. You need to win to continue and be happy. You think your father and I abandoned you, but it isn't true, although we were involved in other matters, we were always attentive to everything that happened to you.

Julia, surrounded by destructive thoughts and forms, didn't listen.

Homer, the other entity, showing concern, said: – Jandira, it is useless. She doesn't listen to us.

Jandira, with tears in her eyes, continued to shine lights on Julia: – My daughter, I know that you often wondered why I died when you were born. It was necessary. I was reborn so that you could be born. We all knew this day would come.

We are here and we will stay until this moment passes. We pray to Heavenly Father that you can win.

Alzira, realizing that Julia didn't react, said: – Since they are here, I will go away for a while.

– Where are you going, Alzira?

– Don't worry, Ciro. I'll be back. I need to try one last thing.

He, knowing Alzira and knowing how she was willing to save Julia, said: – Okay. Go and do what is necessary and what you can.

She disappeared. They stood there, praying and trying to shine a light on Julia.

Meanwhile, as soon as the bus arrived, Julia got on it. In it, due to the time, there weren't many people. She looked and saw

Just Beginning

that one of the benches was empty. She sat by the window and looked out.

Her face was drawn. She couldn't think of anything other than the way she intended to commit suicide. Ciro, Homero and Jandira, fearful, stood next to her, like the figures that laughed and surrounded her, encouraging her to commit suicide.

When the bus stopped at the point where it was supposed to get off, she got up and, still frowning, got off. She entered the building and passed the doorman without saying hello, which was strange: what happened? She never came here so quietly. She always had something to say. It seems that she's not ok.

Julia got on the elevator, pressed her floor number and left. As soon as she entered the apartment, she looked at the door to Sueli's room. It was open: as predicted, she is not here and will only return at night. I have plenty of time to do whatever it takes to have peace. When Sueli returns, it will be too late and I will be free.

She went to her room, lay down on the bed and kept thinking: there is no other way. It's the only way I can stop suffering.

Although they couldn't keep the figures out, Jandira shouted: – No, Julia! This is not the way!

– You think it's over, but you're wrong! It's just beginning! There is so much to live and do!

– Change your range of thought so you can hear us!

Julia felt a gentle breeze pass over her face, but was soon pushed aside by the shapes that, drawn by her thoughts, completely enveloped her.

– You're welcome, they completely involved you, Jandira.

Jandira, looking at Ciro and Homer, almost crying, said: – This isn't right, Ciro! She is under their control!

Just Beginning

– She is not thinking straight! She is suffering a lot from abandonment! Our lights should be brighter than they are!

– Our lights are stronger than them, Jandira. They are simply not stronger than Julia's desire and free will.

– She is suffering, but she chose the path that she thought was the easiest.

– Despite all our efforts, we can do nothing. Unless we stay here until it's over.

– Can we avoid what comes next, Ciro?

– You know that unfortunately we cannot Jandira. As soon as she carries out what she intends, these brothers of ours will take her to the Valley and you know what it is like there. As much as we try to address it, it won't be possible.

– In the Valley, she will suffer a lot, as she has suffered several times. And, like those other times, she will stay there until she understands what she did. Until she understands that, again, despite all the promises she made before she was reborn, she has failed.

– It's sad, Ciro, to think that we were all by her side when she chose the life she wanted to have.

– She was warned that it would be very difficult, but she insisted a lot. She thought she could do it.

– It's true, but apparently, Jandira, she won't be able to do it.

– Let's keep throwing lights and praying. There's still time.

Just Beginning

– Until the last moment, she may regret it. If she does go ahead, we will be here to help her, to comfort her. They fell silent again, just praying and throwing lights.

Julia, without imagining the concern and dedication of her spiritual friends, got up, went to the closet, opened a drawer and took out a pajama. Then she went to the bathroom, turned on the shower, and took a long shower. She finished showering, put on her pajamas, and went back to the living room. She pulled up a notebook, pulled out a page, and wrote in very large letters for Sueli to see, as soon as she entered:

"Sueli, I'm sorry for what I'm going to put you through, but I don't even want to go on living. I can't bear so much suffering anymore.

I want to rest.

Thank you for everything you did for me."

Julia went back to the bathroom, took a knife out of a drawer and went into the bedroom, lay down and thought: With this knife, I will cut my wrists. I will cut one first, then the other. Blood will flow, I will pass out and feel nothing.

Jandira, Ciro and Homero couldn't prevent the tears from falling down their faces. The happy figures approached her.

She took the razor in her right hand and brought it to her left wrist.

When she was about to do it, to the surprise and amazement of her friends and the figures that were there, Julia began to cry and say: I can't do that! I can't! I know it's wrong!

Just Beginning

Very nervous and shaky, she jumped. As soon as she put her feet on the ground, she slipped on a carpet and began to fall.

She tried to grab hold with her arm, but failed and hit her head on a stool in front of the dresser.

Immediately the blood began to flow.

She tried to get up, but failed. Crying, she continued lying down.

Jandira, Ciro and Homero raised their hands and thanked God for that moment. The room lit up. The figures, frightened by the light, leaned against one of the walls and stared.

Just Beginning

16.– Act of despair

That morning, Sueli woke up and, as she did every day, got up and went to the kitchen: I'm going to have a coffee. Julia must have already gotten up and prepared.

As soon as she entered the kitchen, she was surprised: What happened? She didn't make coffee, like she always does. Hasn't she woken up yet?

She went to Julia's room; the door was closed.

She knocked on the door and, when there was no answer, she opened it: she wasn't there and she left without making the bed, this is not what she does. She would never leave the room like that. It seems like she left in a hurry.

What happened? She was worried about the delay in the news from Anselmo. Could it be that he came here and they left together? Well, there's no point in wanting to guess. I'll wait for her to come back and tell me everything. Since she didn't make coffee, I'm going to do it.

She went back to the kitchen. She got herself ready and drank coffee. Then she went to her room. She looked at her watch: it's almost noon! I slept a lot. I made an appointment today to try on my wedding dress! Julia said she was going to go with me, she must have forgotten, but I can't miss it. The wedding day is close and I have a lot to do. I'll get dressed and go out.

Just Beginning

After trying on my dress, I head straight to work.

It was what she did. She dressed, went out and went to the dressmaker.

While trying on the dress, the seamstress asked: – Julia didn't come with you?

Sueli smiled: – No, when I woke up, she wasn't there. I think she forgot that I had to try on the dress today.

– It seemed strange to me, because you are always together.

– It's true, but she is dating someone now. I think she must have gone to see him and you know how it is, when we have a boyfriend, we forget about friends, right?

The seamstress laughed: – It's true, I think that never changes. Man always comes first.

She finished trying on her dress.

She set a new date, went out and started window shopping: – I need to buy some things for the new house. Since I have time, I will enjoy being here.

For more than an hour she went in and out of the stores. She bought bedding and towels.

While waiting for the package, she thought: Wow! I bought a lot! I'm glad the restaurant is close.

It was at that precise moment that Alzira appeared, stood next to her and, in a low voice, said: – Sueli! You need to go home. Julia needs you.

Unaware of what Alzira was saying, Sueli took the last package and left. On the street, she looked to the side of the restaurant and, carrying several packages, began to walk.

Alzira said again: – Sueli go home... Sueli didn't listen to her and continued walking.

Just Beginning

¬Alzira, desperate and not knowing what to do, continued walking by her side and repeating the same words. Sueli, without knowing why, stopped, looked at the opposite side that she was walking and thought: I think it's better to go home.

When I get off work, I will be tired and find it harder to take these packs. That's right, I'm going home! – Alzira smiled and went back to the others. As soon as she arrived, she said euphorically: I think I made it!

– You made what, Alzira? She almost achieved her goal and is now in a terrible situation!

Sorry, Alzira looked at Julia, who was lying on the ground, and saw the large bloodstain that formed around her.

– I got Sueli back home. I hope she makes it on time.

– Even if that happens, what good will it be if Julia still has the same idea? You know she's going to try it again.

– I know, Ciro, but we'll have more time to make her change her mind.

– How? Look!

Alzira looked and saw the figures that, although leaning against the wall, were watching Julia.

– Ciro, it's not over yet! It is not over yet!

Jandira and Homero, who continued the conversation, nodded. Immediately, they turned on their lights and went into prayer.

Sueli arrived at the building. She went through the lobby and the doorman wasn't there. She opened the door to her apartment.

Her eyes went to the table where she could see the open notebook. Since the letters were large, they caught her attention.

Just Beginning

She went there and read what was written. Her body shook, the packages fell to the floor and she ran to Julia's room with the door open. As soon as she entered, she ran screaming: Oh my god! Julia, what did you do?

Julia, with a weak voice, replied: – A madness, Sueli. I don't want to die, help me...

The room now became even brighter and the figures, who were still leaning against the wall, were forcefully thrown. The friends managed to get closer. While Jandira and Homero continued to throw lights on Julia, Alzira and Ciro calmed Sueli down. Alzira said: – Calm down Sueli. You need to help Julia and then ask for help.

As if listening, Sueli took a deep breath, went to the closet, opened a drawer and took a scarf and wrapped it around Julia's head, trying to keep the blood from flowing. Then she said: – Keep calm, Julia. I will ask for help

– Don't leave me alone, Sueli...

We need help. Try to hold the scarf close to the wound. If you do, the blood will stop flowing. Stay calm. She left the room, picked up the phone to call an ambulance.

She realized that it was broken. She thought: broken again? What am I going to do? I can't get out from here.

Oh my god why did that phone break today? I need help, but I can't be away for long. She opened the hall door. She looked both ways.

It's useless, there's no one to help me. Everyone is working at this time. My god, what am I going to do? Alzira, who was by her side, whispered: – Mr. Joaquim...

Sueli, at the same moment, thought: – Wait! Mr. Joaquim, who lives here in front, must be home! I'll ask him to bring help.

Just Beginning

She took a few steps and knocked hard on the door. A few seconds later, the door opened and a boy appeared who, seeing her state of concern, asked: – What happened, girl?

Very nervous, she replied: – My friend! I need help!

Sueli quickly returned to the apartment and was followed by the boy who, as soon as he entered, could see the note that Julia had left and understood what had happened. When Sueli entered the room, she yelled: Julia! No!

The boy approached and saw that Julia was very pale and with her eyes closed. Sueli began to cry.

He put two fingers on Julia's throat and nervously said, She's alive! We need to take her to a hospital!

– Please go to the street and hail a taxi!

– We don't have time for this! My car is parked on the street, let's take it!

Immediately, he wrapped Julia in a sheet over the bed, picked her up, and ran off. Sueli, crying a lot, followed him.

The elevator has never taken so long to arrive. As soon as they arrived, they got out and, when they passed the entrance, the doorman asked: – What happened?

Sueli, still crying and without stopping walking, replied: – She is not well, we are going to the hospital.

As soon as they got to the car, the boy said, Get in and sit in the back seat, keep her head up.

He took a handkerchief out of his pocket and handed it to Sueli, saying, Put that handkerchief over the cut. It's smaller than this scarf and it fits well. Do this until we get to the hospital.

Sueli automatically obeyed.

After getting the two of them settled, he got in the car and got out.

Just Beginning

A few minutes later, they arrived at the hospital. He stopped the car in front of the emergency, got out and ran.

Shortly after, two nurses, carrying a stretcher, came to the car and put Julia, who still had her eyes closed, on the stretcher and rushed inside.

Sueli and the boy accompanied them. When they entered, one of the nurses said: – We will take her to the emergency room, meanwhile you must fill out some paperwork there in the office.

The nurses with the stretcher, accompanied by Teca and Jandira, entered through a door. Alzira and Ciro stayed next to Sueli and the boy, who then went to the counter.

After giving Julia's information and indicating what had happened, Sueli and the boy sat on one of the benches there. As soon as she sat down, Sueli began to cry violently. The boy was startled: – Why are you crying like that?

Sueli, sobbing, replied: – I don't know. Now that they are taking care of her, I think my strength is gone.

– This is how it happens. If you think crying will make you feel good, go on. I will stay here by your side. Sueli wanted to stop crying, but couldn't. The scene of Julia lying on the bed didn't get out of her head. She cried for a long time, until, little by little, she calmed down.

She wiped her eyes with her hands. She took a deep breath and asked: – Will she be okay?

– She is now in the hands of the doctors and God. Everything we could do, we did. Let us have faith and hope.

– Thanks for everything. Without your help, I don't know what I would have done.

Just Beginning

– You don't need to thank me. I'm glad I helped. However, I think it's time to introduce ourselves. My name is Mario, I am the son of Mr. Joaquim.

– My name is Sueli and as you saw, I am your father's neighbor. He is very nice and talkative. That is why everyone likes him. – Mario smiled: – I know. He likes to talk and he is very curious.

– I knew he had a son who lives in Rio de Janeiro, but I never saw you here.

– It's true, I live in Rio. I work a lot, so I hardly come here. My father is the one who visits me.

– I wanted him to move in with me, but he never wanted to. He likes this city. He says that Rio is very big and that he doesn't know anyone.

– You're right about that. In a small town like this, it's easier to meet people.

– I guarantee that, he knows a lot of people.

Now Mario started laughing.

– I believe that. Actually, my father is a great gossip, isn't he? He wants to know everything about everyone's life –. Sueli also laughed: – He's not a gossip, he likes to know things and he also talks a lot about his life.

He likes you and is very proud of you.

– I also like him very much. Thanks to him, I am what I am today. He encouraged me to study.

– I'm glad you were there. If it wasn't for you, I don't know what I would have done.

– The funny thing about this story is that I don't even know why I was there in my father's apartment and I'm here, now, with you.

Just Beginning

– I didn't understand...

– I am in the middle of a very complicated project. I couldn't leave Rio for now. When I woke up yesterday morning, I had an overwhelming desire to see my father. I thought about calling, but I know it wouldn't work.

– Even if he had a problem, he wouldn't say it. You know, he says he doesn't want to bother.

I tried to forget it, but couldn't. At night, seeing that there would be no peace, I decided to come here.

It seems like someone was telling me to come here to help you and this girl.

– I think that this really happened.

– What do you say, Sueli?

– That's what you heard, Mario. I am studying a Doctrine that teaches us exactly that.

– Teach what?

– That death doesn't exist. That when we die, we turn into spirits and return to our true home.

– That we were born and reborn several times to perfect our spirit.

– That we ourselves choose the life that we will live in a new physical body and, the most important thing is that we are never alone.

– All this is very beautiful, but it is only a theory, Sueli.

– You're right, it may just be a theory. So, I am studying and trying to understand and so far, everything I have learned convinces me.

– It's true. I don't know how we got into this conversation, but even if what you're saying is true, what does it have to do with me being here at a time when I couldn't be?

Just Beginning

– I also learned that we are part of a larger group than the one we know.

– I'm not understanding. I know well the group to which I belong. My family, my friends...

– They are the ones you met in this incarnation, but as I said, we were born and reborn many times.

– Many of our friends walked faster and are waiting for us so that we can accompany them.

– Some are reborn, often unnecessarily, just to help us on our learning journey.

– Others remain in the spiritual realm, always by our side, trying to help us.

– During our life, here on Earth, we met several people. Some of us we like as soon as we see them, and for no reason whatosever, there are others we don't like. Some of us get to know each other and become friends, others just pass through our lives for a short time and then disappear.

– They are all part of our spiritual group.

– This is all crazy, Sueli! How can you believe these things?

– You said yourself that you don't understand how you were there, when I needed you and now, you're here, right?

– That's true, but it has nothing to do with everything you said.

– As I understand it, you are saying that I was influenced by a pseudospiritual friend, to drop everything and come here to help a stranger. Is that what you are saying?

Sueli began to laugh: – That's more or less, Mario. All I know is that when I needed you, you were there and I thank you, thank God and, although you don't believe me, I thank my spiritual friends.

Just Beginning

Now it was he who laughed: – You're really crazy, Sueli.

– I understand how you feel with all this talk. At first, it seems complicated, but when you understand, you will see that it's not.

– I don't know. For me, who has always studied science, it's a bit difficult to accept all this.

– For science, everything that happens always has an explanation.

Sueli looked toward the door where Julia and the nurses had entered: – Mario, don't you think it's taking a long time to hear from Julia? Is she fine? Did we come here on time?

– Stay calm. Everything you could have done, you did. Now, she is in good hands and is being cared for. We can only wait.

– Although we don't hear from Julia, to pass the time, can we continue our conversation?

– All right, Mario. Keep talking

– Assuming that what you say is true, I can deduce that we are all working, studying, each one living our life as we do, and suddenly, one or more of our pseudo spiritual friends, approaches us, whisper anything in our ear and immediately we drop everything we were doing to do what they want. Is that what you're saying, Sueli?

– That's exactly what happens, Mario.

– Do you really believe that?

– Of course, I do. It happened to you and me too.

– You were calm working, suddenly, out of nowhere, you felt an uncontrollable needed to see your father.

– You stopped everything you were doing and came here. The same happened to me. Today when I left home, I had planned to try on my wedding dress and then go straight to work. I didn't

Just Beginning

think about going home, but when I went to work, I felt an uncontrollable urge to go home.

– If that hadn't happened, Julia would have died without help.

Mario, when he heard that, fell silent, just thinking about everything she had said.

Sueli continued: – After everything that happened, I can only say that someone there likes you a lot –. Hearing that, Ciro looked at Alzira, who was there and who also smiled.

Mario was silent. After a while he said: – You're right, Sueli. Someone must really like me.

– After everything you said, I think that if it wasn't a great coincidence, all that may be true.

– However, there is something that still bothers me.

– What, Mario?

– I always knew that, just as there is good, there is also evil. If a spirit of good can influence us along the way as you are saying, can another spirit of evil do the same and lead us to do bad things to commit a crime?

– It can. Of course, it can Mario!

– What you say is very dangerous, Sueli.

– I'm saying that it can, but we don't need to follow what it suggests.

– I'm not understanding...

– You yourself said that there is good and evil. Just as we all learned from a very early age what is right and what is wrong.

You really wanted to see your father, right?

– Yes. The desire was so strong that I'm here.

Just Beginning

— Well, if that wish were to kill him, to harm him, would you have come to do what was suggested to you?

— Of course not!

— Do you see the difference? We call this decision, free will. Due to our free will, no spirit, good or evil, can force us to do what we don't want, what we believe is wrong.

— The spirit of good or evil cannot interfere in our decisions.

— They are ours even before we born. We are free spirits, Mario. We only do what we want.

— If they are so powerful, why do they need our help, mere mortals?

— Spirits, because they don't have a physical body, often need to talk to us and for that, they use another spirit with a physical body. I think this is what happened to you and me. Julia needed material help.

— The spirit or spirits as needed a physical body, came seeking our help, and here we are.

— If you remember your past, you will see how many times in difficult times, someone came to help you, often even with a simple word or simply listening to what you needed to say. Strangers, during our life, appear, helping us in some way and then we'll never see them again. In a moment of great suffering, I met a girl who didn't know me, didn't know where I was from, and even so, she offered me her house to live in and helped me a lot.

— Your arguments are strong, Sueli. I need to think about it and investigate.

— Do it, Mario. I guarantee you will not regret it.

— I just have one more question.

— What question?

Just Beginning

– Why did he or they have to take me out of Rio to help this girl? Couldn't they have found someone from here, closer?

Sueli laughed: – Do you remember the group I talked about? Yes, you must belong to our group, mine and Julia's, and you must have been part of our life in the previous incarnation.

Mario also laughed: – Everything is so simple for you.

– But it's simple, Mario. We are the ones who complicate everything.

– That's right, I think it's time to change the subject. This is very serious. You said you went to try on your wedding dress. Are you getting married?

– Yes, in two months.

– Good. Congratulations.

– If you give me your address, I can send you an invitation. Your father will definitely be invited.

– I would like that very much. I work so hard that I don't have many friends and the opportunity to meet other people.

– I think my group is very restricted.

– Are you married?

– No. Although I am thirty–three years old, I haven't yet decided to marry. I don't think I've found my other half yet. Sueli laughed again: – Don't worry, at any moment, when you least expect it, she will appear.

– You know that I want to have a wife, children...

– There comes a time when a man or a woman feels this desire. It is the biological clock.

– Yes, I think my watch is complaining. – Mario said laughing.

Just Beginning

Although they had been talking for some time, neither took their eyes off the door Julia had gone througj.

At one point, he asked: – What happened in the life of this girl, for her to take such a drastic attitude? You who know her, do you know what the reason could have been, Sueli?

– She had a very painful life. As she says, it looks like she came marked.

Nothing in her life has worked. Every time she thought everything was fine, everything fell apart.

Until yesterday, everything seemed to be going well. She was going to live with the man she loves, and move with him to Recife.

Everything was so good that she quit her job. Something very serious must have happened.

– We don't need much to imagine what it was.

– Did the man abandon her?

– I don't know, but everything points to that.

– It's so sad. So young and so beautiful...

– You're right, it's sad. Besides being young and beautiful, she is also a great person, a great friend.

– If he really abandoned her, it must be very sad, but many people are abandoned and don't take such extreme action.

Sueli immediately remembered Nilson and what it was like when she discovered that he had abandoned her.

She felt a knot in the throat. She said: – It's true, Mario. Many people are abandoned, but I think that abandonment is always very painful. When this happens, people think that it's over and that there is nothing left for their lives, but it's a mistake. Life goes on, other people will appear, other loves will come.

Just Beginning

I believe that these bad moments are just moments and they serve for our learning, to show us that we shouldn't and can't put our happiness in the hands of another person. We are free to love, live and, most importantly, begin over. Life is a constant new beginning. Every time we think it's over, over time we will see that it was actually just beginning. It would be nice if everyone understood that.

Only then would much suffering be avoided.

Mario, who listened attentively, when she stopped speaking, said: – You are right about some things, Sueli.

– Looking back at my past and the people I know, I can say that life is made up of good and bad moments.

– I think that one day we all thought that everything was over and we wanted to die. Not only due to abandonment, but also due to lack of work, of money. There are many reasons that can cause this desire.

– I confess that I myself have already gone through some of those moments.

Sueli, who still remembered the moment when she was in love with Nilson, said: – I also went through this and, like everyone, I also wanted to die, but thank God, I didn't go through with it. I, probably with the help of my friends, spiritual friends, got that idea out of my head and today when I look back and remember everything I went through, I can only say that, even though I thought it was over, it was really just beginning.

– At this moment, I'm going to begin a new stage in my life. I'm going to marry a wonderful man who I love and who loves me too. With him, I will build my family and do everything in my power to make him happy.

Mario was going to say something, but the door Julia had entered through opened and one of the nurses came through it.

Just Beginning

They both got up at the same time and went to the nurse who, smiling, said: – You don't have to worry anymore. We took care of her and everything went well. She is in the bedroom. She will be hospitalized overnight for observation.

– Not so much because of the cut on her head, but because of her emotional state.

– The doctor wants to talk to someone in the family.

– She has no one. She only has me, I'm her friend.

– Then it would be nice if you could come here tomorrow morning. The doctor wants to talk to you, but it can't be now.

– He's getting ready for surgery.

– It's okay. I'll come to talk to him. Now, can we come in? – Sueli asked, distraught.

– You can come in, but it must be for a short time. She needs to rest. They gave her an injection. She should sleep soon. Sueli looked at Mario and asked: – Shall we go in?

– No, Sueli. I don't think it's a good idea. She doesn't know me and due to the circumstances, my presence can embarrass her, and I don't want that.

Sueli thought for a moment, then said: – I don't think so. If it wasn't for you, we might not have arrived on time.

– Still, I'd rather not go in. If you want, I can wait here to take you home.

– Do you want me to stay?

– Well, as you don't want to come in, if you want and you can, I would like you to wait for me not to take me home, but to work. With everything that happened, I ended up forgetting about it. I'm late.

Mario smiled and Sueli accompanied the nurse.

Just Beginning

As soon as she entered, she realized that Julia was very dejected. She approached her, moved, asked: – Are you okay? Julia began to cry: – Sorry, Sueli, for what I put you through.

– Don't worry about that, the important thing is that you are ok.

– I don't know what happened to me. After discovering that Anselmo went to Recife with his wife, without telling me anything, as if I didn't exist, I was desperate, I just wanted to die and almost went crazy.

– Don't talk or think about it. Now you need to rest. The nurse said you're going to sleep soon. Rest well.

– I'll be here early tomorrow. Don't worry, everything will end well.

– Why does nothing work for me, Sueli?

– I told you not to think about it. Sleep and dream of angels.

– Especially with your guardian angel, I think she had a lot of work. Sueli said laughing.

Julia couldn't bear it and began to laugh too: – You're right, Sueli. For me to be alive, it must have been a lot of work.

– I'm sleepy... – Sueli kissed Julia's forehead.

– That's good. Enjoy, sleep well. I'll come here tomorrow.

Julia immediately fell asleep. Sueli looked up and thought: Thanks to you, God bless you for all your work.

Alzira, Ciro, Jandira, and Homero smiled. Alzira said: – We are the ones who are grateful for all the help we had. Lights were thrown on Sueli, who, feeling the light, left the room and found Mario who was waiting for her.

– How is she?

Just Beginning

– A little scared and under the influence of tranquilizers, but okay. I'll talk to the doctor tomorrow. They left. Mario left Sueli in front of the restaurant and went to his father's apartment.

Even before Sueli left, Julia was already asleep. Alzira, looking at Jandira and Homer, said: – It's fine now. I know you are involved in some important matters. From now on, Ciro and I will continue by her side.

You can go back to your duties. We can only thank you for helping us.

– Are you sure you don't need us to stay here, Alzira?

– Yes, I am, Jandira, but if I need you, I will not hesitate to call you again.

– Then let's go. Like you said, we are involved in some important work.

– You can go in peace, Jandira. I know that your project involves enormous help for those incarnated.

– Then it must be completed.

Smiling, they disappeared.

17. – Friendly visit

As soon as Jandira and Homero disappeared, Ciro and Alzira looked at one of the walls of the room.

The figures around Julia were still there, but, frightened, they leaned against the wall and stayed there. Alzira and Ciro, pretending not to see them there, turned to Julia, who was sleeping.

– Is it time, Alzira?

– Yes, it is. We knew the time would come. So far, she's done well, but we know that at any moment, the suicide wish will come back with great force. She has little left to recover from the past.

– Only then can she move on. We are committed to helping her and staying with her until she is done.

– Now, she needs to remember what happened in order to feel stronger.

True, but can she go on, Alzira?

– We will help her as much as possible and hope she gets it, Ciro.

Alzira ran a hand over Julia's hair and spoke softly: – Wake up Julia... Julia opened her eyes. She looked around and realized that she was in the hospital room.

When she saw them there, she said: – Are you doctors?

– No. My name is Alzira and his is Ciro. We are your friends and we are here to help you.

Just Beginning

– How can you be my friends? I never saw you in my whole life!

– Yes, we are your friends and we will make you feel much better.

– Thanks, but the only way to help me is to let me go. I'm fine now.

– We wish we could do that, but we can't. The doctor hasn't discharged you yet. You need to be patient.

– He will come here soon to see how you are.

– I'm great. Can you help me get out of here?

Alzira smiled and asked: – Do you remember what you did Julia?

She started crying and saying, I remember, and I know I almost went crazy. However, if you knew my life, you wouldn't ask that question.

– Alzira, while adjusting Julia's head on the pillow, asked: – Do you want to talk about that?

– We are here to hear what you have to say.

Julia looked at the two of them for a while, then said: My life hasn't been easy. Since I was a child, I have suffered non-stop.

Every time I think that everything is fine, that I can finally be happy, something happens and everything goes back to the way it was, just loss and suffering.

– When you thought about committing suicide, did you think you had found a way to end your suffering?

– At the time, I thought I had.

– Why didn't you go all the way?

– I was afraid.

– Afraid of what?

Just Beginning

– What comes after death, afraid of hell.

– Do you think there is something after death?

– I don't know, but I was afraid. People say that there is and that there is no salvation for those who committed suicide.

– Do you think so too?

– I don't know, but what if it's true? I didn't have the courage to check it out.

– Will you try again?

– Never again! So, when I learned that suicide is wrong, I also heard, throughout my life, that people say that our life belongs to God and that only he has the right to take it away.

– Do you think they were wrong?

– I don't know. That is what I learned and that is what everyone says, but if that is true, that it was God who gave us life, I only ask that he take me as soon as possible. I don't want to go on living.

– Will you give up like this, without waiting for better days that will surely come?

Julia began to cry desperately and, between sobs, answered: – Wait for better days?

– That's not going to happen!

– Why not?

– Better days may come for anyone but me. I don't understand why everything goes wrong for me.

I'm a good person, I have never hurt anyone. From the day I was born, I've always been alone! I never had a family, nobody!

– You were never alone, Julia.

– You don't know me. I've always been alone, since the day I was born...

Just Beginning

– You were born in a place where people took good care of you, gave you shelter and even affection. You weren't alone.

Then when you grew up, with the help of Neide, you went to the house of Teca and Altair. They, for a while, showed you a home and the peace of family love.

– You said it very well, for a while! What good was that time if it was taken away from me?

– It was necessary, Julia.

– Necessary for what?

– For you to learn to value a family.

– How can you say that? I have always valued a family, much more after meeting Teca and Altair!

– It wasn't always like this. Ciro and I are here to help you. We are here to show you that you have never been alone.

– That you always had friends by your side who did everything possible to help and facilitate your trip and who will still help a lot.

– After Teca and Altair, Neide stayed by your side. She helped you study, graduate, and get a job.

– She made you able to support your life and take care of your life alone. Then, when you needed a place to live, you were instructed to find Sueli.

– I don't understand what you're saying.

– I know, but in time you will understand. We will continue.

– Even in Teca's house, there were Margarida and Jonás who were always by your side. As you can see, you never were alone.

– It's true, they were good friends, but there was also Aunt Rosa who, out of sheer malice, took everything from me!

Just Beginning

Alzira looked at Ciro and they both looked at the figures who, after being thrown, were allowed to approach again.

They were still leaning against the wall, but still, they paid attention to the conversation.

Ciro said: – There are always two sides to everything, Julia. Just as there is good, there is also evil.

Right and wrong, light and dark.

Friends and enemies. During our spiritual life we go through all phases, on both sides.

The good serves to help us walk and the evil to be able to make our decisions.

Right or wrong to give us the opportunity to choose which path we want to take. Friends to help us on the journey and enemies to help us forgive and be forgiven.

– I think I always chose the right path and was always a good person. I always thanked my friends and I always forgave my enemies.

– Did you really forgive, Julia?

– Yes.

– Even Aunt Rosa?

– Yes, even Aunt Rosa. I forgave her and insisted on not remembering her or everything she did to me.

– Do you see that you still haven't forgiven Aunt Rosa? If that had happened, every time you remembered it, you would have no pain,

Pain and resentment. Forgiveness must be sincere. From the bottom of the soul. Forgetting, wanting not to remember, simply postpones the moment that needs to arrive and that, for many, takes too long to arrive. There is always a reason for everything.

Just Beginning

– If Aunt Rosa acted like she did, it was because it was important for you to lose everything at that time.

– ¿Important? You don't know what you're saying! I really lost it all! The house, the school, the nice clothes I wore, but mostly Teca and Altair! I was alone! I was a kid! She could have had a little compassion, but she didn't! Do you really think I can forgive Aunt Rosa from the bottom of my soul? Sorry, but it won't happen.

Even if I wanted to, I can't.

The figures that remained there began to move.

Ciro looked at Alzira and said: – Only forgiveness brings peace to our spirit. Without it, we won't be able to continue our journey towards Divine Light and we will wander aimlessly.

When we ask for forgiveness and forgiveness from the bottom of our soul, just remember those we love and by whom we were loved and they will appear and lead us to the Light, to peace and happiness. Never again will we have to wander aimlessly.

We will never feel lost again. God is our Father, and he loves us very much. Therefore, he always gives us a new opportunity to begin over.

The figures looked at each other and began to cry and ask for forgiveness. Immediately, other figures appeared in the room and hugged one by one. All crying, stayed hugging for a while.

Then, still hugging, they followed those who led them with great affection. Those who led them thanked them with their heads and disappeared. Alzira and Ciro smiled.

Julia, who didn't see that scene, only remembered the words that Alzira had said.

Very nervous, she asked: – I don't understand what you're saying. Who are you? How do you know so much about my life?

Just Beginning

– Who we are, doesn't matter, Julia. You just need to know that both Ciro and I are here to help you.

– You're scaring me.

Nervous and scared, Julia tried to get up, but couldn't.

Alzira, in a calm voice, said: – Calm down, Julia. Everything will be fine.

– Nothing is going to be fine. You know everything about my life, so you must know how I was lied to.

The man I trusted and would do everything for, left me without saying a word.

Again, I thought my suffering phase had passed and that now, finally, I would be happy, but I was wrong.

God doesn't want me to be happy. I think he hates me...

Alzira looked at Ciro and they both laughed. He then asked, Do you really think God doesn't like you and hates you?

– I can only believe that.

– God doesn't hate you, Julia. He is the Father and creator of us all.

– If he doesn't hate me, if he is the Father of us all, he must choose his children so that their lives are so different from each other. Why has my life been the way it is? Why does nothing work for me, while for other people everything always works well? Why do some people, like me, have nothing, while others have money they can't run out of, beauty, and a wonderful life?

– What if I tell you that it was you who chose this life?

Even with tears running down her face, Julia couldn't stand it and laughing said: – You must be joking or trying to fool me.

– Why do you say that, Julia?

Just Beginning

– How could I have chosen a life like mine? If I could choose my life, today I wouldn't be desperate for what I almost did. I would have a lot of money, so much that I couldn't spend it.

I would be traveling the world, visiting different places.

It would be beautiful, so beautiful, having many men who wanted to seduce me. I would have everything I wanted, without having to ask for it or work for it. I would have people serving me and my will would be law!

– Was that the life you wanted to have? What if I tell you that you already had that life? That you had the life you described?

Julia, very nervous, almost shouted: – You really must be joking! Why are you doing this?

– We're not joking, Julia. We are your friends. You have already had a life like the one you described and the result wasn't what you wanted.

Because that life that didn't work out, you chose the one you live today.

– This is all crazy! Am I going crazy?

– No, Julia. You're not going crazy! Let's go Julia. Let's go for a walk. Julia, confused and scared, asked: – Where are you taking me?

– Don't be afraid. I said everything will be fine. Let's go!

Julia spread her arms. Ciro and Alzira, each to one side, took her by the hands and she got up.

When she realized that she was floating, she looked and saw that she was on the bed. She saw her body on it and also, that there was a silver cord that held her body which was lying down.

She despaired: – Am I dead? Sueli couldn't save me? Oh my god! How did I do this madness!

Just Beginning

– Calm down, Julia. You're not dead. Your body is asleep, but your spirit is fully awake.

– You mean I'm dreaming?

– More or less – Alzira replied, looking at Ciro and smiling.

– What is this cable I'm looking at?

– This cord ties your spirit to your body. It shows that you are alive. Julia looked up and became even more desperate.

– Don't you have a cord? You're dead!

– Do you think we're dead?

– It seems that you're not, but you don't have the cord.

– You're right, for you, you can say we're dead, but you don't have to be scared.

As you can see, only the body dies. The spirit is still alive. Don't you think we're pretty much alive?

– Until now, I thought so, but now I'm very scared.

– There is no need to fear. We are only doing this because it's time to find out about your past.

– Let's go, let's go and don't be afraid because now you are going to sleep and, when you wake up, you will be in another place, at another time.

– I guarantee you will be surprised.

Even scared and worried, Julia tried to smile and fell asleep.

Ciro took Julia in his arms and they disappeared.

✳ ✳ ✳

That afternoon, while all this was happening to Julia, Anselmo, in a car that the company had given him to work with, was going to the airport. Anxious, he thought: Good thing Suzana is coming. In the end everything went well. I know that our life

Just Beginning

from now on will be different. We went through difficult times, but it is all over.

Suzana, when she saw that our marriage could end, decided to give it the value it deserved and Rodrigo will grow up happily in a stable home.

The light turned red and the car stopped. Without knowing why, he remembered Julia: How is Julia?

Did she find out that I left with Suzana? I know what I did was wrong; disappear without saying a word, without saying what was happening, but what could I do? I didn't have the courage to face it. After everything I promised, after knowing that she must have quit her job, how do I go in and say it was all a mistake?

Well now it's done and there's no going back. I don't need and can't worry about her.

She is a young lady, strong, beautiful and intelligent. Soon she will find another job and someone who loves her the way she deserves. Worst of all, I like her, like Suzana. How is it possible to like two people at the same time? If I could, I would have them both. But I had to make a choice. It had to be Suzana, because in addition to loving her very much, we have a marriage, a child to raise. Well now it's done and there's no going back.

He arrived at the airport. He parked the car, entered the lobby, and went to see the panel showing the planes that were to arrive. First, he looked at the board, then the watch on his wrist: the plane was almost an hour away. I'm going to drink a cup of coffee.

He went to a cafeteria, ordered coffee, looked around and saw that there was an empty table. He took the coffee and walked to the table. He sat down.

While drinking coffee, he thought again: – a month ago, I could never imagine that today I would be here living, working

Just Beginning

and, mainly, that Suzana would leave everything to accompany me.

How can life change like that? I came to the conclusion that there is no point in planning our lives.

I think that regardless of our will, I walk alone. I had a life that many people could envy. It was well planned. I had a job and lived in a huge apartment, but I was always alone.

Suzana was hardly ever there and when she was, she only thought about work.

For her, work was more important than anything else. That is why I asked Julia to accompany me.

I know she must be very angry, but there is no reason for that. I, from the beginning, always said that I would never abandon my family.

He finished his coffee and looked at his watch again: only five minutes had passed. It seems that time has stopped! I can't wait to hug Suzana and Rodrigo. I think my anxiety makes time go by very slowly.

He got up and walked away. He looked at the shop windows.

"I need to give Suzana a welcome gift. She has to like it here and get used to living here. It is very different from anything she knows, but I know she will make it. "

In front of him, he saw a flower shop. He went there and bought red roses. He asked the manager to make a bouquet. With it in his hands, he went to the landing site, where Suzana should arrive. He sat down and waited. At that very moment, Suzana, on the plane, looked at the seat next to her and saw Rodrigo sleeping.

"My son. We are changing our lives. No matter how far I go, I will never forget the pain I felt today when I left our apartment.

Just Beginning

The furniture, the paintings and every object were bought with so much love. After a long time, I managed to have the apartment that I always dreamed of, and then all of a sudden, it was all over. I will never forget the day when, without further explanation, I was fired from the job I dedicated myself to so much.

Nothing that is happening to me is fair! I didn't deserve it; I was never a bad person.

Maybe I was exaggerating a bit with Anselmo, but he was always very quiet. He always agreed to earn a low salary. He never had ambition. Unlike me, who always wanted more. Now, I don't know who was right.

Me for wanting so much or him for not caring. For him, living in a two–bedroom apartment was fine. I never accepted it, nor will I accept it!

I studied hard, I struggled to have a good position in the company despite being a woman. I know the reason for being fired. I could never have a higher position than I achieved. I would never be president of the company.

The men of the company would not allow it.

It's not fair, after going through everything I went through to get where I was and now, I'm unemployed, depending on Anselmo's meager salary. It all happened at once, so I didn't have time to wait until I found a new job. I couldn't be alone and without a husband. So, I'm following Anselmo.

Going to a place that I don't know and where I will hardly find a decent job.

Although I live far away, I will keep sending my resume and if a job comes up, I will be right back.

I hope that happens before my apartment is sold. I like it a lot and I don't see myself living anywhere else. That's why I left the apartment as it was. I only took clothes and personal items.

Just Beginning

For now, I won't be able to pay the fee. But, if I find a new job, I'll fix everything rapidly. The most important thing is to return to my home and my life. My mother said there was always a purpose for things to happen. God often makes us walk in strange ways so that we can reach him, and that all is ok. As much as I think, I don't see any purpose for all this that is happening.

Well now there is nothing to do. I am here and I will stay until I need it or discover the purpose of it all. The figure of a woman who was there smiled and said: – You will discover my daughter... you will discover..."

The commander said they were arriving. She adjusted her seat belt and Rodrigo's too.

She put her arm around the boy to protect him. A few minutes later, the plane stopped. She stood up. Rodrigo, half asleep, refused to walk.

She didn't know what to do, as she needed to get the suitcase that was on top and another that contained the child's toys. A gentleman who was sitting in an armchair behind her, took the suitcases: – You can carry the child on your lap.

– I'll take your suitcases –. Suzana smiled, thanked and took Rodrigo.

In the luggage section, the same man took her three suitcases off the conveyor belt and placed them on a cart. She, still with Rodrigo on her lap, tried to push the cart, but couldn't.

Without an alternative, she put Rodrigo in the basket of the car and pushed it, and in a few minutes, she was in front of the exit. As soon as she got out, she saw Anselmo, who also saw her arrive. With the bouquet in hand, he ran to meet her.

They hugged, they kissed. Anselmo took the boy on his lap and kissed her several times. Then they went to the parking lot. Along the way, he said – I'm glad you've come, Suzana. In those

Just Beginning

days when I was alone, I missed you so much. I definitely don't know how to be alone.

– It was also difficult for me. I had to prepare many things. I left the apartment to be sold.

– I didn't understand why you didn't want to bring the furniture, Suzana. The company would pay for the move.

– I thought it was better to leave it as it is. With the furniture and decoration, as beautiful as they are, I think it will be easier to sell.

– I hope it sells out soon. With my salary, it will be difficult to pay the fee.

– I know, but I'll try to find a job. If we can, we can keep the apartment.

– I feel an oppression in my heart just to imagine that it will no longer be mine. You know I planned every detail.

It was the dream of my life. I am very sad about everything that is happening.

– I understand that you are going through a difficult time, Suzana.

– Don't be sad. It will be difficult at first, but I am very good at my job and will soon be able to ask for a raise.

– Everything will be fine! Let's begin a new life and I feel like it will be very good! Now, take the opportunity to get to know the city.

As he drove, Anselmo excitedly showed Suzana the city that, although she was looking, didn't pay much attention to.

She thought: – "My mother always said that we shouldn't be attached to material things. How can we not get attached if we fight so hard to achieve what we dream of? How can I stop

Just Beginning

suffering when I see everything that I have achieved with so much work, escape from my hands without being able to do anything? "

The figure of the woman smiled: – although she didn't pay much attention to what Anselmo was saying, Suzana realized that the landscape was changing. The car entered a pleasant neighborhood, with beautiful houses and imposing buildings.

Anselmo, not realizing that she wasn't paying attention to what he was saying, said: – I had little time to find a house or apartment that wasn't very different from ours. You know I want you to be happy here, Suzana.

– Temporarily, we're going to stay in a not so big one, but that's good. As you can see this is a good neighborhood and the building is new and beautiful and it's facing the beach. You can sunbathe whenever you want.

He stopped in front of a garage door. The doorman opened the door.

Anselmo got in and parked the car in one of the garages. He got out of the car, opened the door on the side where Suzana was sitting, took Rodrigo on his lap and said: – Get out Suzana. Come to see the apartment.

No need to worry about the suitcases, then I'll come get them later.

Suzana got out of the car and they walked to the elevator. The elevator arrived and the two entered. Anselmo pressed the ninth floor. As soon as the elevator stopped, they got out. Anselmo left followed by Suzana. The department was in front.

Anselmo opened the door and walked away for Suzana to enter. The front door led to the living room.

She came in and stood up and thought: Oh my god! The kitchen in my apartment is bigger than this room.

Just Beginning

– Come in Suzana, this is Rodrigo's room and that's ours!

Suzana entered the room slowly and approached Anselmo. He stepped aside for her to enter the room.

She entered silently. He, excited, unaware of her disappointment, took her hand and entered the room that would be theirs. He approached the window: – Come here, look at the view of the sea. I guarantee you have never seen a sea as blue as this! She approached the window and, when she looked, she couldn't help it: – Indeed, the view is wonderful, Anselmo!

– Now, while you stay here looking at everything else, I'll go to the garage to get the suitcases.

She, with her arms propped up by the window and looking out to the sea, said: – All right. Come on, I'll stay here for a while looking out to the sea.

He smiled and left.

She stood there for a moment, then searched and found the kitchen. Another disappointment: my bathroom is bigger than this kitchen...

When Anselmo returned with the suitcases, she was sitting on a sofa in the living room.

– Did you see the rest of the apartment, Suzana?

– Yes, I did Anselmo.

– What do you think?

– It's smaller than the one we lived in when we got married.

– I know, Suzana, but don't forget that we were very happy in that department.

– At that time, we were first married and had many dreams. Some dreams were achieved, but like dreams, they disappeared.

– We lost everything, Anselmo...

Just Beginning

– I know this apartment doesn't come close to our department, but it's just the beginning. Soon we can move.

– The important thing is that we are together, right?

– Yes, Anselmo, you're right. That's all that matters... He hugged her and kissed her passionately.

Suzana returned the hug and the kiss.

The figure of her mother, who was there, said: – I know you think it is all over, my daughter, but actually, it is just beginning...

18. – The dream

Alzira and Ciro, who was carrying Julia asleep on his lap, came to a large garden.

They stopped and looked at the huge house in front of them. Ciro, sitting down and placing Julia on the very green grass, said: – We arrived, Alzira. Where do we start?

– Wake her up. She needs to see this place and remember the life she had here.

– She will be afraid...

– At first she will Ciro, but soon she will understand and pay attention to everything that happens.

Alzira sat next to Ciro and, affectionately, called: – Wake up Julia. We reached our destination.

Julia opened her eyes and, seeing that she was lying on the grass, tried to get up, but couldn't.

Looking at them, very nervous, she asked: – What is happening here? I'm dizzy!

Alzira, holding her hand, said: – Calm down, Julia. Everything is alright. This dizziness you feel will soon pass. Your spirit is still attached to matter, so your energies are somewhat heavy. In a few minutes you will feel good.

– What place is this?

Just Beginning

– We are in another time and in a place that you don't remember at this time, but soon you will remember everything that happened and the reason for choosing to live the life you are living.

– I can't believe I chose such a difficult life, so sad...

– Soon you will understand everything. It's okay now. Get up

Helped by Alzira, she managed to sit up. When she saw that huge house, she was ecstatic: – What a beautiful house!

– Apart from being big, it is very beautiful! Look at that mall surrounded by trees and the beautiful garden!

– I have never seen a house like this, only in movies or books. The people who live here must be very happy!

– Didn't you say that we are in another era?

– What era?

– At the time of the empire.

– Do you mean that we are in the time of the king, the queen, the counts and countesses, dukes and duchesses, princes and princesses?

– That's right, Julia.

– I love reading stories or watching movies about that time. I like to see those beautiful dresses and the dances in the great halls. Every time I go to a museum, I keep imagining the girls coming down those stairs.

– Living in that moment must have been great and romantic. I read about great love stories.

– Yes, there were great love stories, as there are today.

Júlia remembered Anselmo and what he had done: – That love you are talking about, if it existed at another time, today it no longer exists. Today there is only betrayal, lies and seduction.

Just Beginning

– You're wrong, Julia. Besides love, there is another very strong feeling.

– ¿Hate?

Alzira smiled: – That one too, but even hatred is not as strong as love and forgiveness.

– Love and forgiveness are the strongest and most difficult feelings to control and they have always always been the same, at all times. They are part of the spirit.

– Only they, when they are sincere, can make the spirit walk and find the Divine Light.

– Now, enough chat, let's get in.

– I need to apologize, but I will hate Anselmo until the end of my days, for everything he did to me.

For lying to me like he did.

Alzira looked at Ciro, who said: – You don't hate, and you can never hate Anselmo, Julia.

– How can you say something like that? You can't know what I feel!

– You're right, I can't know what you feel, but I know what you've experienced.

So I know you will never hate Anselmo. You've been trying to find yourself for a long time. Someday it will pass.

– Well, this conversation is taking an unwanted turn.

– We'll postpone it for later and get back to it. Now, shall we go into the house?

– Good idea, Alzira. Let's talk about it some other time.

– Now, the best thing you can do is enter the house. ¿Shall we go Julia?

Just Beginning

Julia was surprised: – Enter, how? The people who live in this house don't know us; they won't let us in! – Alzira looked at Ciro, they both began to laugh. He said: – Don't worry about it, Julia.

– As Alzira said, we are in a different moment. They won't see us. Just as we have done with you all your life. We were always by your side, but you never saw us.

They entered the house through the open door. Julia stopped at the door, unable to enter.

– What happened, Julia? Why don't you come in?

– This room is wonderful! Beautiful! Look at the furniture, paintings, and rugs! They look like works of art!

– Look at that stair! It's like the stair I was talking about when I said that I liked to imagine girls in those long–armed dresses. Imagine one of them coming down that stair! Everything here is so beautiful!

– It's really beautiful but keep looking. See what is behind so much beauty and wealth.

Julia, who only paid attention to the beauty of the room, hadn't noticed several people walking around. Some cleaned, others took the coffee plates on the table, and others shook the furniture.

They worked fast.

Admired, Julia asked: – Are they slaves? That no longer exists!

– Didn't I say that we are in another time, Julia? At that time, slavery existed and black people suffered greatly.

– They worked fast because there was a lot of work to do.

– Fortunately, abolition came...

Just Beginning

– It's true. Now let's look at the rest of the house and meet the people who live here.

Alzira looked away at the imposing staircase in front of them. Julia followed her gaze and asked, Shall we go up those stairs?

– Yes, Julia. Everything will begin in one of the rooms of this house. Let's go! Alzira started walking. Ciro and Julia walked beside her.

Julia was so excited that she didn't pay attention to what Alzira said. Seeming to forget who she was and what she was doing there, she ran and started up the stairs. In the middle, she turned and said: – This is all wonderful!

– Only the long–armed dress is missing!

Ciro smiled: – Before we go, if you want, you can wear a long–armed dress and also go down the stairs the way you always dreamed of. Do you want to?

– Can I really do that?

– Sure. Don't forget that you are dreaming. In a dream everything is allowed.

– It's going to be wonderful! We really need to know the rest of the house and who lives here.

Julia kept going up. At the end of the stairs, there was a corridor with a half wall from which you could see the room.

Julia looked over the wall. When she saw the room from above, she said: – It's wonderful! The people who live here must be very happy!

Ciro and Alzira were silent and kept walking. Julia looked and saw that there were doors on either side of the corridor.

She deduced they were the rooms. Excited by everything she was seeing, she followed them both. They entered a room with

Just Beginning

the door closed. Julia opened her mouth and couldn't close it. Alzira realized it and, laughing, asked: – What was that Julia? close your mouth and answer!

Julia took a deep breath and asked: – How did we get into this room if the door is closed?

– You 're dreaming, Julia! Just that!

– You're right, but everything is so real! I can't believe it's a dream!

– It's true. It's very real. Now, look at the room. What do you think? – Julia looked around.

– I can't believe I'm in a room like this! It's wonderful!

– I've only seen one like this in movies! I'm so excited that I don't even know what to say! You said that I chose the life that I live. – You're wrong! If I could choose, I would choose a life like this.

I would live in a beautiful house like this and have a room like this!

– Very good. You can have this life if you want.

– Are you serious?

– Yes, but now, you will meet the resident of this house and this room. It's because of her that we are here.

– She's sleeping. Look.

Julia looked at the huge wooden bed in the middle of the room. A white veil that fell from the top surrounded the bed. For that reason, she couldn't see the face of the resident who owned the room.

Alzira and Ciro noticed her delight. They smiled.

– Now, Julia, you will meet not only the resident, but also her life.

Just Beginning

– She must be very happy...

When Julia looked around, the door opened, and a black woman entered.

She had a breakfast tray in her hands. While she was placing the tray on a small table, lined with a blue fabric like the bedspread and the curtains, Júlia, astonished, asked Alzira: – Who is this woman?

– She is Zefa, the slave, who takes care of the owner of this room. We told you that we were in another time and that you were dreaming, right?

Julia nodded in agreement.

– Well then. Keep watching. Imagine that you're watching a movie whose events took place in the time of the Empire.

After placing the tray on the small table, Zefa approached the bed, pulled back the veil and called softly:

– Wake up, my lady María Inéz.

The girl opened her eyes and when she saw the lady there, she said: – It's still early, Zefa. I need to get some more sleep.

– You already slept a lot. It's time to get up. The day so longed for by my lady arrived.

María Inés stretched her body and sat down: – It's true, Zefa! Today's the big day! Did my gift arrive?

– No. I don't think it will come. When I asked your father, he said he forgot it.

Furious, María Inés got up and shouted: – Did he forget it? How can he do something like that?

– He said that, worried about your mother's disagreement, he forgot it.

Just Beginning

– He couldn't have done that, Zefa! When I saw that necklace at the jewelry store, I knew it was perfect as it would fit with my dress.

My father was there with me and promised to buy it! I need that necklace!

– Please, understand, your mother is very happy and he is happy...

– I don't need to understand anything! I know my mother is sick, but he could go to the jewelry store for a moment or send someone else to buy it!

– Your father is very busy, my lady...

– I know, but I need that necklace! My life depends on it! – Zefa began to laugh: – your life depends on it, huh, my lady?

Walking around the room, very nervous, María Inés replied: – How can you ask that, Zefa?

– Today is the day of the annual dance in the palace! All the important people will be there! Especially Luiz Claudio!

I need that necklace! Only by wearing that beautiful necklace will he notice me!

– Well, lady, don't miss the fact that you are young. No matter what clothes or jewelry you wear, you will always be pretty!

– Everything is always easy for you, isn't it, Zefa?

– It could be for you, lady. Just accept things as they are, that in the end, everything will be fine.

– I don't understand how you can be so calm and always be at ease with life! You always seem happy.

– You have no karma, please, my lady?

– You are a slave, Zefa! How can you be happy!

Just Beginning

– I'm not sad about it. I like this house, I really like you, my lady. Your father has always been a good master.

He never thought of selling Ignacio or any of my children. He always let us live together as if we were a family.

My lady knows that not all masters think that way. They sell their slaves regardless of whether they have a wife and family.

– When your father bought us, Ignacio and I had just met. Then I started liking him and your father let us live together.

– He didn't do it out of kindness, Zefa. He knew you were going to have children, so more arms for farming.

– That may be true, my lady, but he would have arms for agriculture, even though we don't live together.

– You are very naive, Zefa.

– I think there is a reason for me to be a slave...

– What reason, Zefa?

– I don't know, my lady, but there should be a reason. Now, my lady must have coffee.

– Today you will be very busy so please start eating too.

– Okay.

María Inés sat down and began to eat. Julia, silent, looked at everything.

While María Inés ate, Zefa said: – My lady, your father said that he is in the hospital so Ignacio will take my lady there.

María Inés got up again and, very nervous, said: – I can't go, Zefa! I have a lot to do!

Today is the day of the party, I need to dress up. You know how difficult it is to do hairstyle!

Just Beginning

– I know, my lady, but the doctor told your father that your mother has no cure, that she will die soon, that it could even be today.

María Inés, ignoring what Zefa said, said: – I need that necklace, Zefa!

Zefa insisted: – Your mother is very sick, my lady...

– If she is going to die, what can I do, Zefa?

– You could go to the hospital. She's going to be very happy to see my lady.

– I told you I can't get out of here, Zefa! I need to get ready for the party tonight!

– Ignacio will take my lady there very fast.

– I already said I can't get out of here and don't bother me with that issue!

– All right, my lady. Alright...

Hearing that conversation, Júlia whispered: – Mrs. Alzira...

– What Julia? You don't have to whisper; you can speak normally. They cannot see or hear us.

– How can she act like this with her mother? Doesn't she like her?

– She likes her mother, yes, Julia, but she likes herself much more.

Is she like that?!

– Like what?

– Selfish and mean?

– You're the one who says that, but let's keep listening to the conversation.

– Zefa, is Maria Augusta up yet?

– Yes, my lady. She went to the hospital with your father.

Just Beginning

– Why did she go there?

– She went to visit your mother, my lady...

– Why did she do that? She knew she couldn't leave the house! We need to get ready for the dance!

– I know your sister doesn't care about those things.

– I know, but I care a lot and I need her help!

Nervous, María Inés went to the closet, opened the door and took out a green dress. She placed it in front of her body and looked at herself in the mirror.

– It's beautiful, isn't it, Zefa?

– Yes, it is, my lady. The color matches my lady's eyes and her hair as well.

– I really liked this fabric, so I asked my father to buy it and you sewed it very well. Thanks Zefa!

She looked in the mirror again: – It's not good. My necklace is missing! I need it!

Call Ignacio, Zefa!

– For what, my lady?

– Since my father didn't buy my necklace, I'll go there myself!

– You can't my lady...

– Why?

– My lady knows that a lady doesn't walk alone an d does nothing without having a man by her side.

The man from the jewelry store won't sell the necklace to my lady without her father being present.

– It's true, Zefa! How angry I am about all this! Why does it have to be like this?

Just Beginning

Why doesn't a woman have the same rights as a man? If I didn't have a father, what would it be like?

Couldn't I buy anything?

– I don't know, my lady...

– What I wanted most in this life was to be alone! Not having a mother or father! Not having anyone!

– Only then could I decide how to live my life without having to ask for anyone's permission!

– Don't talk like that my lady! Orphanages have many fatherless and motherless children. I think they suffer a lot... – Alzira looked at Ciro.

Both ignored Julia, who was horrified by what she had just heard: – She doesn't know what she's talking about, Mrs. Alzira!

– She doesn't know how sad it is to have no one. If I had had a father and mother like her, I know I wouldn't have suffered as much as I did. She said that she wouldn't go to the hospital to visit her mother, because she couldn't leave the house, but she was willing to go out and buy a necklace! I don't understand that! I don't understand how a person can be so selfish.

I always thought that someone who lived like her could only be happy, but from what I see here, that is not true.

She, despite having everything, thinks she is unhappy...

– It's true, Julia, but don't worry. She will understand and appreciate everything she never did. God is our father and creator.

He gives us the opportunity to assess what really has value.

He has patience and gives us all eternity to make that happen.

– My lady, are you going to bathe? I prepared the bathtub with hot water.

Just Beginning

– It's the best I can do to forget about this unhappy life that I live.

– All right, my lady. I will prepare your clothes.

Julia looked at them and said: – Are you sure she'll understand?

– Yes, Julia. All of us sooner or later understand and find our way.

Now while she's showering, let's go to the garden and breathe fresh air. I think the three of us need it. Isn't that right, Ciro? – He didn't answer, he just smiled.

19. – Spiritual help

Julia immediately opened her eyes. She looked around and saw that she was back in the hospital. She remembered what she had done. Oh my god! How did I go crazy like this? Where was my head?

She remembered Anselmo: he couldn't have done what he did. I didn't deserve it...

– Did you wake up?

Hearing that question, Julia turned her gaze to the voice.

She saw a lady who was smiling. She replied: – I woke up. It seems I slept a lot...

– You really did. My name is Silvia, what's yours?

– Julia, did I sleep a long time?

– When you arrived, you were a little dizzy. You talked to your friend and then fell asleep. You slept for almost two hours.

– Only two hours? I thought I had slept more. I had such a strange dream...

– Do you want to tell me?

– I don't remember very well. I just know that I was in a very beautiful place and that there was a dress like the one a woman used to wear. It was beautiful! I know there were people with me, but I don't know who they were...

Just Beginning

– It seems that the dream was really beautiful!

– Yes, it was. I just wanted to remember more of what happened and those who were by my side...

Alzira and Ciro, who were there, smiled. Silvia continued:
– I think that when we sleep, we leave the body and go for a walk.

– We leave the body? How? – Julia asked suspiciously.

– I'm talking about our spirit, Julia.

– Are you talking about that religion that talks about the dead? Sueli, that friend of mine who was here, said something about it, but I didn't pay attention.

– I have no religion, Julia. I read about all of them. I study each one, but so far, I haven't decided to follow any.

– This one in particular, that you said, managed to convince me more.

– Why this one in particular? Do you like death?

– Exactly what you said. Of course, I like death, especially mine.

– The Doctrine I am studying teaches that death doesn't exist. That our loved ones, who are gone, are waiting for us somewhere, because one day we will go to meet them.

Julia remembered what Neide had said about her mother.

– Do you really believe that, Silvia? Do you think that one day I will find my mother who died when I was born?

– I think so, Julia. Just as I'm going to meet my parents, brothers, friends and my husband as well.

– That's just talking. I think that when we die, everything ends, Silvia.

– It may be a conversation, but thinking about it makes me feel good.

Just Beginning

– I can't believe our life ends when we die and that our loved ones disappear forever.

– It would be very sad. A life is very short.

– A life? Do you really believe that there are other lives after the one we are living?

Silvia was about to answer, but they heard a moan. They looked and, in front of the bed where they were, there was another woman who seemed to be sleeping.

Julia asked: – She's sleeping, Silvia, but she seems to be in a lot of pain. What's wrong with her?

– I don't know. Ever since I've arrived three days ago, she's been sleeping and moaning almost always.

– I think she is really in pain.

– Poor. There is nothing worse than pain...

Alzira and Ciro looked at a lady who was standing next to the lady moaning and with her hands she threw bright white lights on her.

When she saw that they were looking at her, she said smiling: – It's my mother. She has been like this for a long time, but refuses to leave her body, despite being in a lot of pain. I keep throwing lights to see if the pain goes away, but the physical body is sick and I can't.

She doesn't want to die. She is afraid...

Alzira approached and also shining on the lady, said: – And who isn't? When we are in the physical body, we are afraid of everything. Even more so of something unknown like death.

The lady smiled: – It's true. The physical body leads us to forget what our life is like in spirituality.

– That's why we're so scared.

– Her spirit, how is it?

Just Beginning

– It could be better if it weren't for all that fear...

– Her life in the physical body, how was it?

– It was very good. She had an ordinary life. She managed to rescue some outstanding debts.

She had her children and raised them lovingly. The only thing she failed to do was to get rid of her attachment to things and people.

She always liked the things she had at home. She never threw anything away. She kept them even when they were broke.

I would like people to see and praise. This attachment spread to children. She was always super protective and couldn't take it when I died in an accident. She was devastated, she cried every day, I could say every hour.

When I recovered after the accident, already on the spiritual realm, and learned how I was, I tried to do everything possible to make her go back to being the same woman as before, but I couldn't. She wasn't happy before and today, because I died. She never reconciled with the fact of losing me. Her pain, bitterness and sadness were so great that they reached her physical body. She was very strong and determined, after my death, she became what you are seeing.

Her body deteriorated until the moment when there was no turning back, because the disease and some other spirits, suffering from the same disease, came closer and made her situation worse. I'm trying to push them away, but she stops me.

She attracts them. The moment you walked into the room, I was thinking of asking for help, because I don't know what else to do.

– Are you alone by her side?

Just Beginning

– At this moment, I am, but as you know, we are never alone. My father and some friends, although they are not here now, are always aware whether they need to be here.

Alzira looked at some figures in the room. She realized that they were anxious and restless. Then she looked at Julia and Silvia who were talking. Cyrus approached.

Alzira, holding the hand of the lady who was next to her mother, asked: – Don't you want to wake her up so that you can talk and try to convince her that it's time to leave the body?

– I tried but couldn't. I spoke to her, but she is so attached to her body that she doesn't listen to me.

– Then I was going to ask for help. It can't go on like this. She is suffering a lot.

– Do we try again?

– Of course. I will do whatever it takes. I just want her to be at peace. I want her to understand that death isn't the end, that it's only the beginning.

Ciro positioned himself at the head of the bed. Alzira and the lady's daughter were on both sides of the bed.

They spread their arms, prayed, and the room lit up completely. The light was so intense that it made the figures there embrace and lean against one of the walls.

From the hands of the three, lights began to appear directed at her. Alzira looked at the girl and asked: – What is her name?

– Rosalia

– Well. Try to wake her up.

The girl put her hand on the lady's head and spoke softly: – Wake up mother...

Although the woman's body was still sleeping, she opened her eyes and when she saw her daughter there, she despaired:

Just Beginning

– Lucila! Are you here, my daughter?

– It's me, mom. I'm here by your side...

– Am I dreaming? I can't see you! I'm dead!

– No, mom, you're not dead, neither am I.

– What? I saw you being buried. I never settled for your death. You were so beautiful, you were studying, and you had a whole life ahead of you! You couldn't have died like this!

– I know you were sorry, but you were right. Everything that happens is always right.

– Nothing is right, my daughter. I had you, I raised you with all the love, when you grew up and prepared for life, you were taking away from me without me being able to do anything to stop it! This is not right or fair!

– I should have protected you! I should have kept you from leaving the house that day! You were mine and you are mine!

– Don't be like that, Mom. I was never yours. So, like you, I am the daughter of a wonderful father!

You were a wonderful mother.

Nothing you can do could change that day. It had to happen.

It had to happen. I can only thank you for everything you did for me, but now you need to continue and preferably by my side. We have a long way to go.

– You are my daughter! Mine, nobody else's! I can never forget that!

– No mom! I am not yours! You and I are daughters of God!

He created me, just as he created you and all things and people that live on earth and in heaven.

We have been friends for a long time.

Just Beginning

We have been living together many times and will live together again and we will always be helping each other during our walk into the Light.

– I've always controlled my life. Why couldn't I stop you from dying before me?

– Really, you always controlled everything, but just as you could not prevent my death, you cannot prevent yours.

– My death? I don't want to die!

– It's not under your control, mother. You need to understand this to stop suffering...

– I don't want to die. What will happen to my things, my house and everything that I bought with so much work?

I can't leave everything behind! Everything is mine and I won't leave it to anyone!

The daughter looked at Alzira and Ciro and said: – You see? She can't help but hold on to the things she has accomplished. Alzira smiled: – Keep calm. I will talk to her.

Addressing the lady, she said: – Hello, Rosalía, how are you?

When Rosalía saw Alzira dressed in white, she replied: – I'm not well, doctor. I feel a lot of pain.

You need to help me. I need to feel better to be able to return to my house, to my things.

– You will return, but first, I want you to get up and hug your daughter.

She is here and she missed you so much. She wants to receive a hug from you. Rosalía looked at her daughter.

– I really wanted to, Lucila, but I can't get up. I feel a lot of pain...

Just Beginning

You can get up, yeah. Your daughter is here. Lucila, take your mother's hands and help her get up.

Lucila walked over to her mother, took her hands and, with some effort, got her mother to stand up and hugged her.

The two hugged each other and began to cry. The emotion was so great that Alzira and Ciro had to make an enormous effort not to cry too. The figures that were still leaning against the wall looked at each other.

Alzira, seeing that they were interested and moved, said: – Love is the most important thing to exist.

– It makes our spirit vibrate with excitement and happiness.

Addressing Rosalía, she continued: – As you can see, your daughter's love stopped your pain.

– It only depends on you to stay with her, without pain.

Still hugging her daughter, Rosalía said: – I'm worried about my things! Everything I achieved with so much work!

I can't leave it like this...

– The things you have were never yours. What is yours and that no one can take from you is the way you lived, the good you did, and the friends you made. These are the difficult times you went through without losing your faith.

Your need, at this time, is related to your spirit, your well-being, and your spiritual evolution.

The material goods you obtained served to help you during your life in the physical body.

No more than that. Now, you must thank them and get rid of them.

Nothing can come with you. Everything will remain on Earth, so that other people can continue to enjoy them.

Just Beginning

Ciro nodded and Alzira followed his gaze. She saw that the figures were paying close attention to everything she said.

She smiled at Ciro and continued: – All of us, spirits that live on Earth or anywhere else, have moments where we have to choose. Some options are right and some are wrong, but it's all part of improving our spirit.

Sometimes we try not to choose and we just leave it for later. However, there comes a time when there is no escape. That moment has come for you Rosalía and for so many others who, like you, are trapped with the things they have achieved and the people they have loved. You can't take with you the things you have earned.

The people you loved, as well as your daughter who returned before you, are waiting for your return.

Others, who still have their mission, their rescues, will one day return and they'll be waiting for them.

The time for your decision has come. Only you can decide whether to go with your daughter to a place where you no longer feel pain. A place where you will discover the reason why you were reborn or you can continue to suffer in that body that has already done a lot for you, but that now, with the passage of time, is degenerated, worn out.

You can choose to thank it for all it did and let it rest in peace, while you live in eternity. You will have other opportunities to be reborn, to improve even more. But this incarnation of yours is ending, Rosalía, it is only up to you.

Rosalía and Lucila listened in silence. The figures, one by one, moved closer to hear better.

Alzira, now looking at them, continued: – You can also, if you don't want to accept what I am proposing, become a spirit that will wander from one place to another or with others who wander, without destination.

Just Beginning

Leaning against others who are still in the physical body, but who are also attached to things or people, things that have no value to the spirit, without appreciating what is really important for the spirit on its journey.

The good you can do, the friends you can earn, and the love you can give. Material goods are necessary.

Dreaming, desiring and conquering is a way of learning. What is not right is for people to value them so much.

What is not right is to get attached in such a way that it is difficult for the spirit to break free while it is happening to you.

Being rich not always means happiness or being poor sadness. Each one, before being reborn, chooses the life they want to have.

What will be best for your spirit, your learning.

Whichever life you choose, in the end, no matter if you are rich or poor, you will have to answer for what you did with it. They all paid attention to what Alzira said. The figures looked at each other and thought.

Alzira, seeing that they were paying attention, continued: – I just have to warn that in life, both incarnate and disincarnate, there are only two paths, good and evil. It is up to each one to choose the path they wish to follow.

– Whoever chooses to wander can do so. No one will stop you. You will only lose a huge and precious time on your walk and you will be further and further away from those you once loved. What I say is for you, Rosalía –. Addressing the figures, she continued: – Everything I said also applies to you who were attracted to Rosalía and who are also attached to things and money. They are also wasting enormous and precious time that they can use to find happiness and peace, as well as to see the people they love.

Just Beginning

When she finished speaking, she smiled and returned to Julia's side, who was still talking to Silvia.

Rosalía, who was still holding her daughter, moved away a little and, looking into her eyes, asked: Are you telling the truth, Lucila? Can we be together?

Lucila, unable to believe what she was hearing, laughing, hugged her mother.

– Everything she said is true, yes, mother! Let's be together, yeah! Many are waiting for your decision.

– Will this pain go away?

– Of course. This pain is coming from your body, not from your spirit.

Rosalía began to cry: – I was really valuing that which has no value...

– It's true, Mom. You need to be grateful for everything you conquered, the dreams you made and that wonderful body that helped you on your journey, but now, your path is different. All this needs to be forgotten, left behind.

– You're right, my daughter. I'm in a lot of pain and I'm tired of fighting...

– So, mom, are you ready?

– I am, my daughter. I am ready to drop everything that I thought was important, because there is nothing more important than this moment when I am by your side. I feel that now I will find happiness.

At the same moment, Lucila, crying, said: – The moment has come, father. We are waiting. A few seconds later, five entities appeared.

Just Beginning

One of them approached Lucila and, hugging her, said: – At last, my daughter. You did a great job –. Lucila looked at Alzira and Ciro: – I couldn't have done it without your help.

The man looked at Ciro and Alzira, smiled: – Thank you. My name is Valdomiro.

– I disincarnated early so that Rosalía could understand that attachment to things or people is not healthy and that it is bad for the spirit, but it did not help. She, as she always has, remained attached to it. Before being reborn, she understood that this was an obstacle to her evolution. So, in this incarnation, she wanted to get everything she wanted, and then she would lose.

So, she wanted to go through the same thing again, hoping that this time she could win.

Lucila and I promised to be reborn by her side, and we disincarnated in front of her so that she would understand, accept and let go of unimportant things. Neither my disincarnating nor Lucila's made her understand.

We knew that her disincarnation would be difficult. You saw that, even though she suffered with her sick body, she clung to it.

You must have been surprised that she left Lucila alone. It was necessary to understand our work.

Once you have helped your mother, you can help anyone. She will work on our team. Lucila was surprised: – Will I, Dad?

– Go, my daughter. You passed the test with honors. Through our call, you needed to show that you would know how to speak to a brother at the time of disincarnation. Now you are ready to go with us.

– We will understand it well. Don't worry, Lucila. We all passed these tests. Isn't that right, Ciro? – Ciro, also smiling, nodded and said yes.

Just Beginning

Valdomiro, turned to the others who accompanied him, raised his arms and said: – Thank you, my Father, for the opportunity to learn from this work. Thank you for allowing me to be here now and to take Rosalía home.

All those who were there, including Alzira and Ciro, extended their hands, from which rays of white light came out, towards Rosalía. From the tips of Valdomiro's fingers, the lights became brighter and with it, he cut two silver threads that still held Rosalía's spirit to her body. When he finished, he embraced the one who had been his wife:

– You are free, Rosalía. Now we can leave.

Crying, she hugged him: – Did you come looking for me, Valdomiro?

– Of course. I have never stopped being by your side through thick and thin, I wouldn't miss, now, such an important moment, together with the woman who helped me on my journey on Earth, who gave me such happy moments that helped me grow spiritually.

She laughed: – You also had difficult moments, right? It wasn't easy...

He also laughed: – That is part of the marriage. I also had my glorious moments. It wasn't easy for me either. We were both walking and learning. Now, shall we go? See how many are waiting for you here. Rosalía looked where he was pointing: – Did everyone come to pick me up?

– Not all of them, Rosalía. Some wander, others are in the valley, but together we will try to rescue one by one. Crying, Rosalía hugged everyone. Then she hugged Valdomiro and Lucila.

He asked: – Are you still sad about leaving everything behind?

Just Beginning

– No. Only now do I understand what it is to value that which is really valuable. They all smiled.

Together, they thanked Ciro and Alzira and, sending a kiss with the tips of their fingers, they disappeared. At that same time, Julia and Silvia heard a different moan than they had heard until then. They turned and saw Rosalia breathing deeply.

Julia, who was lying on the bed, asked alarmed: – Did she stop breathing, Silvia? Silvia raised her body to see better.

– I don't know. I think we better call the nurse.

The two, scared, pressed the bell next to the bed.

The nurse from the floor, when she saw that the two were calling her, also scared, ran to the room: – What happened? Why are they pressing the bell together?

The two, scared, couldn't speak, they only indicated with their hand the bed where Rosalía was. The nurse went there, put her finger on Rosalia's neck.

Then she looked at them and said: – I'm going to call the doctor, but it seems that she died. Thank God. I was desperate, she suffered a lot, she was in a lot of pain. The drugs were no longer effective. The nurse left the room.

Soon after, she returned with a doctor who, examining Rosalia, looked at the nurse and said: – It's over.

Ask them to come get her. He smiled at Julia and Silvia and left the room.

They couldn't see it, but if they could, they would see Rosalía left happy, along with her family, her husband and her daughter who were happy to be able to make that return trip.

Julia, still scared, said: – I've never seen anyone die...

– Nor I...

Just Beginning

Then two nurses arrived with a stretcher and took Rosalía's body. As soon as they left, Julia lay down and started crying.

Silvia went back to bed and was silent for a long time.

The figures that had approached, when they saw everything that had happened, returned to the corner of the wall and one of them asked: – Is everything you said is true? Can we choose what we want?

The figure of a woman who was there, crying, replied: – Of course it is true! Didn't you see how many came to help carry the woman?

Another said: – I don't know, no. They may be trying to lie to us...

The woman, who was very moved, argued: – Have you never heard of the people of the Light? – They all said yes, with their heads. She continued: – They say they don't tell lies.

– Have you ever seen a light like the one that illuminated this room? – They shooked their heads again, saying no.

– I don't know about you, but I'm tired of wandering aimlessly, to go back to my house and look at the people and everything I had. I want to see my husband and son who came before me. I want to find peace –. Alzira, hearing that, approached.

The figures, seeing her approach, leaned against each other.

Alzira, looking at the figure of the woman, smiling, asked: – Are you being honest about what you are saying?

The figure of the woman, crying, replied: – I am. I want to have the opportunity to be happy, to meet the people I love.

– I want to feel what that lady felt.

– Are you making a decision?

– Yes, I am...

– Look over there...

Just Beginning

The figure looked where Alzira was pointing and began to cry and shout: – I can't believe it! They really came! In fact, several spirits with their own light approached and began to embrace the figure.

She was so moved that she couldn't speak. She just cried. After the hugs and shouts, everyone hugged her, took her away.

Alzira and Ciro smiled.

One by one, the other figures approached and asked what had happened to them. Ciro and Alzira cared for everyone and soon the room was small for many.

After the hugs and tears, they all disappeared. Ciro laughing, said: – When we got to be with Julia, we didn't think that we would help so many brothers. I am very happy, Alzira.

– So am I Ciro. Once again, it has been proven that when help is needed, it always comes.

Silvia, who had been silent for some time, asked: – Julia, why are you here? What happened to your head? Júlia, ashamed, lied: – I was hit by a bicycle, I fell and hurt my head.

– Are you hospitalized just for that?

– Yes. When I hit my head, the doctor told me I should stay a day for observation.

Silvia knew that she had lied, because she heard when Julia spoke with Sueli, but she pretended to believe her:

– I'm leaving tomorrow too. They removed my gallbladder. There were some stones, but now everything is fine.

– I can't wait to go home.

Julia remembered what her life was like and she was silent, just thinking: unemployed and having to move out of the apartment, I don't even know what will happen in my life...

Alzira and Ciro smiled.

Just Beginning

Silvia didn't stop talking. Little by little, Julia began to tire.

After Rosalia's death, she was a bit depressed and said: – I've never seen anyone die, Silvia.

– It makes me think about what we're doing here. We are born, we live and we die. People work very hard, fight and run, and then die. I don't see any use in all this.

– No, Julia! You are so young and you are thinking like an old woman! Life is beautiful and very good!

– Of course, it is full of surprises, it has ups and downs, but even so, it's great to live!

– If you think that way, my life has only had down moments...

– It's impossible, Julia! Everyone has good times and bad times. For example, even though I had bad moments, I refuse to think about them.

– The word is: moments. They pass. I prefer to think about the good ones that happened and wait, anxiously, for the others to come. If, during this trip, something bad comes, it will pass.

– I can't think like that, because I've had few good moments. And, as of now, I just see a lot of bad men coming. I'm tired, Silvia. I don't know why I live or why...

– You can be sure that even if a bad time comes, it will pass and you will still be happy.

– I hope you are right. I've been waiting for this for twenty-three years.

– Twenty three? You are still very young! I guarantee that there are many good times ahead and many bad ones. That's life!

This is living, Julia!

Julia, Ciro and Alzira smiled.

Just Beginning

They continued talking until a girl came into the room with dinner. They had dinner and talked for a while.

Ciro and Alzira decided that it was time to continue telling the story of María Inés to Júlia, who, yawning, said: – I'm tired, Silvia. I think I'm going to get some sleep.

– I think I'm going to sleep too...

In a few moments, Julia and Silvia were sleeping soundly.

20.– Eulalia

As soon as she opened her eyes, Julia realized that she was lying in the garden. Sitting next to her were Alzira and Ciro. She asked: – Are you calmer, Julia?

Julia sat down and, smiling, replied: – I'm a little scared and confused, but I'm fine.

– Scared? Confused? Why?

I was in the hospital talking to Silvia and I saw a woman die.

– Were you afraid?

– Of course.

– Why?

– I don't know. The woman was there, moaning in pain. Suddenly, she took a deep breath and died.

– What did you think?

– I thought about death and why it exists.

– Don't you think death can be a blessing?

– Of course not! We don't have to die. We could live forever.

– You wanted to die yourself. Why did you want that, Julia?

– I was desperate and I still am. I don't know what will happen to my life.

Just Beginning

– That lady who died in the hospital had a long life.

– Like all of us, she had good and bad moments. She suffered and was happy. Often when she thought it was over, she found out later that it was just beginning. Not you, Julia. You are young and have a lot to do.

– Many young people die...

– It's true, but none of them die unscheduled.

– There is always a reason for everything that happens. God is perfect. He is not unfair.

– This is all very complicated.

– Nothing is complicated. Everything is simpler than you can imagine.

– There's something else bothering me.

– What?

– I was in the hospital. Now I came back here. I thought I had a dream, but apparently it wasn't a dream or I am dreaming in chapters.

Alzira and Ciro laughed. He asked: – You are not dreaming in chapters, Julia. You are only learning a story.

– Why don't you tell it right away?

– Why, after being here, I woke up and couldn't remember, in detail, this dream?

– There are many reasons, Julia. Don't hurry. At the right time, you will get those answers.

– I'm not in a hurry, just curious.

– Did you know that curiosity is one of the most used tools for the evolution of the spirit?

– Why?

– That's exactly why.

Just Beginning

– You're questioning, you're curious. Curiosity leads the spirit towards the whys, the search for answers and knowledge, and therefore, wisdom. Before a great invention, the same thought always arises: "If I did this or that, maybe I could do it." Most of the time, the inventor can do it.

– Can I ask one more question?

– Of course.

– Why do I need to know this story?

– First, because the time has come, second, because it is very beautiful.

– Just one more question?

Ciro and Alzira smiled and nodded.

– Why does this happen to me? Why was I chosen?

Ciro replied: – Do you know what causes the spirit to often fail?

– No...

– The presumption. Why do you think it is special that you were chosen?

– I don't know why I thought that, I just know that I never heard something like this happen to another person.

– You are not special nor were you chosen. What is happening to you, happens to all spirits when they are sleeping.

– Everyone?

– Everyone, Julia. It doesn't matter race, class or religion.

– When your body sleeps, your spirit is taken to places where you will study and learn about spirituality or, as it is happening to you, to learn a story.

– Why do you speak of spirits and not people?

Just Beginning

– Because people live for a short time, but spirits live forever, for all eternity.

– We are all spirits, created by our Creator. Our creator is perfect. He has no favorite or special children.

– It may be that what you are talking about is true, but I think there is a difference, yes.

– Why do you say that?

– There are rich and poor people, ugly and beautiful, intelligent and less intelligent. In addition to those who, with a minimum of effort, get everything they want. While others, no matter how hard they try, achieve nothing.

– There are healthy people and other sick people and so many differences that I don't remember now.

– We already talked about that, Julia.

– We talked, yes, but the answer you gave me didn't convince me.

– You said it was my choice. However, if I had a choice, I would never have chosen this life that I lead.

– I would choose a very different one.

– Are you sure about that?

– Of course, I am! Anyone would choose it!

– I know. You would choose to be rich and beautiful to have everything you wanted, etc., etc., etc.

– That's right. My life would be totally different.

Alzira interfered: – We already talked a lot. It's time to continue meeting the people who live in this house. Julia, who was sitting, got up and looked around her.

Just Beginning

– As incredible as it sounds, I can't believe I'm in a house like this! It's really beautiful! Alzira and Ciro smiled and started walking towards the house.

Julia, still looking at everything there, walked beside them.

They entered the house and walked towards the stairs.

As they went up, Julia said: – It's been a long time since we left here. It must already be party time.

– No, Julia. We are in a dream. Did you forget that?

Julia didn't have time to reply. They entered the room. María Inés was sitting in front of a mirror. Zefa combed her hair.

– The little lady's hair is very pretty. My lady will be beautiful for the party.

– I'm not going, Zefa. You forgot that I won't be wearing that beautiful necklace!

– Are you thinking about that, my lady?

María Inés was about to answer, but the bedroom door opened and a girl entered.

When she saw her in the mirror, María Inés got up and nervously asked: – I'm glad you've arrived, María Augusta!

I was waiting for you!

– I went with dad to the hospital. Mom is very sick. The doctor said she could die at any moment.

– I'm very nervous, María Augusta!

– I am too. She is suffering a lot...

– That's not why I'm nervous!

– What is the reason?

– Have you thought about what if she decides to die before the party?

– How can you say that, María Inés? She is your mother!

Just Beginning

– Didn't you say there is no cure? Since there is nothing to do, she can die at any time, as long as she dies after the party! I waited so long for this day!

– I can't believe you're saying that, María Inés. She was a good mother. She looked after us both with great affection.

– How can you be so cold?

– I know she was a good mother. I can't complain, but she is sick, she is going to die, right? – María Augusta, nervous, as she left the room, shouted: – You are a monster, María Inés! – Julia, also nervous, said: – She is right. How can this girl be like this? If she knew how difficult it is to grow up without a mother, I guarantee she wouldn't talk that way. I would have given anything to have met my mother...

– Unfortunately, she doesn't think so, Julia.

– How can she?

Alzira replied: – The spirit, when it is in the physical body, is hardly satisfied with what it has.

– When you have a lot, you don't value it, if you have little, you complain. María Inés is demonstrating this.

– She has a lot and doesn't value it properly. So, she is unhappy and selfish. She is so preoccupied with herself that she doesn't see anything wrong with her attitude. We will continue to see what happened.

Julia didn't understand the behavior of María Inés, but she kept silent.

As soon as María Augusta left, María Inés got up and shouted: Zefa! Go call Maria Augusta! I need her to help me!

– Why do you need her, my lady?

– I don't know! I just want her to come here! She is older and must help me! She needs to find a way for me to get that necklace.

Just Beginning

– Forget the necklace, my lady! You have so many you could choose from.

– Forget? Of course, I won't forget it! My dress, without it, will lose its light, it will look horrible!

– Do you think Eulalia is going to the dance anyway? I guarantee that she will wear a beautiful dress with beautiful and expensive jewelry! She will try to win over Luiz Cláudio and I cannot allow that to happen! Go call Maria Augusta!

– I don't think she's coming...

– Don't argue Zefa! Go call her!

Zefa left and then came back: – My lady, María Augusta won't come, my lady.

– Why not? We need to get ready for the dance!

– My lady, she said she's not going to the party.

– Is she not going to the dance?

– She said she's not going. I just saw a change of clothes and I am going to take her to the hospital. She said that she wanted you to see your mother, that she would go with Ignacio to stay with your mother.

– Maria Augusta can't do that! I can't go to the dance without her and my parents. I really want to go to this dance, Zefa!

– I'll talk to her!

– No way. When I reached her, she was already getting into the carriage.

– Without my parents and María Augusta, I need to find someone to accompany me, but who?

– It would be very nice if I had a brother. I'll talk to her.

– You're right my lady. I don't think you can, no.

Just Beginning

– You better talk to your sister later. I already told you she left. The one down there is Eulália. She wants to talk to you my lady.

– Is Eulalia here? What does she want?

– She said she needs to talk to you my lady. I can tell her to come up, or is my lady going down?

– I know what she wants, Zefa! She wants to see my dress! Help me hide it here in the closet. I'll show her another one!

– Why are you doing this, my lady? She will see it at the party...

– Only at the party, Zefa! Only at the party! Not before!

– Oh God, my lady. Why do you do all this?

– Stop talking, Zefa and help me hide the dress!

They quickly put the dress on a hanger and into the closet.

– Now that we have the dress, you can go down and ask Eulalia to come up. I'm curious why she came here.

Zefa left the room. María Inés thought: – I don't know what Eulália wants, but I'm sure of one thing, I can go to the dance with her family. So, I will be able to see and speak with Luiz Cláudio.

A few minutes later, a girl entered the room. She was crying, she ran and hugged María Inés.

– What happened, Eulalia? Why are you like this?

– I need your help, María Inés. Are you gonna help me?

– Calm down, Eulalia. Stop crying, tell me what's going on.

I am desperate, I don't know what to do.

– Speak!

– I'm in love with José Antônio and he's in love with me. I really wanted to go to the dance tonight, so I could see him.

Just Beginning

– Who is José Antônio? I don't know him. Does he belong to a good family?

– You mean, from the court? No. He is the son of a merchant.

– Merchant?

– Yes. You are prejudiced too, but I don't care. We love each other and we want to be together.

– So, what is the problem?

– Last night, my father told me that today, at the dance, I must let Luiz Cláudio woo me. María Inés felt the blood rush to her head: – Luiz Cláudio?

– Yes. You know that Luiz Cláudio's father is the count. Don't you know?

– Yes. – That's why my father said that I need to marry Luiz Cláudio, because he will receive the title of Baron and if I marry him, I will become a Baroness.

– My father said that if he receives the title of Viscount and I become a Baroness, by marrying a Baron, we can attend the court. So, with that prestige, he would be close to the King, and could gain privileges.

– Why is Luiz Cláudio's father doing this?

– Even though he's a count, he's bankrupt. You know about my father's immense fortune.

– With the wedding, he will receive part of our land, in addition to an amount of money.

– My father really wants to be a viscount and, to achieve this, he is selling me, María Inés!

– I don't want this wedding!

– This has always happened, Eulalia. Many weddings have been held and will still be held for that reason.

Just Beginning

– For us women, we can only obey.

– It's not fair! We are not merchandise, María Inés!

– I think it's not fair sometimes too, but what can we do?

– We have to fight this; we have to rebel!

– How, Eulalia?

– I don't know, but I need to find a way to escape this engagement. I love José Antônio.

– I want to be with him for the rest of my life! How I wish I had been born a man...

– Why, Eulalia?

– Because I would be free! I would be treated like a human being.

– I could work and have my own money!

– It will never happen. The woman, forever, will depend on the man and will have to do what he wants.

– First there are the parents, then the husband and, finally, the children. It was always like this.

– It's not fair! It's not fair, María Inés!

– Is Luiz Cláudio in love with you, Eulália?

– I don't know. We never speak. We only greet each other a few times. I don't care either!

– I love José Antônio.

María Inés could hardly hide what she was feeling: – Have you been meeting with him for a long time?

– Yes. Two months ago. He intended to ask my father for my hand.

– Will he?

Just Beginning

– Yes. Tonight, at the dance. He will make an appointment with my father so he can ask for my hand.

– I don't understand your anguish.

– How can you not understand, María Inés? My father won't allow me to marry him.

– I will have to marry Luiz Cláudio!

– I don't want to! I don't want to! You have to help me!

María Inés, still confused by this revelation, asked: – Help? How? What do you want me to do?

– Today, at the dance, I won't be able to talk to José Antônio. Because of the imposition of my father, I must accept the courtship of Luiz Cláudio. José Antonio won't understand. I want you to distract Luiz Cláudio, so that I can talk to José Antônio and explain what is happening. You are my friend. Can you do that for me, María Inés?

María Inés could hardly hide what she was feeling.

She thought: she's going to marry Luiz Cláudio! There will be a title of nobility!

I can't allow that to happen! I need to find a way to stop this marriage! But for that, it's imperative that I go to the dance!

María Inés, after thinking that, began to cry.

Julia looked at Alzira and asked: – Why is she crying like this? – Alzira smiled and said: – Don't talk. Pay attention, Julia.

Júlia looked again at María Inés, who was crying desperately.

Eulália, without understanding what was happening, asked: – Why are you crying, María Inés?

– I really wanted to help you, but I can't...

– Why can't you help me?

Just Beginning

– I'm not going to the dance...

– You don't want to go?

– I can't. My mom is in the hospital. The doctor said there is no cure and that at any moment she could die...

– I didn't know about that!

– My dad doesn't want people to know. He and my sister are in the hospital. I'm waiting for Ignacio to take me too. He must be coming. As you can see, I can't go. I need to stay with my mother.

– She wasn't going to the hospital, Alzira! She wasn't worried, she wasn't even worried about his mother's illness! – Julia rebelled.

– Pay attention, Julia.

Eulália hugged María Inés: – I'm sorry, María Inés. I couldn't imagine it. We can go to the hospital, talk to your mother. I will say that I need your company and your help. I think she will understand.

María Inés thought for a moment, then said: – You don't have to go to the hospital, Eulália.

– Yesterday I spoke with my mother and told her that I wouldn't go to the dance. She was very sad because she knows about my desire to attend the dance. She told me to go and not worry about her and to come back tomorrow to tell her how it was.

– I said I wouldn't go, because I would rather stay by her side. She insisted.

– I really didn't want to go, but, given what you asked me, I'll go.

– Thank you María Inés! You are really my friend!

– There is another problem for me.

– What problem?

Just Beginning

– I can't go alone. My father and Maria Augusta will be in the hospital...

– No problem, María Inés. I will speak to my father and he will send our carriage to pick you up here so that you can go with us.

María Inés looked at her and, pretending disinterest, said: – I think there won't be any problems then.

– I'll be ready waiting for the carriage.

– You can wait and thank you again. María Inés smiled.

– Now I have to go. Time to start getting ready for the party. I want to look beautiful!

– You are beautiful, Eulalia.

– Can I see the dress that María Inés will wear?

– I don't have a new dress, Eulalia. Knowing that I wouldn't go, I didn't worry about it.

– It doesn't matter what dress you wear, because you are beautiful even dressed in rags.

– Thanks my friend. Now I will accompany you to the carriage. Let's go Zefa!

Zefa, who was there all the time and who opened her eyes wide to each lie of María Inés, silently obeyed. As soon as they left, Julia, also wide-eyed and open-mouthed, looked at Ciro and Alzira, who smiled.

– I can't believe that she, with lies, got everything she wanted!

– She's very smart, Julia. She has always been... – Alzira said looking at Ciro who smiled.

– She is not smart! She is evil and double-faced! Do you still say that God exists? How can he exist and let a person like her have

Just Beginning

everything she has, while others who have never hurt anyone have nothing? – Julia said with disgust.

– God exists and because he is God, he cannot be unfair. He gives everyone the opportunity to learn, evolve and walk.

– But, for that to happen without privileges, he imposed some Laws. Among them is the Law of Action and Reaction.

– In other words, the law of return.

– What does this law say?

– That whatever a spirit does, whether in the physical body or on the spiritual realm, it will receive back with the same intensity.

– It doesn't matter if it's good or bad.

– Are you saying that she will be punished by God?

– No, God is love and does not punish any of his children.

– I don't understand what you want to say.

– God doesn't punish his children. They themselves, by recognizing the evil or good they have done, determine what their punishment or reward will be. Each of us is responsible for our actions.

– Everything you say is very complicated.

Alzira looked at the door. Ciro and Julia followed her gaze.

María Inés came screaming: Liar! Liar!

– Calm down, my lady...

– Calm down Zefa? Did you hear what she said?

– What, my lady?

María Inés changed her tone of voice and spoke, imitating Eulália: – Even if you are dressed in rags, you are beautiful! Liar! Liar!

Just Beginning

– She was glad that I didn't have a new dress! Didn't I tell you she came here just to see my dress?

– I want to see her face, when she sees how beautiful it is! Too bad I don't have the necklace, but it doesn't matter, I'm still going to make my dad buy it and at the next dance, I'll wear it!

– My lady, Eulália didn't come for a dress. My lady came to speak of the boy that her father wants her to marry.

– She won't marry him!

– Didn't you say so, my lady? She and her father knew that if he wants her to do it, she can not do anything...

– She won't marry him because I will be the one to marry him!

– My lady?

– Me, Zefa! I will marry him and become a baroness!

– She spoiled everything Eulalia said! I don't understand how a person can be like this. Is she going to the dance?

– Will she be able to marry Luiz Cláudio?

– We won't tell you Julia. If we do that, we will say the end of the movie and I guarantee that you wouldn't like it.

– Will I have to watch to the end? Why?

– There is no reason. Just to get distracted. Ciro replied, laughing.

– It's okay. You said there is the Law of Return.

– I want to see what will happen to this bad, lying, selfish and double–faced girl!

– You'll see, Julia. But, it won't be now.

– It won't be now?

Just Beginning

– No! You have been away from your body for a long time. Your energies are weakening. You need to go back. We will continue with this story another day.

– You can't do that!

Alzira and Ciro smiled.

Julia jumped on the bed and was surprised: Wow! – I thought I was going to fall. She rolled over in bed and went back to sleep.

21.– A true story

Sueli, although she was late to the restaurant, was worried about Julia and didn't sleep well. She woke up and slept several times. As soon as the day cleared, she got up and went to make coffee.

As the water boiled, she thought: I never imagined that Julia would take such an action. Why did she do that?

Having been through something like that with Nilson, I understand what she felt when she found out that Anselmo had left with his wife. The feeling of abandonment is horrible, but it can't make you take such an extreme action. She will be discharged today.

I'll look for her and try to talk to her. She's a good girl, she's just lost.

Julia also woke up. She looked at the bed next to her and saw that Silvia was still sleeping. She thought: Another strange dream again? I never dreamed so much as now.

Again with people I can't recognize. I remember well that, as in the other dream, I felt that I was living in another moment and that there was that beautiful dress. Now I'll wait for Sueli to arrive. She said she would come to take me home. I need to think what I'm going to do with my life, which is very complicated.

Just Beginning

The waitress came into the room, bringing the coffee. While Silvia was waking up, Julia sat on bed and began to drink coffee. Silvia woke up: – Good morning.

The waitress and Julia responded to the greeting.

– I'm glad I'm leaving today. I miss my home and my children. The waitress laughed and asked: – Don't you miss your husband too?

– I don't have a husband. That bastard left me when my youngest son was a year old and never came back. Julia marveled: – Is it true? What did you do?

I was desperate. I had three young children, without a profession, and lived in the back of a house, paying rent.

– I looked for the bastard everywhere, but I couldn't find him. No one knew where he had gone. I cried a lot.

– He left me without money. The food he had bought began to lack. Seeing that I would have nothing to feed the children, and that the only thing I knew how to do was take care of the house, I took the three children and went out to look for a job. One was eight, the other six, and the youngest was two.

– Oh my god! Did you find a job?

– No, Julia. Who gives a job to a woman with three children? I came home crying and not knowing what was going to happen to my life.

– What did you do? Didn't you have a family?

– When my parents died, I was a girl. My siblings and I were raised by our uncles since I was four.

– We were never in the same house together for long. There was always a problem that forced us to move from one house to another. That was one of the reasons I didn't study, so I didn't have a profession.

Just Beginning

The waitress who was still there asked: – Didn't they help you?

– My siblings and I were not very close. We hardly knew each other. Because they were raised like me, they were not in good financial shape either and also had their families to take care of.

– Even so, every time I went to their houses looking for something to eat, I would leave with a package of rice or beans, things like that, and with the same speech: – Silvia, you must work to take care of your children.

– I, ashamed, left with food in my hands and a deep feeling of defeat, of sadness, because they thought I didn't want to work as a profiteer. That was not true, Julia. I have nothing to do.

– I tried to get a job but couldn't. I started collecting food, cans, glass and paper from the household trash.

A lot of food is thrown away, I was able to enjoy it and give it to my children. With the money I got, I bought bread. I was very hungry, but my children ate what was necessary for their growth. I couldn't pay the rent.

– Two months after my husband left, the owner of the house told me that I needed to move, because he needed the house. I knew it was a lie, because he had many houses, but I also knew that he had the right to rent it. I was desperate not knowing where to go with the children. That morning, I went out to find something to sell.

– At the end of the afternoon, I got some money, went to a bakery and bought bread.

– At home, while the children ate, I tried to find a way to stay and take care of them.

– The only way I found was to leave each child in different houses, but I didn't want that. I knew what I had suffered and

Just Beginning

didn't want the same for them. I didn't want to separate my children.

– We were a family, and we would be together. The only way to solve it, so that we didn't suffer more, would be death.

– I went to the closet, took a glass with rat poison, I put water in a pot, some sugar and the poison.

– I put them in glasses and was going to give them to the children.

– Oh my god! – Julia said horrified.

– You're right to react like that, Julia. Today, when I remember that day, I'm also horrified.

– But my despair was too much. I didn't see a solution, a way to go. It was over and I didn't have the right to let my children suffer, going from one house to another.

– What happened? How are you alive? I hope your children are alive too.

Silvia laughed: – They and I are very well, Julia. Today they are adults and married. Only the youngest still lives with me.

– He's finishing college.

– College? What happened? Did you win the lottery?

Silvia laughed: – That couldn't happen to me, Julia. I had almost no money to buy bread, how would I have to buy a ticket?

– Tell me Silvia! How did you change your mind? I'm getting anxious!

– Me too. I need to serve coffee in other rooms. – The waitress spoke anxiously.

– Okay, but it was you who interrupted me, Julia.

Julia smiled. Silvia continued: – I never had a religion, I always thought that God was unfair throughout my life.

Just Beginning

– After thinking about it a lot, I came to the conclusion that he didn't exist. I never thought of him again, not even then.

– Just when I was going to kill my children and kill myself, Lea, my neighbor came into the kitchen.

– When I saw her, I dropped the pot with the poison on the table. She, without suspecting what was happening, said euphoric:

– I found a solution for you, Silvia!

– I looked at the pot, I felt a tightness in my heart and a lump in my throat. With great difficulty, I asked: – What solution, Lea?

– You know that I have been working in the same house for more than ten years. Don't you know?

– I do.

– My bosses are judges. It has been two years since he retired and she is retiring this month.

This afternoon, when I was doing the dishes for lunch, she came into the kitchen. I was surprised because she never went to the kitchen.

I dried my hands with a kitchen towel and looked at her: – Okay, Doctor. What is it about?

– She sat down in a chair next to the table and said: – As you know, I'm going to retire.

Joel and I don't want to stay here in the city. We intend to go and live in the place that we have in the country.

You know how nice it is there.

– Yes, I know, it's beautiful!

I need to know if you can join us.

– I can't. You know I have a husband and children. Are you going to fire me?

Just Beginning

– I didn't want that, Lea. You've been by our side for so long you are like family, but don't worry.

I'm going to earn enough money that, if you put it in the bank and don't spend it at all, you won't have to go back to work.

– Thank you, Dr. Vitória. I am very sad because I can no longer work here. I really like you and Dr. Joel.

– I'm worried, Lea.

– About what, Doctor?

– My husband and I got married very early. We had no children, but that never bothered us.

– We had our job, which we love. However, now that we need to stop working, we regret not having adopted one or more children. Today we wouldn't feel so alone.

– We would have grandchildren and children running around the house, doing mischief.

– We believe that on the farm we will have a more peaceful life and finally we will be able to rest, enjoy nature.

– I think you'll find all that at the farm.

– We believe so too. However, since you cannot accompany us and we cannot be alone because of our age, we need someone that can live with us and take care of our home. We don't know anyone trustworthy.

– Do you know someone you can recommend us?

– At that moment, Silvia, it seemed that someone was shouting your name in my head. Immediately, I almost shouted: – I know, doctor! A girl! She lives in the back of my house.

I'm sure you'll like her.

– Well. Ask her to come talk to me tomorrow.

– She only has one problem...

Just Beginning

– What problem?

– I told her about your situation, Silvia, what your husband had done.

– Did you mention the children?

– Of course, Silvia.

– What did she say?

– At that moment, Dr. Joel entered the kitchen. He was looking for the woman. She told him what I had said about you and ended up asking: – What do you think Joel?

– He didn't answer, he left the kitchen. He came back a few minutes later.

He hugged the woman and said: – Fine, my old woman. Finally, we are going to have children running around the house.

– She looked at me and smiled: – I couldn't stop a tear from running down my face. She was also excited. He said: – Given this girl's situation, Lea, stop what you're doing and go find her with the children. Today.

– She will sleep here at home.

I didn't expect him to speak again, Silvia. I took off my apron and uniform and ran out. It seemed like everything was working. The bus that I always take didn't take long today. At the stops, the bus usually stops, there wasn't anyone.

I got off the bus and ran up the street. I went out down the hall and didn't even go home.

I wanted to arrive soon to give you this news. Come on, grab the children's clothes and let's go.

They are waiting.

Julia and the waitress felt a chill in their body. Julia asked: – What did you do, Silvia?

Just Beginning

– I looked at the pot in the sink, then at my children and started crying.

– Because you were happy that you didn't do that crazy thing?

– That too.

– That too? Why else would you be crying?

Silvia began to cry and replied: – I cried that day and now I am crying, because, at that moment, I finally believed that God exists and that he never abandoned me. They were more than parents to me and my children.

– The children grew up healthy and happy. They studied.

– The two oldest will graduate. The oldest is a doctor and the other one is a lawyer. The youngest wanted to be a journalist. Can you believe it?

– Dr. Joel is seventy–eight years old and Dr. Vitória is seventy–six, but they are healthy.

– They say they won't die until my son graduates. Every time they say that, my son says he won't study hard for a long time. My older children are married. The little one and I are still living with them.

– I continue to take care of them with all affection. After all, they are the parents I never had.

The waitress, who was still there, hearing Silvia's story, began to push the cart and said: – I still think I have problems. What happened to you was a miracle...

Julia, looking at her wrist, said: – I also thought I had problems. You are right. It really was a miracle... – Alzira looked at Ciro and the figure of a lady who was next to Silvia. All three smiled.

Just Beginning

Silvia smiled and, looking at Julia's arm, said: – As you can see, there is always a path other than death. Miracles exist.

Julia was embarrassed when she realized that Silvia knew what she had done. Silently, she placed the tray where she was drinking coffee on the nightstand, lay down, and closed her eyes.

Seeing Julia's reaction, Silvia said: – Now is not the time to sleep, Julia! We need to change and pack our things. The doctor will arrive and discharge us. My son is coming to get me. I think that girl who was here yesterday is coming to get you. Isn't she coming?

– She must come. She knows I have no one.

– You are the one who thinks you have no one. I guarantee you have a lot more company than you think. We are never alone, Julia. Doesn't my story show that?

Hearing that, Julia got up, went to the closet, grabbed her clothes and went to the bathroom to take a bath. Silvia smiled and got up too.

When the doctor arrived, they were ready.

He took Silvia's file, which was at the end of the bed, and looked: – You're fine. You can go home, but be careful, don't make any effort, take the medicine I prescribed and come back in seven days.

He turned to Julia. After looking at her chart, he said: – You are in perfect health. I spoke to your friend and gave her my instructions. I hope you follow them all.

Saying that, he smiled and left.

Two nurses came to the room and accompanied Julia and Silvia.

When they reached the hospital lobby, Julia saw Sueli running towards her. They hugged.

Just Beginning

– Thank you, Sueli, for coming to find me. Even more so in the morning. I know that, right now, you should be sleeping.

– Stop it, Julia. I'm glad you're fine.

After the hug, Julia looked at Silvia, who was hugging a young man and a woman. She smiled and thought: This must be Silvia's guardian angel.

They left the hospital, took a taxi, and went home. Throughout the trip, Sueli talked about work and Eduardo all the time. Julia realized that she didn't want to talk about what happened.

At home, Sueli wanted to take Julia to the room, but she refused: – No, Sueli. I don't want to go to bed. I'm fine.

– We need to talk about what happened.

– Save it for later, Julia.

– There's no point putting it off for later. The doctor said he left instructions and wants me to follow them. What did he say?

– It's okay. Sit down, while I make our lunch, I'll tell you.

Julia sat down. Sueli went to the refrigerator, took a piece of meat and began to speak: – He is worried about you and asked me not to leave you alone.

– Worried? why?

– He said that everyone who tries to commit suicide once, if they fail, will try several times until they succeed.

– He said that you have depression and therefore you should go to a psychologist or psychiatrist, because depression can lead you to try to commit suicide again. He said you need help, I agree.

Julia got up and, disgusted, said: – I don't need a psychiatrist! What I did was crazy!

I know why I did it! Sorry and it won't happen again!

Just Beginning

– I told him that, but he insisted. I don't know what to do. I am your friend, I want to help you, but, as you know, my life is busy. I don't have time for anything. When I get married, I will move out of here and hand over the apartment.

– I'm fine, Sueli! That won't happen again! I need to find a job and I don't think it will be difficult!

I am a professional! I studied hard for this! You can stay calm.

– How can you be so sure you're okay?

– I've been having some strange dreams. I spoke with a woman who was hospitalized with me. She told me her story.

When it was over, I saw that my life, no matter how bad the thing I'm going through is, is not even close to what it was. She told me about hope. She said that we are never alone and that we always have help when we need it.

– Does she follow the same Doctrine as me?

– I don't know. She didn't say. Before it all happened, she said that she had no religion. Now after everything is settled, I don't know.

– She said that her story proves that God never abandons us and that we always have spiritual friends who help us in difficult times. I'm believing that, Sueli! I need to believe!

– All right, Julia. I have some books that you should read. For the moment, that's all I can do for you.

Since I can't be by your side all the time, I need to believe what you're saying. I need and will trust you and my spiritual friends. They will help you, just as they helped me, to find a new path and avoid doing something as crazy as what you did.

– I'm sure of that, Sueli! Now I'll help you with lunch.

Just Beginning

– Then, you need to go to work. You can go and don't worry about me. I'm fine!

– I bought this medicine that your doctor prescribed. He said to take it after lunch to make you feel good.

– You should take it every day until you find help.

– It's okay. Today I will rest and tomorrow I will look for work. I told you, I don't need a psychiatrist or a psychologist!

Alzira and Ciro smiled and threw white lights on them.

As soon as lunch was over, Sueli left, saying: – I need to go to work.

– Today, we will receive a number of tourists who came to the city. I can't stay here with you.

– The doctor said that this medicine that you took will make you sleep. Promise me that as soon as I leave you will go to your room, lie down and go to sleep.

Julia smiled: – You don't have to worry about me, Sueli. I'm fine. You can go relax and, to make you feel better, I promise that in the evening I will have dinner at your restaurant. Then we can come back here together. What do you think? Can I go?

– Of course you can! You don't even have to wait until tonight. As soon as you wake up go there. You're right, I'll be much more relaxed.

– I am going! Now go, Sulie.

Sueli left and Julia went to the room, looked at her arm, which was bandaged, and lay down: – As much as I think, I can't see myself in the situation Silvia was in. Without a husband, profession or money and having three children to feed.

It's good that I didn't have a child with Anselmo.

In that sense, my life is easier.

Just Beginning

I know I'm going to get a job, find a place to live, and forget about it.

May he be happy with his wife!

She laid her head on the pillow, smiled and thought: Who am I trying to kid? I really want him to die! He acted like a scoundrel! My life is over!

Soon after, she was sleeping.

22.– The dance

Some time after sleeping, Julia opened her eyes and saw Alzira and Ciro smiling. She was lying, again, on the grass she already knew.

She smiled: – Am I here again? I'm getting used to this place and you.

I've always had a hard time falling asleep. Today that no longer happens. I Just put my head on the pillow and the dream comes. Are you responsible for this?

– Partly, yes, Julia. You are going through a difficult time in your life. Your body needs to rest and we are helping you a little. You had a busy day today, right?

Julia smiled at Alzira.

– Yes, I did. I heard a story that moved me very much and made me think about my life. I don't understand how Silvia told her story to strangers.

– We know Silvia's story, he said: – because both you and the hospital waitress needed to listen.

This is how the spiritual realm works. It's always present and acts according to the circumstances.

Just Beginning

– Sometimes it makes people say what others need to hear. Other times, it puts in the life of a person another person who can help materially with money or a job.

– They always help us, incarnate or not.

– It's still difficult for me to understand everything you say, but I am getting used to that and to your presence.

– I just wish that when I woke up I could remember you.

– Even if you think you don't remember, you can be sure that you do remember the most important things.

– Now, since you like the story so much, shall we continue with ours?

Before Julia answered, they heard a noise. It was a small carriage that was pulled by two horses and stopped in front of the front door. They approached the door. A black man got out and ran toward the house.

He spoke to another black woman who was cleaning the room. She heard what he said, covered her mouth with her hand, and hurried up the stairs.

Alzira, Ciro and Júlia accompanied the black woman who was crying.

They entered María Inés' room. The black woman, very nervous and crying, could hardly speak. María Inés was in front of a large mirror, looking at her dress.

As soon as Zefa entered, seeing that she was anguished: – What happened? Why are you crying? Sobbing, the black woman replied: – Your mother died, my lady...

– What?

– Ignacio came from the hospital. Your mother died and your father asked my lady to go there. Ignacio will take my lady there.

Just Beginning

María Inés, after the first impact, looked at herself in the mirror again.

– Now that I'm ready to go to the dance? Couldn't she have died tomorrow? What am I going to do? Eulalia's carriage must be arriving.

Zefa, who heard everything, said: – It's your mother, my lady. I'm going to the hospital...

María Inés, very nervous, shouted: – I know Zefa! I know! But it's not fair! I waited so long for this day!

– I'm ready to make a dream come true!

– There will still be many dances, my lady. Your mother will no longer be here...

– Couldn't she have left tomorrow? I don't want to miss the dance!

– She couldn't, my lady. The time of birth and the time of death are already decided...

– All right, Zefa. I need your help to take off this dress.

– I can't go with this dress on.

– Okay, my lady...

María Inés turned her back and Zefa began to unbutton her dress. When she was on the last button, María Inés turned and shouted: – Wait, Zefa! Button all the buttons again! I know what I'm going to do!

Zefa stopped and, surprised, asked: – What will my lady do?

María Inés looked at the black woman who had brought the news and said shouting: – Go talk to Ignacio and tell him to go back to the hospital and tell my father that, when he got here, I had already left in Eulália's father's carriage...

Just Beginning

The black woman's eyes opened and Zefa, crying, asked: – Is my lady going to the hospital naked? Is my lady going to the dance?

– I will, Zefa! I can't miss this dance! I waited so long for it! My father must bring my mother here.

– Tomorrow I will be with her all day so that people can see me, but not today! Today I'm going to the dance! – Julia also opened her eyes and mouth wide. She looked at Alzira and Ciro and asked: – Is she going to do this?

– Keep looking, Julia. You don't want to know the ending of the movie, do you?

– No! I don't!

– Go, Zefa! Button up my dress! The carriage must be arriving! – Looking at the other black woman, she shouted: – Black!

– Go relay my request to Ignacio!

The black woman lowered her head and ran out of the room. Zefa buttoned her dress again and smoothed Maria Inés's hair.

She looked at herself in the mirror again.

– I look beautiful, Zefa! I know that I will seduce and marry Luiz Cláudio! – They heard a noise: – The carriage has arrived, Zefa! Let's go down!

They went downstairs and were followed by Julia and her companions. Maria Inés passed silently by the room, where some slaves were crying.

Pretending not to see the slaves, she got into the carriage and, accompanied by Zefa, left. When they arrived at Eulalia's house, she, with her parents, was already waiting for her. The carriage stopped and María Inés got out.

Just Beginning

Zefa got out right behind. Eulália's mother approached: – How are you, María Inés? Eulália told us that your mother is in the hospital. We hope it's not serious.

María Inés looked at Zefa and said: – She is fine. My father preferred that she stay in the hospital for a few days.

The doctor said it's for observation only. She is very happy that I am going to the dance. She knows how much it means to me.

She is also very thankful to you for allowing me to accompany you.

– There is nothing to be thankful for. I know that if the situation were the other way around, your parents would do the same for Eulalia.

– I also know how important this dance is to her.

– Don't worry, we are happy for you.

– We will use two carriages. In one carriage it will be , my husband and Paulo Octávio. In the other one, you and Eulália.

– Is it okay like that?

– It's great! Thank Mrs.!

– Well, enough thanks. It's time to go. Get in the carriage.

Before getting in, María Inés said: – Zefa is accompanying me. Could she stay here, until we get back?

Eulália's mother looked at Zefa: – Of course she can and, if you prefer, as soon as we get into the party, the coachman can go back and drive her home. When the party is over, we will take you, María Inés.

– Thanks once again. I think she better go home.

– Then, when I arrive, my bed will be ready waiting for me.

– Ok let's do that.

Just Beginning

María Inés approached Zefa and, with a low but strong voice so that the others wouldn't hear, said: – Go home and don't dare comment with the coachman or the blacks of the house what happened to my mother!

– All right, my lady. As an agreement I won't say anything...

They got into the carriages and left. Zefa, with her eyes, remained standing until the carriages disappeared. After that, she cried. Forty minutes later, the carriages passed through a beautiful portal and continued along a path surrounded by trees and palm leaves. In the distance, you could see a lake.

María Inés and Eulália watched and were delighted with all that beauty. Julia was delighted too, but she was silent, just enjoying it.

Soon after, the carriages stopped in front of the palace entrance. Two pages, one from each car, got out and helped the passengers out.

María Inés, Eulália and her mother adjusted their dresses. They entered the hall and were escorted by two richly dressed pages into the dance room.

The entire room was lit by several huge chandeliers, with lighted candles lighting the room.

They noticed that the tables were decorated with white tablecloths. On each of them there was an arrangement of field flowers, with small white candles in the center, which helped the lighting and completed the beauty.

María Inés and Eulália, although they were excited, for being there for the first time, with much effort and pride, followed the pages and managed to reach the table indicated by them. They sat as if what was happening was normal in their lives.

Just Beginning

On the contrary, Julia was ecstatic. She screamed: Everything is so beautiful! I've seen dances like this in movies, but I never imagined it would be so impressive! It's nice! Beautiful.

Alzira and Ciro were silent, they just smiled.

After sitting down, María Inés looked around the room and thought: – There are many beautiful dresses here, but no dress is as beautiful as mine. Eulália's dress is cute too, but it's not close to mine!

Although I am wearing this beautiful necklace, I cannot forget the wonderful necklace that I saw at the jewelry store. I hate my dad for not buying that necklace! I can never forgive what he did!

Paulo Octávio, who was sitting next to her, said: – You are very beautiful, Miss María Inés.

– Yes, my dress is beautiful!

– I'm not talking about your dress, but about all of you.

– Thank you!

– I was glad to know that you would come to the dance with us.

– I was also happy to come.

María Inés didn't pay attention to what he said. Her eyes roamed the room looking for Luiz Cláudio. Eulália was also looking for someone, looking for José Antônio.

Eulália turned to María Inés and spoke softly: – I'm worried, María Inés...

– Why, Eulalia?

– It is almost time for the duke to enter the room and so far José Antônio has not arrived.

– Are you sure he will come? He is not part of the court.

Just Beginning

– He said he would do his best to come. Although he is not part of the court, his father has a lot of money and donates a lot.

– Surely, he must have received an invitation.

María Inés, without listening to what her friend was saying, still looking around the room, said with no interest in the conversation: – Okay... – Paulo Octávio, tried several times to talk to her, but María Inés didn't pay attention.

Her only concern and attention was focused on the door through which Luiz Cláudio had to enter.

A few minutes later, she saw that he was accompanied by his parents, two girls and a boy who she knew were his brother and sisters. A page, as it had happened with Eulália's family, accompanied them to a table on the other side of the room, which was in front of her. Her heart was pounding.

Eulália also saw them when they entered, but felt nothing. What she really wanted was to see José Antonio walk through that door.

After sitting around the table, Luiz Cláudio's father, touching the brim of his hat, greeted Eulália's father.

The ladies just smiled.

The sound of a cornet enveloped the entire environment. Everyone stood up.

The duke and duchess entered. Smiling, they sat down at a table that had been reserved for them. The table was on a high level. From there, the duke could see everyone present and everyone could see him.

A very tasty dinner was served. There were crystal goblets and fine porcelain plates that came from Europe. Black people, very well uniformed, served everyone.

Just Beginning

Seeing all this, Julia screamed: – I can't believe I'm here! Seeing everything! I met a duke and a duchess! – Alzira and Ciro looked at her.

Putting her hand over her mouth, she continued, speaking in a low voice: – I know, it's just a dream, right? Alzira laughed: – That's right, Julia. It's just a dream.

After dinner the duke got up and began the dance. A piano and several violins began to play a waltz.

Couples were forming and occupying the center of the room. Luiz Cláudio got up and walked to the table where they were. Leaning down, he invited Eulalia to dance. He looked at the father who nodded.

They went to dance.

María Inés was furious: He can't be with her! He is mine!

As they danced, Luiz Cláudio, shaking Eulália's hand, said: – You look beautiful, Miss Eulália. Eulália, who, at each turn, looked at the door waiting for José Antônio to enter, didn't listen. He, realizing that she was absent, shook her hand again and said: – You are a beautiful lady...

Hearing what he said, she blushed and, embarrassed, said: – Thank you. You look so good, too.

– Do you know the agreement between our parents?

– Yes, my father told me.

– What did you think of this agreement?

– You know I need to obey my father.

– I'm in the same situation. But I will only accept this agreement if you are really determined to get married.

We are young, we have a whole life ahead of us, and I don't want this life to be unhappy.

I have a proposal for you.

Just Beginning

– Which one?

– Let's pretend we're okay, so our parents continue to discuss their agreement.

We will see each other for a while.

So that we can get to know each other better. When the time comes, I will tell my father that I don't want to get married and I want to go to study in Paris.

– Our parents won't accept it! There is a lot involved.

– I know, money, land and bonds, but what do we have with that?

– Unless, during that time, who knows, we fall in love and get married...

– I can't marry you.

– Why not?

– I'm in love with another one...

He, laughing and shaking her hand, said: – I want to go to Paris! As you can see, this marriage cannot happen. Let's just pretend!

She also laughed: – Okay. We can do that. When the time comes, we will find a way to reject this marriage.

They laughed and turned happily around the dance room.

Although María Inés danced with Paulo Octávio, she never took her eyes off them. When she saw that they were dancing and laughing, and they seemed happy, she was furious: they are laughing, they look happy! This can't be happening!

I need to do something to stop this marriage!

Paulo Octávio, without imagining what was happening, while they danced, said: – I have been thinking a lot about you and

Just Beginning

I would like to talk to your father so that he will grant me your hand. My family and I would be happy.

– I know my parents would be happy, but I, in particular, ask you not to do that.

– Why not? I belong to a good family. I know that the union of our families will make everyone very happy –. Nervous about that conversation, María Inés, who was still looking at Luiz Claudio and Eulália who seemed happy, replied:

– Our families can be happy, but not me! My heart belongs to another! Excuse me!

Without any more preambles, she walked away, leaving the boy alone in the center of the dance room, returned to the table and looked at Eulália and Luiz Claudio, who were dancing happily. After the end of a song, Luiz Claudio, holding Eulália by the hand, accompanied her to the table to the joy of her parents and the sadness of María Inés.

Eulália sat next to María Inés, who asked in a low voice so that the others wouldn't listen: – What happened? You seem to be happy!

– I am very happy, María Inés.

– Why?

– We can't talk here. I'll tell you everything later. Although she was irritated, María Inés smiled.

The dance continued. Paulo Octávio did everything possible and impossible to please María Inés.

As they danced, he shook her hand and said: – I've been in love with you for a long time.

– Can we talk about it?

– I'm sorry, sir, but my heart belongs to someone else.

– I see, I would still like to see you again.

Just Beginning

– If you want, I can talk to your father.

María Inés, furious, stopped dancing and shouted: – No!

Nervous, she went out into the garden. Tears of hatred fell down her face.

This can't be happening! Eulália said that she wouldn't marry him!, that she is in love with someone else! It's a lie! She is happy with him ! Liar! Liar!

– Are you crying, miss?

María Inés turned around and saw that the interrogator was Luiz Cláudio. With tears streaming down her face, she tried to hide it.

– No sir. It must have been a stain that fell into my eyes.

– Yes, you are crying. What happened? I saw you run out of the hall. Was Paulo Octávio inconvenient to you?

– No. He wants to marry me...

– Are you crying about that? He's a good guy and from a good family. I know he will make you very happy. María Inés cried again: – I can't marry him. My heart belongs to someone else.

– Someone else?

– Yes. Someone that I can't forget for a minute.

– Lucky! – Said Luiz Cláudio laughing.

She looked up and said immediately: – You...

– Me? – He asked, perplexed.

– Yes sir. It was because of you that I came to this dance.

– I never thought you were interested in me. I'm happy because I think about you a lot too. I thought about talking to your parents, but something happened that changed my mind.

– I know. Your marriage to Eulalia, imposed by your parents.

Just Beginning

– How did you know that?

– Eulália told me. She is unhappy because she doesn't love you! She is in love with someone else!

– I know that.

– Do you?

– Yes. She told me a while ago while we were dancing.

– I don't think so! While dancing, you looked so happy and in love... – He laughed: – This is great!

– I'm not understanding.

– We made an agreement. We will deceive our parents and, it seems, we will succeed.

– An agreement?

– Yes, we will pretend to be in love, but we won't marry. After our parents understand each other, we will say that we don't want to get married.

– They won't accept it. You will be forced to marry.

– When the time comes, I will speak with my father and tell him that I cannot marry Miss Eulalia.

He loves me and only wants my good. He doesn't want his child to be unhappy for the rest of his life.

My father has financial difficulties, but nothing too serious. With my marriage, everything would be easier, but he is smart and will find another way.

I wanted to go to Paris, but given what you said, I think I'll change my mind.

– I don't understand...

– I became interested in you as soon as I met you at Colonel Cintra's house.

Just Beginning

However, I never imagined that you were interested in me. Given what you said today, I don't want to travel anymore.

After everything is settled between Miss Eulalia and I, when I am free of that engagement, I will speak with my father, who will speak with your family and we can get married. What do you think?

María Inés began to shake: – Do you want to marry me?

– Yes, that's what I want the most.

Saying this, Luiz Cláudio took María Inés's hand and kissed it for a long time.

– Now, I have to go back to the hall and take Miss Eulalia to dance. We need to keep up appearances.

Don't talk to anyone, not even to Miss Eulália, what we talked about, because if someone finds out about our plans, they will be harmed.

María Inés, moved, only managed to agree with her head.

Before leaving, Luiz Cláudio said: – Until we can tell the world about our love, can we meet without anyone knowing? I would very much like to be able to talk to you in a quieter place.

Again, she nodded.

– Well. I'll be waiting for you, at 2, by the lake near your house, alright?

She smiled. He returned to the hall and went to the table where Eulalia was and invited her to dance again.

After a while, María Inés also returned to the hall and, smiling at Paulo Octávio, said: – I'm sorry for my behavior. I would like to dance with you.

He, without understanding what was happening, but without worrying about it, got up and, taking her by the hand, led

Just Beginning

her to the center of the dance room and began to dance. María Inés was happy.

Seeing that, Julia, looking at Alzira and Ciro, shouted: – It can't be! It can't be!

– Can't be what, Julia?

– How can she, being selfish, evil and double–face as she is, be with the man she wants? How can she get what she wants?

– How can her plans always work?

Alzira looked at Ciro and replied: – Although it may often seem the opposite, everything is always fine, Julia.

– It's not fair! It's not fair! She doesn't deserve it!

– Keep looking, Julia.

Julia looked around her. After a while, she asked: – Is it true that they can't see or hear us? – Ciro smiled: – Yes, Julia. It is true.

– Can I dance in that hallway?

Alzira looked at Ciro and smiled: – Yes, you can, Julia, and if you want, I can dance with you.

– Yes, I do!

– So, let's go.

While Alzira was smiling, they began to dance. Julia was happy and every time Alzira passed, she smiled and waved a hand.

Minutes before the dance ended, Luiz Cláudio said goodbye to her family and María Inés.

Eulália's father, shaking his hand, said: – I would very much like to welcome you to my house for dinner tomorrow.

– It will be my pleasure, sir.

Smiling, Eulalia held out her hand for him to kiss. Gently he, looking into her eyes, took her hand and kissed it. He did the

Just Beginning

same with Eulália's mother and María Inés, who shook when she felt the touch of his hand.

When the dance ended, one of the carriages took Eulália and Paulo Octávio home. The other, with Eulália's parents, took María Inés.

The carriage stopped in front of her door. After getting out of the carriage, María Inés said: – As much as I look for it, I can't find the words to thank you for taking me to the dance. I'm very happy.

Eulália's mother smiled: – We too. You are a very nice company. Tomorrow I will go to the hospital to visit your mother.

Only now did María Inés remember her mother. She hid it: – I know she will be happy with your visit. Thanks again –. Smiling, she walked away and waited for the carriage to disappear at the end of the road.

She entered the house and, as if she were levitating with such happiness, she climbed the stairs and went to her room. As soon as she entered the room, she saw María Augusta leaning on her bed and Zefa sitting on a stool:

– What are you doing here?

– I waited for you, my sister.

– for what?

– To see your happy face when you get home from the dance.

– As you can see María Augusta, I am happy! Zefa! Help me take off this dress. It has already fulfilled its mission –. Zefa got up and began to unbutton the buttons at the back of the dress.

María Augusta, furious, got up and shouted: – How could you do that, María Inés? – María Inés, pretending not to understand, asked: – Do what?

Just Beginning

– Do not play dumb with me!

– I don't understand what you mean, María Augusta. What have I done?

– How could you go to the dance even though you knew that our mother had died?

María Inés looked at Zefa and glared at her: Why did you tell her? Dirty, with a black tongue!

– I didn't say anything, my lady...

– You didn't tell her?

– She didn't tell me! – Maria Augusta screamed.

– If it wasn't her, who was it?

– You!

– Me?

– Yes, right now. I didn't know, but I suspected it. Ignacio had time to get here, before you left to go to the dance!

– When he returned to the hospital saying that you had already left, I didn't think you were going to do what you did! – María Inés, realizing that there was no way to argue, tried to justify:

– I couldn't help going to the dance, Maria Augusta! You know how long I've waited for this day!

– Your mother died! Didn't it move you in any way? Your mother, María Inés!

If she had been a bad, distant mother, I would have understood, but no! She was a wonderful mother!

She was always by our side, she always gave us affection... – María Augusta stopped talking, she couldn't help crying. María Inés took advantage of that moment: – Exactly, since she was a wonderful mother, I'm sure she would be sad if I had stopped going

Just Beginning

to the dance because of her. She knew how important this dance was to me.

María Augusta, with her hands, wiped her eyes and walking towards the door, very nervous, said: – You are a lost cause!

You are selfish, mean and spoiled! You only think of yourself! Tomorrow, early in the morning, Mom's body will come here.

Some people have already been notified, others will be. The priest was at her side and still is. Dad is in his room. I hope you show up in the room and even lying, you show some pain! I hate you, María Inés!

She left the room, closing the door.

As soon as she left, María Inés looked at Zefa and shouted: – Are you crazy, Zefa? How can you say I don't like my mother? I really like her, but what difference would my presence make or not? She was already dead! As for me, I loved the dance! Luiz Cláudio is interested in me. Tomorrow afternoon, we will meet at the lake. You'll go with me!

– I can't, my lady...

– You can't, why?

– It will be at three o'clock. My lady has to be present...

Desperate, María Inés: – Do you see how my mother's death disturbed my life?

– She could have died tomorrow, then I would have already met Luiz Cláudio. I'm very unhappy, Zefa...

– You could meet him another day, my lady... – María Inés began to cry desperately.

Zefa approached: – Cry in a moment, my lady. You are still half naked.

Just Beginning

Meet him another day. Now it's time to sleep. It is very late and my lady is tired... – María Inés obeyed. She put on her nightgown and went to bed.

Julia, nervous, looking at Ciro and Alzira, said: – She is really bad! Her sister is right! How can she be so selfish? How can she not feel pain for the death of her mother! She deserved the punishment!

– What punishment, Julia? – Alzira asked, looking into her eyes. Julia looked at her, was about to reply, but stopped.

Alzira continued: – What do you think if, in a next incarnation, she had no mother and no family? Do you think it would be a good punishment?

– What do you mean? Julia asked concerned.

I do not want to say anything. You said she deserved punishment; I'm only suggesting this one.

Julia, still looking at them, asked: – Are you saying that I was that girl and that, therefore, I chose the life I have today?

I'm not saying that. Who says you are that girl...?

Julia walked away and, walking, said: – It can't be! It can't be! I would never be like her!

– Don't get nervous, Julia, or jump to conclusions. You need to know the story to the end.

– You will have to make a very important choice, so you must pay attention to the rest of the story.

– Now, go back to your body, you've spent a lot of time outside of it.

– No! I want to see what will happen to her!

Alzira smiled. Julia jumped up and said: – No! I want to see what will happen to her! She looked around and saw that she was in her room.

Just Beginning

What crazy dream was that? Why can't I remember it?

These dreams are driving me crazy. This time, I can only remember that I was at a dance, in a beautiful green dress, and there were people next to me, but who were these people?

She looked at her watch: almost six in the afternoon! I overslept! I need to get up to shower and go to the restaurant. Sueli must be worried.

She did. She got up and went to the restaurant.

23.- New life

Suzana woke up. She looked to the side and saw that Anselmo wasn't there.

She remembered that she was in the apartment and in Recife: how could my life have changed so much? If my mother were here, she'd say there must be a reason. But what reason can it be?

I am out of work, living on Anselmo's low salary, I fought and studied hard so that that never happened. I am living in this apartment, which costs a third of my salary. What path am I taking, mother?

– You will find out, my daughter. You will find out. – My mother would have told me that were she by my side.

– Good morning, Suzana! Did you sleep well?

– Good morning, Anselmo. I slept very well.

– Great. I'm going to work. I prepared the coffee and the table. Enjoy this city that has beautiful places.

Imagine you are on vacation and go to the beach with Rodrigo. He will like it. After all, you haven't had a vacation in a long time.

Enjoy! When you go through the concierge, talk to the doorman and see if he knows someone to help you here at home. –

Just Beginning

She laughed and asked: – Have you finished giving orders, my lord?

He, embarrassed, also laughing, replied: – Excuse me, Suzana. It's true. It seems that I am talking to a woman who doesn't know how to act. You know what you want and how to do it. I just want you to feel good and don't regret having come here. I spoke to my boss and he said that I was expected to stay here for a year or two, but if I can get everything in order, we will be back before that. As you can see, it will depend on my work.

I'll do my best to make sure everything is okay before then, and then if you want, we can go back. Suzana, still lying down, smiled: – Don't worry about me, Anselmo. I understood and accepted my situation.

I chose to stay with you, with our son, and with our marriage.

Like you said, I'm on vacation. For a week, I will enjoy the beach, walk around the city and of course find someone to help me. You know I don't know how to do housework. I've always worked outside, I know I couldn't handle it alone. After this week, I will look for a small school to enroll Rodrigo in and I will try to find a job.

We will stay here as long as necessary, but work hard to keep this time as short as possible.

I want to go back to my city.

– Glad to hear that from you, Suzana. I promise we will be back as soon as possible. Now I need to go. Seize the day.

– Stay calm. I'm going to enjoy my vacation, Anselmo left. She got up, passed by Rodrigo's room, who was still sleeping.

– Let's begin a new life, my son.

Just Beginning

She went to the kitchen, had a coffee and went to the window where she could see the sea: it is really beautiful!

That blue with green hues and those white waves that hit the sand fill anyone's eyes. The only good thing about this apartment is that it is in front of the beach...

She heard Rodrigo waking up, so she went to the room.

She woke up the child: – Today, we are going to the beach, Rodrigo! You'll love it! We cannot stay long, because here, the sun is very intense. But still, let's enjoy it.

She gave the boy coffee, she put on a bikini and shorts.

In a bag she put water, two towels and sunscreen. She took an umbrella from her clothes, put the bag on her shoulder and the umbrella between her arm and her body. With the other arm, she took Rodrigo's hand and left.

She took the elevator down and, as she passed through the lobby, spoke to the doorman: – Good morning.

– Good morning ma'am.

– I moved here yesterday and I need someone to help me with the housework. Do you know someone?

– Yes, I do! My lady! She worked for two years with a family from the south.

They went back there, and she was out of work. I was desperate.

– Well. When can I talk to her?

– I'm leaving here at two. I live far away, so it won't be possible for her to come today, but tomorrow, if you want, she will.

– It's okay. Tell her to come wanting to work, because if we arrange everything, she will start tomorrow.

– You will like her. She's very hard–working. Not afraid of work, no!

Just Beginning

– Okay. Now I'm going to enjoy the beach. Good morning.

– Good morning ma'am.

Still holding the child, she reached the street. She looked and saw the sea, took a few steps, crossed the street and reached the beach. She looked at the sea and thought again: it is really beautiful!

She took off her sandals and stepped on the very white sand. She saw that some stones, inside the sea, formed a kind of pool, where adults and children played. She went in with Rodrigo and they were playing for a long time.

The boy soon became friends with other children. Suzana looking at her son playing happily smiled.

After a while, she spread one of the towels on the sand, from where she could see Rodrigo, and lay down. As soon as he saw his mother getting out of the pool, the boy also got out.

– I'm thirsty, mom.

She gave water to Rodrigo who began to play in the sand next to her.

She stayed there for a long time and thought: – When will I be able to get used to this life as a housewife, without having to think about numbers, how to talk to the boss and without taking orders.

After half an hour, she looked at the sun: – It's time for us to go. The sun is very hot. I don't want Rodrigo to get burned.

She got up, picked up the towel, the umbrella and went back to the apartment.

As soon as she entered, showered and bathed Rodrigo, after that, she turned on the television. There were cartoons playing that she knew were his favorite. She went into the kitchen and opened the refrigerator.

Just Beginning

Inside were the leftovers of the dinner Anselmo had prepared the night before. She heated the food, gave it to Rodrigo, had a glass of water, returned to the living room, sat on one of the sofas and, laughing, began to eat and think: – "Yes, I think I can get used to this life. On second thought, Anselmo has always been a good husband.

His only failure is having such a low salary. I would like to have a life like this, living in an apartment like mine. Life is strange. I need to work and receive a large salary like before to live in a better apartment like the one I used to live in. For that to happen, I need to work hard and I can't stay like this, as I am now, relaxed.

Why can't we get everything we want? Life is strange, even... "

After lunch, the boy wanted to sleep. She put him on the bed and looked: You are so handsome.

I can count the times I put you to bed. Since you were born, I have never been by your side, I haven't followed your growth. When I left home to go to work, most of the time you were sleeping, and when I came back, you were already back to sleep. On the weekends, I always had work to do. All this for what?

To end up living in an apartment like this? Was it worth it?

She sat on the sofa in front of the television. She changed to a channel where a movie was playing. She lay down on the sofa and watched. She fell asleep without noticing.

Rodrigo woke up an hour later. She opened her eyes, looked at the child who said: – Mother I'm hungry... She stretched, yawned and spoke aloud: – Wow! I don't remember sleeping in the afternoon my whole life!

She remembered her mother and thought: Is this the reason for everything that happened in my life, mother?

Just Beginning

Valuing little things that I never valued? Play with my son on the beach, take care of him and put him to sleep, sleep in the afternoon, be by his side when he wakes up, be present in his life, sunbathing, and breathing fresh air?

Her mother, besides her, smiled and said: – That's one of the reasons, my daughter.

Rodrigo insisted on saying that he was hungry. She went to the kitchen, followed by him.

She took milk and an apple from the refrigerator and said: Rodrigo! Don't you think this apartment looks very sad?

It has no curtains, no paint, no decorations. Let's go shopping! Since we have to stay here, let it be in a happy environment!

The boy, showing happiness, shouted: – Let's go, mom! So can we have an ice cream?

– Of course! I'm also in the mood to do something that I haven't done in a long time. To have ice cream on a stick.

– It will be even better here! We can have ice cream looking at the sea!

– They left. Suzana asked the doorman where she could buy photos, curtains and decorations: – At the square there are some stands and street vendors that sell handicrafts that are very beautiful. These other things, I don't know where they are sold.

Only downtown I think.

– Thank you.

Suzana took the boy's hand and walked along the shore. In some stores she saw handicrafts.

She was delighted with some ceramic pieces. At the same moment, she imagined where she would place them. She bought

Just Beginning

three and, when she was paying, asked: – Who makes these pieces? They are beautiful and very cheap!

– There are many people who make art. They leave the pieces and, once a month, they return to receive the ones that were sold and leave more.

– Where do they work?

– In their houses.

– Are they only sold here in the city?

– I don't really know.

Suzana realized that the man was upset by so many questions. She paid, left and kept walking. She walked some more, observing the crafts. She bought two more pieces and decided to go home.

She passed by a store, where she saw blouses and dresses made with lace.

She took one of the blouses in her hand and asked: – Is this lace on this blouse made by hand?

– Yes ma'am. All the lace is made by craftsmen.

– Do they work for you?

– They leave the pieces and come back at the end of the month to see how many were sold.

– Could you give me the address of a craftsman?

– For what? Do you want to be our competitor? Do you want to open a store?

– No! I just want to make a special request. A dress for a party that I intend to go to.

– Why are you asking me if I'm going to open a store?

– You are from the South, come here, with a lot of money, open a shop, offer more money to the craftsmen and harm us.

Just Beginning

Suzana thought for a moment and said: – I don't want to fight you. I just want a dress for the party...

– Tell me how you want the dress. I'll talk to the craftsman. Come back on the weekend, I must have an answer.

– It's okay. I will think clearly how I want it and I will come back here –. Suzana paid for the blouse, left there, and went home to make dinner.

She didn't know how to cook, so she went to a butcher shop. She went in and bought ground beef. She left and kept walking and thinking: I don't know how to cook, but I can fry potatoes and braise ground beef.

I'm glad the maid is coming tomorrow.

She started to sauté the meat and put a pan with oil to fry the potatoes.

While doing this, she thought: this woman was so nervous that all she could do was lie.

Why were she and the man so nervous when I commented on the craftsmen? Do they exploit these people? I wasn't thinking about that, but now, I would like to meet a craftsman and learn how they work.

The next day, in the morning, after Anselmo left, the doorman intervened saying that his wife was there to talk to Suzana. What she accepted.

Soon after, the doorbell rang. Suzana opened the door. A very young woman said: – My husband said you need a maid.

– Yes, come in.

The woman entered. Suzana pointed to the sofa in the living room and they started talking.

– Have you ever worked with a family?

Just Beginning

– Of course. Here we start working very early. I started at the age of ten, taking care of a little boy.

– I worked for five years, then I got married and stopped working.

– Did you marry at fifteen? – Suzana asked admiringly.

– I did. Here one gets married early too. If not, she never gets married again.

– Have you studied?

– No. My father said that a woman does not need to study. She just needs to learn how to cook and take care of the children.

– Can you read?

– No, but I know how to take good care of the house. If you want, you can ask my mistress.

– Even with young children, I always worked as a maid or cleaning.

– Do you have children?

– I have three: two boys and one girl. Because of them, I have to work.

– My husband's salary is very small. I need to help him, my youngest son is eight months old.

– The doctor, at the clinic, said that I needed to breastfeed him until he was seven months old.

– Now, I don't have to.

– Sorry, but how old are you?

– I'll be twenty in two months.

– Twenty?

– No, I'm still turning twenty.

Suzana looked at her and thought: She seems to be older, but she is still a girl and already has three children...

Just Beginning

– Well, are your children in kindergarten?

– No. There are only a few nurseries here for many children. I couldn't find a place for them.

– How are you going to work? Do you have a mother to take care of the children?

– I have my mother, but she also works with a family and lives far from here.

– If you come to work here, who will take care of your children?

– A girl who lives near my house.

– How old is she?

– Ten, but she's smart, she knows how to take good care of children.

– Doesn't she go to school?

– No, she has five brothers, she needs to help her mother. The father went to São Paulo and never returned.

– My God... – Suzana thought and asked: – How many brothers do you have?

– I have six brothers. My little brother is seven years old.

– How old is your mother?

– I think thirty–six or thirty–seven years.

– Oh my god! – Suzana thought again.

– Did you work even when you were pregnant and when the children were newborns?

– No, I couldn't. I couldn't leave the house, but I was making crafts and earning some money.

– Do you sew?

– I do. Me and all my brothers, only my children cannot work.

Just Beginning

Suzana got up, went to the room and brought the blouse she had bought: – Do you make this kind of lace?

That is easy. We all do it. We have more beautiful and better made lace than this one.

– Do you just make the lace?

– Some women make the lace, others sew.

– How much do you sell a shirt like this for?

– Two thousand cruzeiros more or less.

– Two thousand cruzeiros? I paid twenty–eight! You are being exploited!

– We know, but what can we do. If I don't sell to them, who are we going to sell to?

– It's better to earn a little than to earn nothing. There is always someone who sells cheaper.

– The woman from the store and the man from the stand said that you leave the pieces and come back once a month and that they only pay for the pieces that were sold. Is it true?

– Yes, it is. That is how it is here...

– I knew something was wrong! Let's do the following. You will work here at home, but today, now, I want you to take me to the place where you live and where the craftsmen are.

– Why do you want to go?

– I want to know about the work and talk to the craftsmen.

– I live close because of my husband's work, but the town where my family live is very far from here.

– By bus it takes more than an hour.

– It's not important. Let's take a taxi there.

– Do you really want to go?

Just Beginning

– I want to and I can't wait. As the taxi should take less time, we can return after lunch.

– Well, whatever you want, I'll do it, but I need to talk to my husband...

– Go down and talk to your husband. Meanwhile, I am going to prepare my son so that we can go.

– The girl came down. Susana took a bag, Rodrigo's things, water and a packet of cookies and left. When she got to the ground floor, the doorman said: – My wife said you want to go to the village.

I just wanted to know if you are going to let my wife work at your house.

– Yes, she is going to work, but now I have to go to the village to see the work they do there.

– Then it's okay. You can go.

They went out into the street, took a taxi and left.

After more than half an hour, the taxi finally reached a small village.

The main street was narrow and the sidewalk was no more than six feet.

She noticed that there were many children running and playing on the street. The women were talking outside the houses. The smell of burning wood was strong, showing that the food was prepared on a wood stove.

You could see the smoke coming from all the houses. For her, who had always lived in a big city, everything was new.

– You can stop here, boy.

The taxi driver stopped and Lindalva, smiling at a woman who ran towards the car, said: – Here is where my mother lives, Mrs.

Just Beginning

Suzana got out of the taxi, helped Rodrigo out and stared at the house and the two women hugged.

– What are you doing here, Lindalva? Did something happen to you or the boys?

– No, mom, it's okay. This lady is from the south. She moved here now and I'm going to work at her house.

– She bought a lace blouse, she liked it, but I told her that we have much more beautiful laces than that.

– She came here to see more –. The woman looked suspicious.

– Nice to meet you, lady.

– The pleasure is mine. I hope you don't mind showing me the other works.

– You can't get in. Don't you see that the house is simple?

Suzana smiled. All the surprise that could have happened had already happened during the trip. The taxi went through places I never thought existed.

The house was very simple, but very neat and clean. Several children, curious, when they saw that the car stopped, began to approach.

As soon as Suzana entered the house, they also entered and they were looking suspiciously at that stranger.

– Get out of here guys! The girl just came to see the crafts! – The woman yelled at the children. Suzana smiled and the children, still suspicious and curious, left.

Suzana realized that there was only one room in the house, she thought: – "Everyone sleeps in one room and I still complain about the apartment Anselmo rented."

Just Beginning

The woman showed a chair that was next to a table made of rough wood: – Girl, my name is María do Rosário, but everyone calls me Rosa. Sit down, ma'am. I will get the products.

– Thank Mrs. My name is Suzana and I am delighted with the work that is being done here in the Northeast. The woman entered the room and returned shortly after, carrying several pieces of lace in her hands.

Suzana took one piece after another and, delighted, said: – You were right, Lindalva! They are beautiful! Directing her eyes to Rosa, she asked: – How did you learn to make such a beautiful lace?

– With my mother and she with her mother. Almost all women do this type of work.

– Is there any other type of art, here in this village, besides lace?

– Yes, there is. We have an artist for all tastes. Some use wood, others clay.

– If you take one of them in hand, I know you will like it. There is no work here in the Northeast, so everyone has to do what they can. With our art, we can earn a little money to feed the children.

– Lindalva said that you sell such a beautiful work at a very low price. I paid much more for an expensive blouse.

– Why do you sell them so cheap?

– It's better to sell them cheap and have some money, than to sell them expensive and have no money.

– You're right. I would like to take some of these pieces and see other types of art, could I?

– Sure you can. Come, I'll take you everywhere –. Suzana took a few pieces and then left. She went to various houses.

Just Beginning

And in each of them, she was delighted with the works. She saw dresses, blouses, sheets, and pillowcases.

She saw various pieces of wood and clay. All handmade. In each house that she visited she was more delighted. She bought several pieces and then said goodbye. She and Lindalva got into the taxi and returned to the city.

Along the way, she began to think of an idea.

24.– The ceremony

Julia left the restaurant and walked to the apartment.

As she walked, she thought: these dreams I'm having are touching me. I really wanted to remember something else. Why can't I remember?

Alzira and Ciro, who were walking beside her, looked at each other, smiled and spread their hands over Julia, who stopped walking. Wait, I was dancing in that beautiful dress and I was with Anselmo! Was I dancing with Anselmo?

She kept walking and thinking: I knew that what Sueli said about the spirit going out and going for a walk, when we sleep, has nothing to do with reality! Of course, I dreamed of Anselmo! Everything that is happening in my life is because of him! I could only dream of him, who else? What Sueli said was unable to convince me.

She was walking and thinking until she entered the building. When she passed the entrance door, the doorman said: – Good evening. How are you? Were you cured?

She, realizing that he wanted to know what had happened, replied: – Good evening. I'm fine, but don't address me formally!

– It's not the same. But I couldn't address you informally.

– Miss! Do you see? It got better.

Just Beginning

Laughing, she continued walking towards the elevator. As soon as she entered the apartment, she looked at the shelf where Sueli's books were. She stopped, picked up one, then the other, read the back cover, but neither caught her eye.

This story about spirits, reincarnation is boring. I'm not in the mood to read these things. I'd rather watch television. She went to the kitchen, had a glass, poured milk, and went back to the living room. She turned on the television, lay down on the couch, and watched a comedy show. She watched for a few minutes and, without realizing , fell asleep.

She woke up in the living room at the exact moment when María Inés, in a black dress, was coming down the stairs. Seeing Ciro and Alzira who were there in that house, Julia said: – Am I dreaming again?

– Again, Julia. Aren't you curious to see what happened to María Inés?

– I am! Of course I am! But first, I wanted to ask a question.

– What question?

– When I was awake, I managed to remember something about what I dreamed of. I wore that dress that María Inés wore to the dance and danced with Anselmo. Did it really happen?

– What do you think?

– I was with you watching the dance, next to you, how could I be in two places at the same time?

– I think I was wrong. I must have dreamed of Anselmo for everything he did to me and for thinking of him so strongly.

– It can be. It can be Julia. Now let's see what's going on.

Look around.

Julia looked and saw that the walls of the room were lined with purple fabrics. In the center, on a table was a mortuary coffin,

Just Beginning

surrounded by candles and a large crucifix. From where she stood, she couldn't see the face of the person in it. Some people were crying.

Others spoke in small groups. Beside her was Maria Augusta with red and puffy eyes, and a man Julia didn't know. She was getting closer when she saw María Inés walking towards the coffin, screaming and crying desperately.

She threw herself on the coffin and said: Mother! Why did this happen? How are we going to live without you?

The people who were there, when they saw the despair of María Inés, began to cry with sorrow for the girl.

Zefa, who also had red eyes, looked at Maria Augusta, who made a great effort not to slap her sister in front of everyone who was there.

Julia was also upset: – How can she be such a liar?

She didn't care about her mother's death at all, she only thought about the dance!

Alzira and Ciro fell silent, looking at María Inés, who at that moment hugged the crying man:

– Dad! Why did this have to happen? She was a wonderful mother! She dedicated her life to make us happy! How are we going to live without her?

– I don't know what it will be like, my daughter. I lost the woman who was by my side for more than twenty years.

– I don't know how I'll go on living... – They were hugging and crying.

Julia was distressed, said: – He seems to be a good man...

Alzira looked at Ciro, smiled and said: – Yes, he is a good spirit, Julia.

Just Beginning

– You irritate me with this spiritual story. To me he is just a man, not a spirit!

– You're right, Julia. For now, he is just a man.

Julia smiled and looked at everyone: – You said that life goes on and that death does not exist, so why is there always so much sadness at funerals? The way you talk, it should be a party.

– It's about tradition and lack of faith, Julia. People are sad and cry because, as they have just heard, María Inés's father believes that he will never see his wife again. He said he suffered a loss.

– His wife died!

– Like many people, yourself included, when a relative or friend dies, as you like to say, they think that they have suffered a loss and that they will never see those who left before them. If they believed in life after death, they would know that this is not true. Everyone, without exception, regardless of their level of education, financial life, religion, race or sex, will one day have to walk this path. Some go earlier, others later, but everyone will go through this experience.

– That's true...

Julia looked everywhere. Curious, Ciro asked: – What are you looking for, Julia?

– For everything they said, in that coffin, there is only the body, because the spirit, after death, is liberated. Isn't that what they said?

– Yes, that is correct.

– So, I'm looking for María Inés's mother.

– She's not here, Julia.

– Why not? As she is free from the body...

Just Beginning

– I already told you that the energy of the physical body is different from the spiritual one. When the spirit leaves the body through death, it is carefully brought to a place, where its energy gradually adapts to the new environment.

– Can't María Inés's mother stay here?

– Some spirits, attached to things, money or people, sometimes insist on being next to the body.

Others, due to the evils they practiced, are forced to stay and watch their bodies decompose.

Many even feel pain as if they still have the physical body.

How awful!

– It's true and no matter how much you think about it, you can never imagine how awful it is.

However, normally, when the spirits are liberated, they want to go home. Especially the mother of María Inés, who is a spirit of light and who only returned to Earth to be able to help her daughter of many lives.

– Did she abandon her daughter?

– No and from what I know about her, she would never leave her. She hopes that one day, her daughter can make her decisions and get back on her path. She just needs some time to adjust to her new life.

– Goodness...

María Inés spent almost half an hour hugging her father and crying desperately. She only stopped when Maria Augusta approached, hugged her and spoke softly: – You can stop all this scandal. People have seen all your pain! Go to the kitchen, have a glass of water, compose yourself, and come back.

Just Beginning

María Inés was silent. María Augusta greeted Zefa and asked her to come. Zefa approached, took María Inés's arm and said: – Come on, girl. Come with me. I will give you a cup of water.

María Inés, wiping her eyes with an embroidered handkerchief, followed by María Augusta's eyes, began to follow Zefa. As she walked, people, feeling sorry for her, touched her arms and hair.

She realized that many of those people were at the dance. When she saw Eulália and her family who had just arrived, she cried again desperately. She ran to Eulalia, hugged her and said it out loud so that everyone could hear:

– When she died, I was at the dance! If I had known, I would have stayed by her side. I knew she was sick, but I didn't think she was that sick. Nobody told me...

As soon as María Augusta saw and heard that, she took the arm of the black woman who had been caring for her since she was born and said:

– Come on, Filó! Let's get out of here or I'll throw up or hit this liar pre !

They left there, under the gaze of Julia, who said: – If I were her, I would do the same. This girl really deserves a good beating!

María Augusta and Filó went to the garden and sat on one of the benches.

María Augusta, irritated, said: – I don't understand why María Inés is like that. Since I was a child, even when she played pranks, my parents never saw or pretended not to see, just like my dad is doing now.

– He knows that when Ignacio left the hospital, there was time to get here, before she went to the dance.

Just Beginning

– How can he believe that she didn't know that mom had died?

– Don't be like that, my lady. She was always very evil.

– Every night, I thank God for your mother. Maria Inés didn't choose her. Poor Zefa, I suffered a lot for her.

– My lady treats her as if she were an insect. Although she denies it, she likes to do it.

– I know, Filó, it's just that María Inés doesn't know. She just cares about her, she didn't care about anyone.

Meanwhile, María Inés continued to hug Eulália. Behind her shoulders, she saw Luiz Cláudio arrive with his family. She released Eulalia and went to meet t hem, he hugged the lady, who, surprised, hugged her too.

Thanks for coming.

– I would never stop coming and saying my last goodbye to your mother, María Inés. She was a wonderful person.

– We will miss her a lot. With her ideas and parties she always managed to raise a lot of money for the orphanage.

– Since she decided to found the orphanage, she never let the children lack anything.

– Like I said, she was wonderful.

– That's right. That is why I am so desperate, defenseless... – She said that, looking at Luiz Cláudio. He released the lady and held out her hand, which he kissed gently.

– I'm sorry lady.

– Thanks for coming.

– I couldn't help coming. I had a date at two, but something happened so I imagine it should be postponed.

Just Beginning

– It's a pity, but who knows, this commitment may not be postponed until tomorrow...

– No, I can't tomorrow. I already have another commitment made –. María Inés, although she was very angry with this situation, smiled.

Luiz Cláudio, touching the brim of his hat, walked away and went to talk to some friends who were also there.

As soon as he left, María Inés looked at the clock on the wall and, accompanied by Zefa, returned to her father.

As she walked, pretending to wipe her eyes, she said to Zefa.

– Why did they have to schedule the funeral for three?

– Couldn't they have scheduled it earlier?

– They couldn't, my lady. You can enter before twenty–four hours.

– I don't know why it has to be like this! Has the person died for all this? Everyone, as soon as they died, should be buried instantly!

– People did it to be able to be a little closer to people they like.

– I like my mother, but I don't like being here. I prefer to meet with Luiz Cláudio. She really died.

– What's the use of staying here crying?

– My lady cries...

– Of course I do, Zefa! Have you ever thought what people will say if I don't cry? They will think that I am not feeling the death of my mother!

– Your sister is not crying and you know she likes your mother very much...

Just Beginning

– María Augusta was always like this, okay! I am still going to do something for everyone to find out what she really is like.

– She is not evil, no, my lady. She is very good to all of us.

– Didn't I take care of you?

– Take care, my lady. Take care...

A lady approached María Inés and began to talk about her mother.

María Inés hated that conversation, but she had to keep up appearances.

A drumming and voices began to echo. Júlia marveled: – Who plays and sings at a funeral?

– It's the blacks. They are, in their own way, mourning the death of their lady, whom they loved very much.

– She always treated them like human beings. She never let her husband separate the families.

– She never allowed them to live in subhuman conditions. She always tried to give them the best health and education conditions. She made her husband build a school and taught the children and adults they wanted. Therefore, they suffer the death of the woman who has always treated them as humans.

– That, at that time, was not common.

– Playing and singing?

– Yes, Julia, it's part of their culture. They celebrate sadness and happiness through music. At this time, they sing and play for their lady to accompany Xangô.

– Who is Xangô?

– In their religion, Xangô is the god of justice. All, when they die, are brought into the presence of Xangô so that he can judge and say where this soul will go.

Just Beginning

– Does this Xangô exist?

– In their culture and for them, it does!

– But does it really exist?

– It exists not only for them, but also for us.

– What?

– Each of their gods represents nature. What is more important to human survival than nature? They worship Oxalá, who is the greatest god, the creator, who for us would represent our God.

For them, the forest, lightning and storms, wind, justice, sea and rivers are valuable and essential for the survival of the Earth. For each of these elements, there is a god.

– Everything you said is really essential, but do you need a god?

– Long before they knew Christianity, these people recognized all this as essential to their lives.

It is the tradition of a people and therefore it needs and must be respected. God, our God, is not a jealous or vindictive being. – He created a place where he could place his children, giving them all the conditions so that they could, with a human body, live. Then you know how important nature is and you won't mind that some people respect and adore it.

There are spirits of great light that are born in the midst of this town and that, also because they were born there, worship their gods.

Also, there are those spirits who claim to be Christians and who practice inconceivable evil and injustice.

For the evolution of the spirit, it doesn't matter what religion you follow. Everyone must follow the same path.

Just Beginning

Everyone must overcome their learning difficulties, and everyone is responsible for what they do.

All of us are subject to the major Laws, the laws of love, the laws of forgiveness, the laws of free will, and the laws of action and reaction.

So, let's listen and enjoy those drums and voices.

Julia continued to listen to the voices and, without realizing it, her feet began to follow the sound.

Luiz Cláudio, after talking with the other boys, decided to leave that heavy environment and went out. As soon as he left, Alzira said: – Come on Julia, let's see where Luiz Cláudio is going.

Júlia, who was involved in music and was still on her feet, nodded. When Luiz Cláudio walked out the door, he saw María Augusta, who was still sitting and talking with Filó. He approached and touching the brim of his hat with one hand, said: – My condolences, miss.

– Thank you sir.

– You must be very sorry about your mother's death. Sorry, I shouldn't have said that, because you clearly are.

– Don't worry. I am really sorry about my mother's death, but she was suffering a lot.

– I think it was better for her then.

A tear began to form in her eyes. It was quickly dried with a small, embroidered handkerchief.

– May I sit next to you?

–Yes.

Maria Augusta stepped aside for him to sit down. Filó, who was sitting next to her, got up.

– Sit down, Filó. You don't have to get up.

Just Beginning

– If my lady doesn't mind, should I bring water? I even have a baby water bowl.

– You can but come back soon.

Filó ran towards the house.

– Take a seat, sir.

Luiz Cláudio sat down: – We spoke a couple of times, but I always admired you.

– Thanks, but I don't have much to talk about.

– Your sister went to the dance, why didn't you go?

– I was in the hospital with my mother.

– Your sister didn't go to the hospital?

She wanted to talk about what María Inés had done, but she lied: – My mother was fine and she knew how much María Inés wanted to go to the dance, so she asked her to be very beautiful and have fun.

– Still, I don't think she should have left her.

– Don't judge my sister, sir. She is very young...

– Sorry, I shouldn't have said that.

María Inés saw when Luiz Cláudio left, she thought: I'm going to talk to him so we can organize a new meeting. Accompanied by Zefa, she left the house. As soon as she left, she saw that Luiz Cláudio was sitting next to María Augusta and that they were talking.

She was furious: – Look, Zefa! My holy sister wants to steal my boyfriend!

– They are just talking, my lady...

– Just talking? Why is she alone with him? Where is Filó?

– I don't know, my lady. Filó must have gone to do something your sister asked her...

Just Beginning

– You see? She asked Filó to leave so she could be alone with him! Liar! Fake!

With that saintly face, at the first opportunity, try to rob my boyfriend!

– Is my lady in love with him?

– Not yet, but I'm going to go out and marry him! Let's go there!

– Wait, my lady. You can't get there this way. You're very nervous! I think you should wait a little...

– I can't wait anymore! I'm leaving right now!

– Don't go, my lady!

When María Augusta saw María Inés approaching, she got up: – Excuse me, sir, I need to get in to be with my father.

He also got up and bowed. As she walked away, he smiled and thought: – I'm going to convince you too... – María Inés passed by María Augusta and, angrily, pretended not to see her sister.

She approached Luiz Cláudio: – I had to go to get some air. It's very hot inside.

– That's right. That's why I went out too. Do you want to sit down, miss?

María Inés, vibrating with happiness, but trying not to show it, sat down. She sat down immediately. As soon as she sat down, she looked at Zefa and said: Zefa! Go get juice for me and Mr. Luiz Cláudio!

– I'll be there, my lady.

Zefa ran out and María Inés smiled: – Did you talk to my sister?

– Yes. She is a very nice person.

– Do you think so?

Just Beginning

He began to laugh: – Sorry, I didn't mean to be inelegant. She is definitely not a nice person.

– She is cold and distant.

– Since she was a child, she has always been this way. Very blunt, with time I got used to it, but what were you talking about?

– Nothing important, only the comforts. In fact, while I was talking to her, I was thinking of you.

– Thinking of me? Why?

– What could you do to make that meeting of ours, which had to be postponed, take place? – She shuddered: – Did you find a solution?

– I found it, but I don't know if you will agree.

– May I know what the solution is?

– I thought that after the wake and burial of your mother, I will return and we can meet at the lake.

– Didn't they invite you to dinner at Eulalia's house?

– Yes, and I can't miss it.

– Are you really going to marry her?

– Not! I'm just going to marry you! You know there is an agreement between my father and Miss Eulalia.

– For a while, I need to keep up appearances, but I will definitely not marry her.

– How are you going to do that?

– Our parents are in negotiations. When they're done, I'll say I don't want to get married.

– I'm just worried about Eulalia's reaction.

– I don't want her to suffer.

– It's very noble, but you shouldn't worry. Eulalia doesn't want this marriage.

Just Beginning

– She is in love with Mr. José Antônio.

– The merchant's son?

– Yes.

– Her father will not allow that marriage.

– That is her fear, but she said that she won't marry you and that if she needs it, she will run away to be with the man she loves.

– Do you see how everything is getting easier for us, miss?

– With her refusal, I will be free to marry!

– Are you talking seriously?

– Of course! I just don't hold you in my arms right now, because people might not understand.

I've always been in love with you, and with each passing day, that love grows stronger.

– I can't believe what you're talking about, sir. You never showed any interest in me.

– You've always interested me. You were the one who never looked at me, like you are doing now.

– We need to meet!

– I know that today, with the death of your mother, is not a good day, but, if you don't mind, I would like it very much.

Well sir, it's really not a good day, but what good is staying home crying?

My mom won't come back, will she? If I knew my tears would bring her back, I would cry non-stop, but since this is not going to happen, we can meet, yeah. What did you plan?

– The procession and burial must end before four o'clock.

I think by five o'clock you must have returned to your father and sister.

Just Beginning

– I'll go on horseback and wait for you at the lake, as agreed. I won't be able to stay long.

– You know I need to keep up appearances. So today, at eight o'clock, I'll have to go to the duke's house for dinner.

– However, if you agree, I will be very happy!

– I don't know sir, what if I don't have time?

– There will be. I know there will be! I need to take you in my arms if only for a minute!

– Promise that you won't make me wait in vain –. María Inés was stunned: – I don't know what to do.

– You know that it isn't correct for a modest lady to agree to meet a man alone, especially in an isolated place like the lake.

– I need to ask a question:

– Which one?

– Do you like me?

She thought little and replied: – I think so.

– I also like you very much and I intend to marry you.

– Then there is nothing wrong with this meeting. If we like each other, why do we continue with such formalities?

– Why don't we call each other by our names? I would like you to call me Luiz Cláudio and me to call you María Inés. Do you see any harm in that?

– Not! Of course not!

– So well. From now on, when we are alone, we will call each other by our names.

– Okay? María Inés?

– Yes, Luiz Cláudio... – she said, smiling.

– I'll be waiting for you, María Inés. Today we are going to start a romance that will make us very happy.

Just Beginning

– I'm already very happy!

There were several carriages. Others began to arrive.

He, touching the brim of his hat, said: – I have been here for a long time. It's almost time to start the procession to the church.

– I think it's time for us to go inside.

– Just to keep up appearances, I will support Eulalia. I hope you don't mind.

– It's okay. You said such beautiful things that I even forgot where I am. G o in first and I'll go later. He returned to the living room, went to where Eulalia was, and stood next to her.

María Inés waved her hand to Zefa, who was far away.

Zefa approached. María Inés spoke excitedly: – He loves me, Zefa! He loves me!

– Go easy, my lady. If you take...

– How can I go easy? Didn't you understand what I said? He loves me and wants to get to know me!

– Okay, but now it's almost time for the break to end. My lady, go stand next to your mother.

You need to say goodbye...

– I hope this funeral ends soon! I can no longer bear to be here with all these people wanting to cry for my suffering!

– Aren't you suffering my lady?

– Of course I'm suffering, but what good is spending all this time here? Wouldn't it be better if she were buried soon?

– Let's go in, my lady...

Shortly after they entered, the coffin was closed. María Inés's father stood to one side, crying a lot. Maria Augusta was at his side, crying softly. María Inés wept and sobbed non–stop.

Just Beginning

People hugged her, saddened by her suffering. But inside, she thought: I hope it ends soon! The sooner the better, since I will be able to spend more time with Luiz Cláudio.

He, along with Eulália, also thought: How can she pretend so much?

– I also think she doesn't have a shred of feeling –. Julia spoke, shaking her head from side to side. Alzira looked at Cyrus, they both smiled.

The procession reached the church. After the priest's sermon, the body was buried next to the altar. María Inés was relieved when it finished and everyone started saying goodbye.

When Luiz Cláudio approached Eulália, shaking her hand, she smiled. Despite everything, she was happy.

Seeing that, Julia, who was looking at everything in silence, couldn't help it: It is unbearable!

Again, Alzira and Ciro smiled. Julia looked at them and asked: – Can I ask one more question?

– Of course you can. We are here for you to learn.

– Was she buried inside the church and near the altar?

– Yes, Julia.

– Why? Is she holy?

– No. At that time it was customary. People who had possessions or titles were buried in this way.

– The more money and the bigger the title, the closer to the altar they were buried.

– And the poor, where were they buried?

– Far from the city. Blacks go even farther.

– Was there all this inequality?

– Inequality has always existed and will always exist.

Just Beginning

– It's not fair or right!

– Everything is always fine, Julia.

– Are you trying to say that inequality should not be fought?

– I'm not saying that Julia. I'm just saying that everything is always fine.

– That there is always a reason for what happens.

– In addition, yes, we must fight for people to love and respect each other. Each one is where they belong. – Each one lives the life they chose.

– Here comes the lady with this election story again.

As much as you say that, I will never agree. I will never believe that anyone can choose to live in poverty!

– Okay, but now It's time to go back to your body, wake up.

– No, I do not want to! I want to see what will happen to María Inés! I want to know if she is going to meet and marry Luiz Cláudio.

– You will know, don't worry, but now you need to go back. If you don't go back, I've already explained what happens to your physical body.

– The energies?

– That's right.

Like the other times, Julia woke up with a jump. She rolled over in bed and went back to sleep.

25.– The delivery

That morning, Julia woke up excited. She didn't remember the dream.

She got up determined to find a job. She took her resume and went to some companies and an employment agency. She handed in the resumes and returned home.

When the elevator door opened for her to enter, she found Mr. Osvaldo exiting.

– Good morning, Julia! How are you?

– I'm very thankful.

– My son was impressed and worried about you.

– Your son?

– Yes. He lives in Rio and helped Sueli take you to the hospital.

– I saw a boy, but I didn't think it was your son. Is he here?

– No. He left this morning.

– Please thank him for me and sorry for the inconvenience.

– It's ok, I was just worried.

She smiled. He got out of the elevator and she got in.

When she entered the apartment, she saw that Sueli's room was locked, which meant that she was sleeping. She went into the

Just Beginning

kitchen, took some bread, and buttered it. She took out a box of milk from the refrigerator, filled a glass with milk and went to her room.

She didn't want to wake her friend up.

After eating and drinking the milk, she put the glass on the sink so as not to make a noise. She'd wash it later.

When she returned to her room, she looked at the bookshelf and saw Sueli's books. Since she had nothing to do, she took one of them and carried it to her room. She lay down and began to read. As she read, she became more excited about the story.

She spent the rest of the day reading.

When Sueli woke up, she was amazed and happy to see Julia reading.

– What book are you reading, Julia? Julia showed the book cover.

– This book is beautiful! You chose well. I know you are going to like this story.

– I'm already enjoying it, Sueli.

Sueli smiled and got ready to go to work. She left and Julia continued reading and stopped to make dinner. She ate quickly and continued reading.

When Sueli returned home from work, she saw that the light in Julia's room was on. She approached: – Are you still reading, Julia?

– I am, Sueli. This book is really good.

– Didn't I tell you?

– It's a pity this is just fiction.

– Fiction, why Julia?

– The character has two spiritual friends who support her, all the time to help her in difficult moments.

Just Beginning

– It would be great if that were true.

Sueli laughed: – We all have spiritual friends, Julia!

– Can you even believe that?

– Of course. I believe that our friends and family who left before us, if they can, will help us.

– If they can? What do you mean by that?

– The spirit, after leaving, is not always in a position to help us. They first need to understand what happened and they try to help themselves. Many succeed quickly, others take longer.

– I even think that many of our friends haven't even been reborn and we don't remember them, but they still help us.

– Friends we don't know?

– Yes. When they help us choose the life we want to live, when we are in the physical body, even if we are not reborn, they stay by our side for the entire time we live. They do this so that everything goes well.

So that everything goes according to plan.

– I can't believe this story that I chose this miserable life that I live. I would never have chosen something like that!

– All right, Julia. Now I'm going to bed. Today was a very tiring day. I think you should sleep too.

– I'll be there shortly. I'll finish one more chapter.

– Good night, Julia.

– Good night, Sueli.

Sueli went to her room and Julia continued reading.

She read for a while longer, until she felt her eyes close.

She thought: I'm halfway through the book. I don't want to stop, but I'm sleepy. I'll save it for tomorrow. She lay down and soon fell asleep.

Just Beginning

She was again in the garden of María Inés's house and with her, Alzira and Ciro.

– Today it took you a long time to sleep, Julia...

– It's true. I was reading a book.

– I know about that. I was reading with you.

– What are you talking about?

– You were reading with me?

Julia laughed: You're kidding!

– I'm not kidding, Julia. Just because we are not in the physical body, do you think we have stopped liking and enjoying the good things on Earth?

– I don't know. I never thought about it... – When the spirit returns to the spiritual realm, it brings back memories of the good and bad moments it had when it was reincarnated.

– Have you ever imagined how that artist who dedicated himself to any type of art, such as singing, acting and playing, would feel if he could no longer do these things that he loved so much? The same goes for those who like to read.

– What would they look like if they couldn't do that anymore? I, in particular, have always liked reading.

– Ciro has always liked acting, so he stays with the actors helping in any way possible.

– I never imagined this could happen.

They both started laughing. Ciro continued: – There are many things that neither you nor other spirits in the physical body imagine. Now look who leaves the house!

Julia looked and saw María Inés who, accompanied by Zefa, left the house. She was in a hurry: – Come on, Zefa! Hurry up!

Just Beginning

– We arrived late! I thought Maria Augusta and dad wouldn't go to their rooms!

– We're leaving, why, my lady?

– It's none of your business, but I'll tell you anyway. I'm going to meet Luiz Cláudio!

– Will my lady meet him alone?

– I will! What? Is it too much?

– My lady knows that she can't meet a man alone! It's dangerous!

– Dangerous, why?

– They like to fool the girls...

María Inés, who was walking quickly, holding her dress to be able to walk better, began to laugh: – Zefa! You know me since I was born, do you think someone can fool me?

– I don't know, my lady. There are still dangerous boys. Can I stay together with my lady?

– Of course not, Zefa! How can we speak knowing that you are looking at us and listening?

– As soon as we are far from the house and no one can see us, you will stop walking next to me and wait until I return. Don't worry! Nothing will happen to me.

– Besides, Luiz Cláudio loves me and said that he will marry me!

– Won't he go home with my lady Eulália?

– Of course not! She is only doing the will of her father, but before marrying she will say that she no longer wants to.

He will marry me!

I'll be a baroness!

– Take care, little one!

Just Beginning

– Stop talking, Zefa! We are already here! No one else will be able to see us from the house. I'm going to the lake to meet him!

Stay here and don't you dare look at us!

– I am old, my lady, take care of yourself...

María Inés, still holding the dress, continued running towards the lake. Shortly after, she saw Luiz Cláudio walking impatiently from side to side. When she saw him, she ran even faster.

As soon as Luiz Cláudio saw her, he ran too. As they approached, he unexpectedly hugged her and kissed her. At first, she wanted to avoid him, but she failed and kissed him back.

Before leaving, he, looking into her eyes and with a passionate voice, said: – I thought you wouldn't come.

I was desperate.

– Why?

– I am in love and I feel that I can no longer live without your company.

– Are you telling the truth?

– Of course I am! If not so, do you think I would be here?

– Come on! I need another kiss.

Before she had time to think, he took her in his arms again and kissed her. After the kiss, she walked away but said: – Wait, Luiz Cláudio! We should not and cannot do that...

– Why not? I love you, María Inés! I know you love me too! I intend to marry you! Unless I'm wrong and you don't love me. Am I wrong?

– You're not! I love you!

He walked away: – No, you don't love me, if you loved me, you wouldn't doubt my intentions. So I'm leaving... She, desperate

Just Beginning

to see him leave, shouted: – I don't doubt it! I know you love me and I'm happy with it!

– Then prove it...

– How?

– Come here.

He hugged her and kissed her again, passionately.

Emotionally, María Inés returned the hug and the kiss. Slowly, he made her lie down on the grass. He continued with affection, which made her give up without resisting. Soon, she totally gave herself up. Zefa, who didn't obey María Inés, from a distance, saw everything that happened.

Crying, she said: – My God, my lady is lost...

Júlia was also surprised: – I never thought she would give up like this, so fast! I thought she was more mature!

– Situations always repeat, Julia. Several times he engulfed her and she could never resist.

– How old is she?

– Sixteen years.

– Did you say she's only sixteen? How could she resist? He is to blame!

– As you can see, you're right, Julia. He is guilty and responsible before the spiritual realm.

– As I said, situations are repeated so that the spirit can free itself from all ties and understand that it is free and that, therefore, it cannot be enslaved in any way. Again, she didn't resist, but she will have other opportunities.

– In another incarnation, she will have to pass the same tests. I hope that this time, she resists what is to come.

Just Beginning

– We will be by her side so that she has the strength and is free forever.

– I hope she can! I don't like her! I think she's pedantic, selfish and doesn't have a shred of sentiment, but I think that shouldn't have happened. It's just a girl! Even more so if we consider this moment in which she lives...

– She will still have a chance to win. It will depend only on her free will, her decisions.

– It's just a girl! How do you want her to make decisions?

– Although it wears the body of a girl, it is an old spirit. She can choose, Julia.

– Even though she was just a girl, as you say, especially at this moment when we are watching, she knew what was right and what was wrong. Everyone learns this very early.

– She's in love with him...

– No, Julia. She fell in love with his position. She doesn't accept that he marries Eulalia.

– This fight between the three has been going on for several incarnations and these same situations always repeat.

– It will never end?

– We hope so, but that will only happen when each of them understands that their spirit is free and that they cannot be imprisoned for anything or anyone.

María Inés and Luiz Cláudio continued embracing for some time. Then he got up: – Now I have to go.

– Are you going to have dinner?

– As we agreed, for some time, I need to keep up appearances, but don't worry, Eulália is nothing to me. Tomorrow, at the same time, I will be here and we can love each other again.

Just Beginning

María Inés also got up and happily said: – I will wait anxiously. He, after hugging her and kissing her again, walked away.

Heart pounding with happiness, she watched until he disappeared into the trees. Then she returned to Zefa: – Come on, Zefa!

– What did you do, my lady?

– Nothing happened, Zefa, I'm just the happiest woman in the world! I'm getting married, Zefa! I will be a baroness!

– Now let's go home!

– It's okay, my lady... it's okay...

María Inés didn't realize that Zefa was sad and worried.

When they entered the house, they found Maria Augusta who was in the living room playing a sad song on the piano. As soon as they entered, she asked: – Where were you, María Inés?

María Inés, who didn't expect to find her sister, for a second didn't know what to answer, but she soon recovered:

– I was very sad and decided to go to the lake with Zefa. Before that beauty and that clear water, I felt very good.

– And are you playing the piano the day our mother was buried?

– I'm playing in honor of her. This song was the one she liked the most.

– I'm going to my room.

– Go, María Inés.

María Inés got out and started up the stairs. María Augusta looked at her for a few seconds and went back to playing the piano. When she entered the room, María Inés threw herself on the bed: I'm so happy! He really loves me!

Just Beginning

Zefa looked and shook her head, said: – I will prepare your bath, my lady.

– I don't want to bathe, Zefa!

– Why?

– His scent is still on me! I don't want it to go away! – Zefa shook her head again and thought: my lady is crazy...

26. – The wait

Julia, shaking her head from side to side, woke up speaking:
– It's a girl!

When she opened her eyes, she was surprised to hear her own voice and thought: What girl am I talking about? She glanced at her watch: two thirty in the morning? Why did I wake up at this time?

She continued lying down, trying to fall asleep again. After rolling from side to side unable to sleep, she decided to get up and have a glass of milk.

She went to the kitchen. When she opened the refrigerator, she saw that there was a cake that Sueli had prepared.

She took a piece, poured milk into a glass and sat on a chair by the table and began to eat.

As she drank the milk and ate the cake, she thought: For the first time in my life, I woke up to my own voice. What was I dreaming of? Why can't I remember?

When she finished eating, she placed the glass on the sink and returned to the room.

She straightened the pillow and went back to bed. Minutes later, she was at María Inés's house at the exact moment when a

Just Beginning

carriage stopped in front of the front door. Eulalia got out of it. One of the house slaves opened the door.

Eulália entered quickly and asked: – Is María Inés at home?

– She's there in her room, my lady.

– I need to talk to her! I'm going there!

– Wait, my lady. I need to tell her first.

– Hurry up! I'm in a hurry!

The black woman ran up the stairs. When she got to María Inés's room, she knocked and rushed inside.

María Inés, who was sitting in front of the mirror, while Zefa was combing her hair, asked: – What happened to you?

– My lady Eulália is downstairs, she wants to talk to you my lady.

María Inés got up and asked: – Eulália, here? What does she want?

– I don't know, my lady. I just know that it is very important!

– Important? Let her come in. Tell her to come here.

The slave came downstairs and, shortly after, Eulália, crying, entered María Inés's room.

– What happened, Eulalia? Why are you like this? – Eulália cried so much that she couldn't speak.

María Inés was also nervous: – Stop crying, Eulália! Tell us what's going on!

Eulália, who couldn't stop crying, handed an envelope to María Inés, who immediately opened it and read:

"Dear Miss Eulalia:

It's with a broken heart that I write these lines. I am embarking on a steamboat to France tomorrow.

Just Beginning

My father found out about our meetings. He was nervous because although he made a lot of money as a merchant, he has not yet succeeded in obtaining a title of nobility which is his greatest desire.

He told me that if I keep insisting on seeing you, your father won't let him get what he wants. So, for that reason, he demanded that I stay away from you.

He also said that if I don't fulfill his wish, he will disinherit me, which I can't imagine. I agreed to go to France and stay there for a while.

I hope you understand my position and forgive me. I'm weak.

Thinking of being poor terrifies me. Again, asking your forgiveness, I say goodbye.

Jose Antonio."

María Inés, with the letter in her hand, looked at Eulália and asked: – What does this mean, Eulália?

– What did you read María Inés? He is leaving! He's going to leave me!

– He was afraid of being disinherited! Of becoming poor!

Eulália, crying, hugged María Inés and continued: – Yesterday afternoon, this letter arrived through a messenger.

– I was devastated and cried for hours. I only stopped when I remembered that Luiz Cláudio and his family were coming to dinner.

– Were they there? – María Inés, curious, asked: – Yes and, in the end, it was fine.

– Why?

– Luiz Cláudio is wonderful! He realized that I was not well and made me tell him what had happened.

Just Beginning

– I told him and, when I finished, he, holding my hand, said: – Don't be like that, miss. You are a beautiful and intelligent lady.

"You didn't deserve it, but when we get married, I'll do everything in my power to make you happy." María Inés, laughing inside, knowing that it was just a matter of keeping up appearances, asked: – Did he say that?

– He did and I confess that it made me see him differently. He is very affectionate, María Inés.

– After dinner, when they left, I was thinking that maybe it's not so bad to marry him.

– Are you thinking about that?

– I am. As I was so disappointed with José Antônio, I think this path will not be so bad –. María Inés said, and this time, sincerely:

– Don't trust, Eulalia. Men lie.

They talked a while longer. María Inés looked at her watch and began to worry, because the time when she planned to meet Luiz Cláudio was approaching and Eulália was not leaving.

With remorse, she said: – Excuse me, Eulalia. My teacher will arrive for painting class.

Eulália, who was sitting on the bed and was no longer crying, got up and said: – Don't worry, María Inés.

– I also need to go.

Thanks for listening. Only you have so much patience with me. When I get married, I want you to be my maid of honor.

– I will Eulalia! Of course I will!

They said goodbye and María Inés accompanied Eulália to the carriage, where a black woman was waiting for her. After the carriage disappeared, María Inés, accompanied by Zefa, returned to her room.

Just Beginning

As soon as she entered the room, she began to shout: – Are you getting married? Is she getting married? Poor thing, he's going to marry me, Zefa! He loves me and I have already shown him how much I love him! He's going to marry me! Only me! I'll be a baroness!

Julia, who followed everything, looked at Alzira and asked: – Is he going to marry her?

– Do you want to know the end of the movie, Julia? We will follow it and soon you will know –. Alzira replied, laughing.

Julia also laughed and turned her attention to María Inés, who, looking at Zefa, said: – I need to change my dress, Zefa!

– I want to look pretty to meet him!

– Okay, my lady...

After preparing meticulously, María Inés happily left her home and went to the lake.

As soon as she got closer, she noticed that Luiz Cláudio wasn't there yet.

– It's strange that he hasn't arrived yet. What was it that made him late, Zefa?

– I don't know, my lady. He should have been there...

María Inés continued walking and, when she reached the shore, Zefa spread a rug that was used for that. Maria Inés sat down and looked in the direction he was supposed to come.

Time passed but he didn't arrive. Worried, she said: – Something must have happened, really, for him not to come, Zefa. Did he have an accident?

– I don't know, my lady. Let's go home, he's not coming anymore...

Just Beginning

Although she was worried, María Inés decided to follow what Zefa said and returned home. She walked up the stairs with her head lowered and slowly, which she rarely did.

In her room, she lay down and looked up, trying to understand what had happened. After a while, she got up: – When he comes tomorrow, he will tell me what happened!

I'll be there every day, until he comes. Or rather Zefa, since Ignacio is your husband, you can talk to him and ask him to try to find out if Luiz Cláudio had an accident. You have to tell him not to tell anyone.

– Go black! Go right now!

– Ignacio is not here at home at the moment. Every day, he goes to pick up your father, my lady...

– It's true. I'd forgotten about that, but ask him, tomorrow morning, find a way to go out and investigate!

– Okay, my lady. Grandpa will talk to him.

María Inés spent the rest of the day trying to paint, but was unsuccessful.

She thought about the moments she spent with Luiz Cláudio and why he didn't come to meet her. That night, she had trouble sleeping. She was anxious and constantly looking at her watch.

The day must clear. I have to know if Luiz Cláudio is okay. What happened?

In the morning, when Zefa entered the room to wake up María Inés, as she did every day, she was surprised to see that she was already awake: – Are you already awake, my lady?

– I couldn't sleep! Has Ignacio gone to find out if Luiz Cláudio is okay?

– He couldn't, my lady.

Just Beginning

– He didn't?, why?

– Your father didn't leave today and told Ignacio to take care of his garden. He said it was so withered. Ignacio will be late.

– Taking care of the flowers?

– My lady, you know how much your father likes flowers and that he lets only Ignacio take care of his flowers. Don't you?

María Inés was furious: – It can't be! Cannot be! I'll be crazy if I don't know what happened to him and why he didn't come to meet me!

– Didn't my lady say that she was going to wait for him at the lake today?

– I did and I will! I know he will come!

– Okay my lady. Tomorrow, Ignacio will do what you asked for.

– That's what I'll do! At the appointed time, we will go to the lake, Zefa! Zefa smiled when she saw happiness return to her face.

In the afternoon, through the window, María Inés saw when Ignacio got into the carriage.

– Goodness! I can't take this lack of news anymore!

– I'm sure he had an accident! Ignacio will confirm that to me!

– He went to see, my lady.

Maria Ines, nervous, left the room and walked from side to side in the garden. She was in and out of the house several times. Almost two hours later, she saw the carriage approach. As soon as it stopped and when Ignacio got out, she, trembling, asked: – So, Ignacio, did you manage to find out what happened to him?

– Nothing ever happened to him, no, my lady.

Just Beginning

– How come? Why didn't he come to meet me?

– I don't know, my lady. I was talking to people to know about him, when Joca, my friend said he was in the cafeteria.

I went there and saw him. My lady Eulália was drinking tea.

– What are you talking about, Ignacio? Was he with Eulalia?

– Yes, my lady. Then they left and went to sit there in the square. He, Sinhazinha Eulália and Zefinha. – María Inés was possessed!

– Eulalia lied to me! She said she didn't like him, but she was lying! Liar! Liar!

– After she was abandoned, she decided to stay with him! I know he's doing this just to keep up appearances, but she's trying to get involved! Liar!

– I'll talk to my father and ask him for permission to go to her house! She will have to explain herself!

– Don't do that, my lady. Calm down and think clearly.

– How to stay calm, Zefa? Didn't you hear what Ignacio said?

– That liar is trying to take Luiz Cláudio from me! I won't allow it!

– Is she the one taking him or is he the one staying with her?

– It's not him, Zefa! She is the one who wants to be with him, but I won't allow it! I won't!

Immediately, she entered the house and went to the office where she knew her father was. Although she was very nervous, she took a deep breath and said: – Dad, could Ignacio take me to Eulalia's house?

– The father who was reading, looked up.

– Why do you want to go there, my daughter?

Just Beginning

– I am very sad and I would like to spend a few hours with her.

– Why don't you talk to your sister?

– María Augusta is also sad.

That's right. Your sister stays at the piano all the time. Okay, go ahead, but don't take too long. She, kissing her father, said: – I won't be long!

She ran out and, getting into the carriage, said: – Zefa, let's go to Eulalia's house! That liar will have to tell me what's going on!

Reluctantly, Zefa got into the carriage and Ignacio made the horses walk.

When they reached Eulália's house, María Inés got out of the carriage and went quickly to the door. A slave opened: – Is Eulalia at home?

– No, my lady. She left with Luiz Claudio.

– Did she go out with him?

– She did. He took her and her mother to the cafeteria for tea.

– Did she go with her mother?

– Yes, my lady. They will get married.

María Inés wanted to kill the slave, but stopped: – Okay, when she comes back, tell her that I was here and that I need to talk to her.

– All right, my lady. I will.

Maria Inés, trying to appear calm, returned to the carriage.

As soon as she got in, she said, he just keeps up appearances, I know he loves me, Zefa!

Just Beginning

Zefa looked at her, but was silent. The one who could not remain silent was Julia: – María Inés doesn't understand what is happening? Doesn't she see that he no longer wants to be with her?

– She is doing what most people do, when they are abandoned, Julia. María Inés understands but refuses to accept the fact.

– You know? I feel sorry for her.

– She is really pitiful, but she chose her own path.

– Here comes the lady with this story of choice.

Alzira smiled.

– I do it because it's important. Now is the time for you to return.

– I know, the energies, right?

– That's right. You know, you don't have to worry because you will know the whole story.

Julia, knowing there was no point in arguing, smiled and immediately opened her eyes and looked at her watch. Wow it's late! I slept a lot!

Without remembering the dream, she got up and, after drinking coffee, went back to her room, lay down, and read the book again.

Just Beginning

27.– The rudeness

It has been over a month. Julia kept looking for work.

Sueli's wedding was coming up and she knew that after it, she would have to move. Although she kept dreaming, she didn't remember and forgot the dreams she had had.

After spending a good part of the day helping Sueli with the wedding preparations, that night, tired, she went to bed. Shortly after, she returned to the house of María Inés and next to Alzira and Ciro.

As soon as she opened her eyes, she said: – I haven't been back here in a long time...

– You've come every night, Julia.

– I don't remember, not even being here now.

– Because what happened didn't matter much.

– What happened?

– María Inés couldn't find a way to talk to Eulália. Her father didn't give her permission to leave.

– Every day she will wait for Luiz Cláudio at the lake.

– He didn't come?

– No. Besides, it doesn't matter what happened. What matters is what will happen now. Let's go to María Inés's room.

Just Beginning

When they arrived, Zefa helped María Inés, who said worriedly: – calm down, my lady.

– This nausea will pass soon.

– I'm feeling bad, Zefa! I think I'm going to die!

– No little one. It will be fine soon. My lady is not going to die for nausea, but I think she can die for something else.

– What are you talking about, Zefa?

– I think my lady is expecting a child!

– You're crazy, black! How can I be expecting a child? Where did you get that idea from?

– I already had four children, my lady. I know how it is...

– How did this happen?

– The black woman saw when my lady slept with Luiz Claudio.

– Were you spying on me, black woman?

– I was, my lady, but I was afraid it would happen and it did. Now you see the consequences...

– It can't be Zefa! It was only once!

– You only need once, my lady. The black woman saw that my lady's body was not fine at all. She saw that the blood was not there. María Inés, crying desperately, asked: – You're right, but I thought it was just a delay.

– What am I going to do, Zefa?

Julia looked at Alzira: – Is it true? Is she really expecting a child?

– Keep looking, Julia.

María Inés stopped crying: – This is very good, Zefa!

– Good? why?

Just Beginning

– Now Luiz Cláudio will have to marry me! I will tell my father and he will make him do it!

– Watch out, my lady. He can say that you are lying. No one has seen the two of you together, only me, but the word of a black is worthless.

– I need to find Luiz Cláudio! He has to know what is happening!

– You really need to do it, my lady...

– That's what I'll do. I need to find a way to get out of the house. I'll think something –. At that very moment, they heard the sound of a carriage approaching the house.

They looked out the window and saw Eulalia's carriage stop in front of the front door. The coachman got out.

The door opened and a slave appeared. The coachman handed over an envelope and left.

At that moment when she saw the carriage approaching through the window, María Inés came down the stairs. At the top of the stairs, she asked: – What envelope is that?

– I don't know, my lady. The coachman left without saying anything...

María Inés finished coming down and, nervous, took the envelope that was addressed to her father: – I'll take it to my father. With the envelope in hand, she went to the office and handed it to her father.

The father took the envelope, looked at it, and put it aside.

– Aren't you going to open it, dad?

– No, María Inés. For this size, it must be an invitation to a party, since we are mourning, we will not be able to attend.

– I know, dad, but I'm curious what it's about.

Just Beginning

The father, handing her the envelope, said: – All right. I'm busy and I'm not interested in parties. Open it and see –. María Inés took the envelope and, always followed by Zefa, quickly left the office and ran to her room. She walked into the room, ran to the bed, sat down, and opened the envelope.

She read it, turned white as wax, and began to shake and cry.

– What does it say? My lady? What is it for?

– They are getting married, Zefa!

– They? Who, my lady?

– Eulália and Luiz Cláudio!

– My lady knew this was going to happen...

– No, Zefa! He said he was just keeping up appearances!

– Oh, but it's not what is happening.

– No, Zefa, this is a wedding invitation!

If he only kept up appearances, he wouldn't have gotten to that point! They are getting married, really!

– I just want to know what Eulalia did to make him do it!

– Is it because she did something or maybe because she is pregnant?

– Of course she did something! He said that he loved me and would only marry me! I need to find out what he did!

– My lady, you have something else to worry about. If he marries my lady Eulália, what will my lady do when this child that is there in your womb is born?

– I need to talk to him, Zefa, and tell him that we are going to have a child! He will be happy and will want to marry me!

– All right, my lady. Do it...

María Inés went to the office where her father was.

Just Beginning

She came in and, with a smile to disguise what she was feeling, said: – Dad, Eulalia is getting married and she wants me to be her godmother.

– I need to go to her house to explain to her that, because I'm mourning, I won't be able to go to the wedding.

– She knows it.

– I know, but I need to explain it to her in person. Can I go with Zefa and Ignacio there? I promise I'll be back soon.

The father smiled: – All right, my daughter, you can go. I'm sorry you can't attend her wedding. I know how happy you are with this marriage.

She was always your friend.

Without hiding her happiness, María Inés kissed her father and went to meet Ignacio, who was taking care of the garden.

– Ignacio! Prepare the carriage. Let's go.

Ignacio looked at Zefa, who nodded.

– All right, my lady. Grandpa is getting ready.

– It's okay. I'm going to my room to change this dress and I'll be back in ten minutes. She ran and changed her clothes rapidly. She returned and got into the carriage.

When they got to the center of the city, she asked Ignacio to go around the square.

As she was passing in front of a tavern, she saw Luiz Cláudio talking and drinking with many other people.

She made Ignacio stop the car: – Ignacio, go down and go to the tavern. With a signal and taking care that the other boys do not see, call Mr. Luiz Cláudio. As soon as he comes to see you, tell him that I'm here and that I need to talk to him. Tell him to hide it, I don't want others to see me.

– If the sir doesn't want to come, my lady?

Just Beginning

– Why wouldn't he? Of course he will come, but if he doesn't, tell him it's urgent.

Ignacio got out of the carriage and went to the door of the tavern. María Inés, from afar, followed all his steps. Luiz Cláudio knew him, he knew he belonged to her family and, when he saw the black man standing there, he smiled.

Ignacio, somewhat embarrassed, but having to obey María Inés's order, made a sign with his hand that said they needed to speak.

Luiz Cláudio approached. Ignacio gave him the message from María Inés. Luiz Cláudio looked where the carriage was, put his hand on the brim of his hat and bowed. María Inés smiled and saw that Luiz had said something to Ignacio and, to her surprise, she saw Luiz Cláudio return to the tavern and Ignacio walking back.

He approached: – My lady, he told me to tell you to wait for him, he will approach you.

She sighed in relief. She waited for almost half an hour, when she saw him saying goodbye to his friends and walking towards her. As soon as he approached, he said: – How are you, miss? I am happy to see you here.

She was surprised to see that he called her miss, but trying not to show her nervousness, she said:

– I'm also happy to see you, sir. We need to talk.

– Here in the square? Wouldn't you rather go somewhere else where people can't see us?

– No. Let's talk here. Our conversation will be quick.

After saying this, María Inés turned to Zefa and Ignacio, who were accompanying the conversation: – Get away.

– I need to speak with Mr. Luiz Cláudio.

Just Beginning

The blacks walked away. She, turning to him, her voice trembling, spoke immediately: – I am expecting a child.

– What?

– What you heard. I am expecting a child.

He, trying to hide his surprise, smiled: – Congratulations! I just don't understand why you are telling me that...

– How can't you understand! You are the father of that child and you need to take responsibility before my father. You need to marry me... – He began to laugh nervously: – Me, the father? You must be mistaking me for someone else.

I can't marry you. I'm going to marry Eulalia. Our parents have already decided everything and we agree. – She despaired: – You can't say that! You know that you were the only man I had and that this child is yours!

– How can I know that? I never spoke to you about that topic or anything like that.

– We have never been together and I will marry Eulalia and then we will go to Paris, where I will study.

– Aren't you going to take responsibility for your son?

– What son? This child can be anyone's but mine.

Excuse me, miss, but I must go to my girlfriend.

– I'll tell Eulalia what you did.

He, who was walking away, turned and, laughing, said: – You can tell her! I will say that it's a lie, that you harassed me and when you saw that I didn't accept you for loving my girlfriend, you got angry and invented this son! Who do you think she and everyone will believe?

In the end, if you do that, you will be defamed throughout the city and in front of our friends.

You will be forced to leave here or go to a convent.

Just Beginning

– What did she do that you want so much to marry her?

He, with an ironic smile, replied: – She never tried to convince me or gave in. She is a decent lady –. María Inés began to cry: – What am I going to do?

– I don't know, miss and I don't care. I'm sorry that some fun times ended like this. Excuse me. Now I need to go. If you want, after my wedding, we can meet at the lake, without anyone seeing us, of course... Touching the brim of his hat again and bowing again, Luiz Cláudio walked away.

María Inés, trembling and white as wax, watched him go.

Zefa, although she was not listening to the conversation, realized that it had not been pleasant for María Inés, she approached and, motionless and in silence, stood next to the carriage.

María Inés, crying, looked at her and asked: – What am I going to do, Zefa?

Zefa, returning to the carriage, replied: – I don't know, my lady. I only know that we have to go back home.

– Ignacio, let's go home!

As soon as Zefa and Ignacio got into the carriage, he made the horse start walking. María Inés couldn't stop crying.

Julia, disgusted, said: – He is a scoundrel! How did he do that? He knows what happened! – She looked at Alzira and stopped talking and asked: – Why are you crying?

– Because, for several incarnations, Luiz Cláudio has been going through this same situation and has failed.

– Right now, for us, his friends and companions on the journey, all we can do is to cry and lament.

– Again, his time to redeem himself has not yet come, and therefore his evolution is delayed.

Just Beginning

– Do you cry for him, even after all this evil he just did?

– Yes Julia. Just as we cry for other friends who are on the road, when they miss the opportunity for redemption.

– As for María Inés, who is the victim for me, what will you do to help her? What will she do?

– It's not over yet. She will have a chance at redemption and we will stand by her side so she can be a winner, but we can never interfere with her decisions. This is only up to her.

– From what I see, your help is not worth much! Why didn't you stop Luiz Cláudio from doing what he did?

– Choices and free will, Julia, and, like I said, there is nothing you can do against them.

She had the opportunity to choose. She didn't make the right decision. Now, she will have to bear the consequences.

She will still have her chance. We can only wait.

– They said they will be by her side until she makes the right decision and redeems herself.

– We will be with her and everyone who is part of our group.

– Group?

– Yes. A group of spirits was formed, all with equal opportunities. You must have heard about the parable Jesus told about talents, right?

– Yes, many times. Don't forget that I was raised in a Christian orphanage.

– When God created us, he didn't want us to be like puppets who are doing nothing.

He gave us all the feelings of good and bad so that we could choose the path we wanted to follow.

Just Beginning

As in the parable of the talents, some made good feelings multiply, others took a little longer, and many almost stopped. During the walk, some decided to continue, others preferred to stay with those who were late, trying to help them. Although they knew there was little they could do, as you said, in times of difficult decisions, they spoke words of encouragement and sent lights to calm them down and stop them to make them think. That is what's happening now. Although he hasn't seen it, Luiz Cláudio has figures at his side who, with his behavior, attracted them to him. These figures are part of our group and they have chosen to be left behind, far behind. Whenever we can, we try to talk to them and make them reflect. We tell them that they are wasting a lot of time, but it's almost never possible to make them reflect, as they are hiding in a very dense energy that we cannot pass through.

– So, they cannot see or hear us. They prefer to be with those who think like them.

– Those who don't value the good feelings of others cannot see the friendly spirits who, like us, are with María Inés, Luiz Cláudio and Eulália. All, without exception, have spiritual friends by their side who, although they delay their evolution, refuse to abandon those who are late.

– Why do they do it, why don't they move on?

– Because they know that one day, no matter how long it takes, everyone will find the true path and redemption.

– And thus, everyone can go together towards the Divine Light.

– How to know who is part of the same group?

– All those who meet in the physical or spiritual realm, no matter how fast this meeting is, are part of our group.

– In one way or another, if we find them, it is because we can help or be helped. God is perfect, Julia.

Just Beginning

– It is very complicated for me.

Alzira looked at Ciro who, laughing, continued: – When you return to the realm, you will quickly understand.

– Will I go back?

– Of course you will! Everybody comes back!

– I'm scared. I don't know if I'm ready.

– You won't go back until it's time and you're ready. Unless...

– Unless?

– Unless you cut that day short by suicide.

– I'll never do something crazy like that again!

– We hope this does not happen, because if it happens, you will suffer a lot and even lose an incarnation –. Julia said laughing: – Also because, if that happens, will they be late because of me?

– For that reason too. We have a lot to do.

– Now, I want to know what will happen to María Inés. They are entering through the door of the house. So far, she hasn't stopped crying.

Júlia looked when María Inés was still crying and showed a lot of anger, then she said: – He's a scoundrel!

– I'll find a way to get revenge!

– He won't marry Eulalia! I won't allow it!

– Do nothing, my lady. Let God take care of him.

– I'll do something Zefa! I can't wait for God, he takes too long!

– Don't talk like that, my lady. It is sin...

– Sin is what he did to me! I will get revenge!

Just Beginning

Unable to stop crying, she got out of the carriage and ran toward the house. She ran up the stairs. Maria Augusta, who was in the garden, saw when she arrived. From her sister's condition, she realized that something very serious had happened.

In addition, she hurried to go to María Inés's room.

As soon as she entered, she saw that her sister, lying on the bed, was crying profusely: – What happened, María Inés?

– Why are you crying like that?

– What are you doing here, María Augusta? This is my room!

– I saw you when you arrived and I realized that something was happening. What happened?

– Tell your sister, my lady!

– Why?

– She could help you my lady...

– Help how? – Maria Augusta asked, desperate.

– No one can help me, Maria Augusta. I'm lost...

– What happened, María Inés?

– Tell her, my lady. She is your sister...

– Okay, I'll tell you. Maybe you have a solution, Maria Augusta.

María Augusta breathed a sigh of relief, sat on the bed and looked at María Inés, who told everything and ended by saying:

– As you can see, he was a scoundrel who lied and fooled me. If I didn't have that child, there would be no problem, but how can I hide it?

Everyone will know about my shame and the worst thing is that I cannot say it was him, because he said he will deny me and

Just Beginning

he will say that I got this son to force him to marry me. I don't know what to do...

María Augusta took her sister's hand and said: – I am your sister. I know that sometimes I fight about the things you do, but I love you and I will be by your side.

María Inés, even crying, managed to smile: – What are we going to do?

Maria Augusta got up, walked around the room and then said: – I think we should tell our father. He is a good man and he likes you very much. I know he will find a solution.

– No! We can't talk to him! He will never forgive me.

– We can and must María Inés. He is our father, and it is the only solution. He can send us to a rural town, where nobody knows us. We stay there until the child is born and we will find someone to raise the child.

– When the child grows up, we will make something up and bring the child here.

– Even if dad agrees with all this, which I think is unlikely, what will happen to Luiz Claudio?

– You must forget about him, María Inés. Now, all you have to do is think about yourself and this unborn child!

– Let him marry Eulalia and be happy forever?

Never! As for that child, I don't want him to be born! I don't want him to continue inside of me!

– There has to be a way for that to happen!

– My lady from heaven! Don't talk like that! A child is a blessing from God! The child is not to blame for anything at all...

– This can be a blessing to anyone who wants to have a child! For me it is an obstacle!

Just Beginning

I am not saying that the child is to blame. That scoundrel is the one to blame! I heard that there are some types of tea that can solve my problem! Do you know any, Zefa?

– No, It's just a tale, my lady. If I knew that, I wouldn't have had more children. I wouldn't have had more...

– She's right, María Inés. You don't have to do that. We can manage and this child can be born and loved by both of us. You are not alone, my sister. I am and will always be by your side. We will talk to our father.

– No, Maria Augusta! Our father is sending me to a convent!

I cannot accept this idea! We don't need to talk to him today. With these clothes we wear, it will take a while for my tummy to start showing. I will be able to hide it for a long time. Until that day comes, I will have time to think of a way to get rid of this child and take revenge on Luiz Cláudio.

– Well, let's wait a little longer. Now, the important thing is to stay calm. Everything will be fine, my sister... Maria Augusta left the room. María Inés went back to bed and thought.

Julia, who until then remained silent, following the conversation, said: – Good. I was terrified that she was going to kill the baby...

– You're right to think like that, Julia. If everyone knew how difficult it is for a spirit to be reborn, no one would think of doing it.

Júlia looked at María Inés, who, at that moment, sat up in bed and said: – Zefa, you can take care of your life. I want to be alone.

– I won't leave here, no, my lady.

– Go ahead, Zefa. I'm fine. I just want to think about what I'm going to do.

Just Beginning

Don't worry about what I decide, I'll tell you and María Augusta.

– Okay, my lady, I'll leave, but if you need me, call me.

Zefa left. María Inés got up, went to the dresser, opened a drawer and took out a sheet of paper and a pencil. She sat in front of the dressing table, removed some objects that were on it, put the paper on and thought: if you think that you are going to get married and that you will be happy, you are wrong.

Eulália and everyone will know what he did to me! Since I cannot face this shame nor do I want to go to the convent,

I can't get out of this, and I can't get revenge on Luiz Cláudio, my only way is to die, but first, I'll write everything down. Everyone will know what a scoundrel looks like!

Julia, desperate, screamed: – She can't do that!

– She shouldn't, but she has the right to choose, Julia.

– Will she kill herself and kill the child too?

– Keep looking, Julia. Look at the company she is attracting.

– Where do these black shapes come from?

– They were always here, Julia. Due to their energies that are different from ours and yours, you have not seen them.

– You can only see them now, because Ciro and I made our energies and yours get closer to them. We did it because it's important for you to get to know them to see how they act and how you can prevent them from getting close. Júlia, scared, looked at four figures revolving around María Inés who thought: I can't let this go unpunished. I will write a letter informing them of everything that happened, then I will find a way to kill myself. He will not bear the shame and guilt.

He will never forget me again in his life!

Just Beginning

The figures came even closer. One of them said: – You don't have to! You will regret it and suffer a lot!

– Are you listening to what it's saying?

– Not with our ears, Julia, but with the spirit, yes.

María Inés, without imagining that she was being influenced by evil, began to write.

She used the page on both sides and told the story from the beginning, without saying it, it is clear what she had done to be able to get closer to him. When she finished writing, she read and reread several times to see if she had forgotten any details.

The figures that were spinning happily all the time were by her side, making sure she didn't forget a word.

After seeing that everything was there, she put the paper in the bottom of a drawer, that she knew that Zefa hardly ever moved. She leaned back and thought: Now, I need to find a way to kill myself without feeling too much pain.

To Julia's horror, the figures began to give her many ideas. As they spoke, María Inés, in her mind, saw the scene, until she decided: – I need to go to the lake. If I die there, the impact will be greater.

She got up and got out. On the stairs, she found Zefa who was going to her room: – Zefa, let's go to the lake.

– Why do you want to go there? Are you going to meet him again?

– No, Zefa, I just want to think about how my life is going. Don't worry, I won't do anything crazy.

Zefa agreed and accompanied her. As soon as she approached the lake, she began to look around.

She saw that there were several trees: that's what I'm going to do. Without Zefa noticing, I will leave the house, bring a rope,

Just Beginning

climb up and, after placing the rope on the tree and around my neck, simply throw myself. I think it will be fast and Luiz Cláudio will be lost for the rest of his life! Wait, it won't work. I won't have the strength to tie a knot strong enough to hold me high. I won't be able to do it that way. I need to think of another way.

– Zefa! Let's go back!

– Didn't the lady say she wanted to think alone?

– I already thought enough! Let's go!

When they returned, one of the figures gave her an idea: Zefa! When I was in the room, I think I saw a rat running.

– Ask Ignacio to take a look and kill it. You know I'm terrified of rats!

– A rat, my lady?

– I think it was a rat. I'm not sure, it was quick. It seemed to be very large. Even so, Ignacio can prove it.

– Okay, I'll talk to him.

– Ask him to come over right now. I don't want to risk sleeping and a rat crawling on my bed. They entered the house. María Augusta, seeing her sister, said: – It seems you are fine, María Inés.

– Yes, I am. Thanks for your support. I decided that we will do what you suggested. Just give me some time to take courage.

– I'm glad you decided so.

– I also calmed down. I'll go to my room now–. Maria Augusta smiled.

When they went upstairs, María Inés, looking at Zefa, said: – Zefa! Talk to Ignacio and tell him that he needs to take care of the mouse as soon as possible! Preferably right now.

– Okay, I will, my lady.

Just Beginning

María Inés finished climbing the stairs and went to her room. Zefa turned and went to find Ignacio. Shortly after, Zefa returned accompanied by Ignacio. She knocked on the door and entered.

She entered the room and said: – Here we are, my lady. I never saw a rat in the house.

– I've never seen it either, but I think I saw something running today. It costs nothing to take a look, put in some poison. I don't know! Do anything, Ignacio!

– Okay, my lady.

Ignacio looked around. He looked around and said: – I don't see any rat here, my lady. I don't think there is a rat here.

María Inés was nervous: – I saw something that seemed to be a mouse, Ignacio.

– I'm nervous, scared and panicked. Do you have rat poison?

– Yes, we have some there, my lady. It is there in a shed.

– To make sure that while I sleep, the rats won't attack me, let's do the following: put poison scattered all over the room and you, Zefa, tell Tonha that tomorrow when she comes to do the cleaning not to remove the poison and if a dead rat does not appear in a week, we clean everything.

They both nodded and left. María Inés went to the window and looked at the horizon. The figures were still by her side, talking about the benefit of suicide.

Soon, the slaves returned. Ignacio put poison in the plinth and increased the amount in the corners. When he finished, he said: – Ready, my lady, if there is something here, it will die.

– Goodness. I was not going to be able to sleep.

They left the room. Ignacio returned to the garden.

Just Beginning

María Inés returned to the living room, sat down in front of a canvas and continued painting a landscape that she had begun. María Augusta, at the piano, played a melody.

Zefa, from a distance, looked at the sisters.

After dinner, María Inés went to her room. Zefa arrived later, bringing a cup of tea, as she did every night. She put tea on the nightstand and lit some candles.

As soon as María Inés lay down, she said: – Now that my lady is in bed, I'm going to blow out the candles.

Don't you want to have tea?

– No, Zefa! Do not do that. I'm still afraid of that rat. Leave the candles burning. Zefa laughed: – There is no rat, my lady...

– I saw something, Zefa. I won't be able to sleep in the dark...

– All right, I won't turn it off. Can I go to sleep, my lady?

– You can, Zefa.

Zefa left. María Inés waited a bit and got up. By candlelight she took two pieces of paper.

She put one piece in one hand and the other in the other. With the help of one hand, she picked up the poison that was spread on the ground and placed it in the other.

When she saw that she had a good amount, she went back to bed and put the poison in the teacup.

She went to the dresser, opened the drawer where she had hidden the letter, took it and placed it on the bedside table, poured the poison into the cup. Cup in hand, she thought: he will pay for everything he did! Besides not getting married, being judged by everyone, you will still die of remorse!

More black figures entered the room and approached María Inés. They rejoiced in happiness. When she saw that, startled, Julia screamed: – You are not going to do anything to stop her from doing this?

Alzira, who was crying, couldn't answer.

Ciro, although very moved, said: – We can't do anything, Julia, she made her choice and this has already happened.

– She used her free will and, even, at that moment, we couldn't get close.

– As you can see, she is totally enveloped by those figures that she attracted to herself.

Forgetting her presence and the figures, María Inés drank all the tea in the cup at once. A few minutes later, she felt her heart race and a pain in her stomach like it was on fire. She tried to get up, but failed. After a time of agony, she took her last breath.

Julia, horrified, saw the figures throw themselves at her and laugh, drawing her spirit from her body. María Inés opened her eyes and was surprised to see those figures.

She wanted to ask what was happening, but she couldn't. They, still laughing, took her by her hands and left.

– Where are they taking her?

Ciro and Alzira, one on each side, took her hands and, seconds later, they were in a place that for Julia was scary, dark, muddy, with voices that screamed and cried over and over.

Julia looked around and, terrified, asked: – What is this place?

– The place where all suicidal spirits come from.

– It is awful! Why did they bring her here?

– Life in the physical body is the only place where the spirit can amend its errors and achieve evolution.

– Many want it, but not all get it as fast as they want. Therefore, it is not fair that, in possession of it, the spirit put aside

Just Beginning

all that it has committed and what it has chosen and, before the time, put an end to its life. In this place, you will learn to value life. God is Father and, like every father, when necessary, punishes his children.

María Inés, despite our efforts, has repeatedly committed the same desperate act. She was here many times and was rescued. Now, unfortunately, she's back again.

– She had her reasons. She was still a child, she has been deceived and deluded.

– Nothing is a reason for suicide, Julia, because, no matter how bad the moment seems, there is always a way out and a new way to go. The important thing is to have faith. God is by our side and never leaves us.

The incarnated spirit doesn't know what will happen in the next moment. Therefore, it is only necessary to have faith, to surrender completely into the hands of God, your Creator.

– It takes a long time...

– It doesn't matter how long it takes Julia. God has an eternity to wait.

– María Inés will stay here, for how long?

– A long time, Julia. As much as necessary. Until she understands what she has done, and asks for forgiveness.

On that day, for our glory, we as her friends will be there to take her home.

– Is that day coming?

– Yes. That day always comes for everyone.

– As it happened a long time ago, can I see how she is now?

– You can, but it's time to wake up. You have been away from your body for a long time.

Just Beginning

Julia looked at Alzira and, despite the desperation to be there, said: – Okay, I won't complain.

I know it's no use.

At that moment she saw María Inés running desperately, followed by the figures who brought her. Scared, Julia screamed: – Don't let them catch you!

The scream was so loud that Sueli, from her room, heard her cry, ran to see what was happening. When she saw that her friend was sleeping, she began to shake her: – Julia! Awake!

The third time she called, Julia opened her eyes and began to cry.

– What nightmare was that, Julia? What were you dreaming of?

– I don't know Sueli. I was in a horrible place and I was very scared. The monsters were chasing me...

– Good thing it was just a dream. You are here and very well protected. I was scared when I heard your scream.

– Now, I think that instead of having coffee, I need some fennel tea to calm me down. Get up, I'll make tea.

– Julia took a deep breath: – You can have tea, Sueli. I'm hungry. I'm going to have coffee with milk and eat bread with ham.

Julia got up and went to the kitchen.

When Julia popped a piece of bread in her mouth, she became dizzy and nearly fainted. Sueli, scared, asked: – What is wrong? You're yellow as wax, Julia! Without answering, Julia ran to the bathroom.

A few minutes later, she came back and, embarrassed, said, I must have eaten something bad.

– These fainting spells and nausea... aren't you pregnant?

Just Beginning

– What? Are you crazy, I can't and I don't want to be pregnant!

Sueli began to laugh: – You may not want to, but you can be pregnant, you can...

– Stop it, Sueli!

– I can stop, but if I were you, I'd take a test to be sure. I heard that when a child wants to be born, it doesn't wait to come.

– Don't even joke about it! It would just what I needed! My life is just a mess!

They finished drinking coffee. Sueli returned to the room and Julia left.

On the street, she thought: am I pregnant? It cannot be. However, as Sueli said, it is better to take a test to be sure. I'm not, but if I am, I have time to do something. I really want a son, but now is not the time.

S he then went to a laboratory.

Just Beginning

28.– Free will

After taking the test, Julia learned that the result would be back the next day. She went out to a nearby company to see if there was a vacancy. She gave them her resume and kept walking. After a long walk, she returned home. She was tired. She lay down and, although she wanted to, she could not forget Anselmo.

I still can't accept what he did to me. How could he have been so cruel to leave me without saying a word? If I am really pregnant, what am I going to do, without a job, without a place to live? Sueli says so much that everything is fine, that God is our Father.

What kind of father is this one who allowed my life to be as it was? What kind of God is this keeping me from getting a job?

I'm tired of all this. I don't know why I continue living.

No more suffering. If Dona Neide were alive, I could go back to the orphanage, but even she left me. I'm alone with no one...

Alzira and Ciro, who were there, saw that some black figures began to approach and force those thoughts even more. They tried to drive them away, but failed. The energy that came out from Julia's mind was thick and attracted them.

She spent that day thinking about Anselmo. For a moment she thought about the good times, which made the figures move away.

Just Beginning

During the afternoon, she went with Sueli to do some shopping. That distracted her. In the evening after dinner, under the influence of Alzira, she picked up the book and continued reading.

As she read, the figures remained there, but distant. She finished reading the book and went to bed.

This story is beautiful. It's a pity it's not true. Life is not like romance. She fell asleep and met with Alzira and Ciro, who took her to a beautiful and quiet place.

The next morning, she woke up early and fine. She got up and, still thinking of Anselmo, went to the laboratory and took the result.

She looked at the result and put the paper in her bag. She went out into the street and began to walk aimlessly. She walked a lot until she got tired and decided to sit on a bench in the square.

Alzira and Ciro, who followed her, were worried. Alzira said, she can't go on like this, Ciro.

She needs to cry, scream, act. By taking Julia to visit beautiful and peaceful places, we made her think good thoughts and change her energy.

– By doing this, we managed to keep the figures away, but if it continues like this, it will attract them again.

– Look, they're already getting closer!

– You know that we cannot interfere with her free will, Alzira.

– She needs to decide what to do from now on.

– It's right. We can't interfere, but right now, we can find a way to help her.

– How to help her, Alzira?

Just Beginning

Alzira smiled. She looked ahead and saw a lady approaching.

She was holding a puppy on a hand leash. Ciro also saw the lady. He asked: – What will you do Alzira? – She didn't answer. She stood next to the lady and made her look at the bench where Julia was sitting. In a low voice, she said, Are you tired, Natália? Why don't you sit on that bench?

The lady, without understanding what was happening, looked ahead and saw the bench. She walked quickly and sat down next to Julia.

She tugged on the puppy's collar for it to come over and sit down as well. Julia, thinking about what had happened, didn't realize that she had sat down.

Alzira stood behind the bench and, smiling, looked at Ciro, who, also smiling, came over and stood next to her and behind Julia and Natália. Alzira, still smiling, turned to the lady and said: – Look how nervous she is, Natália. Talk to her.

Natalia, who seemed to be listening to what Alzira was saying, turned to Julia and asked: – Are you okay, girl? – Julia, who seemed not to hear, didn't answer.

Inspired by Alzira, Natália insisted: – You are very pale. Do you want me to call someone or do you want to go somewhere? – When listening to Natália, Júlia turned: – I'm fine, just a little nervous.

– Nervous, why? What happened to make you like this?

– Nothing! Nothing happened.

– Nothing? Something very serious must have happened. I can smell a man –. Julia was surprised: – How? What did you say?

– For a beautiful girl like you to be the way you are, I can bet that it's because of a man.

Just Beginning

Am I right?

Julia didn't reply. She began to cry desperately. The hiccups came from deep inside. Natália let her cry. Alzira looked at Ciro and said smiling : – Now she will be okay, Ciro. Natália put her arm around Júlia's shoulder and brought her head close to her.

Natália, in silence, stroked her hair. Desperate, Julia snuggled close to her and continued crying.

Alzira and Ciro stayed there the whole time. After crying a lot, Julia, who seemed to remember where she was, turned away from Natália and, with an embarrassed smile, said: – I'm sorry, ma'am...

– You don't need to apologize. You were in pain and needed to cry and if you hadn't cried, your heart might have exploded.

– You don't know me, and you still tried to help me...

– Indeed girl. Wait. My name is Natalia. What's yours?

– Julia

– Julia? That's my daughter's name! Like you, she is also very beautiful.

Julia smiled. Natália continued: – As I was saying, Julia. I am a calm person, I don't even like to talk a lot.

– The only one I speak to is Duke, my puppy. Isn't it beautiful?

– Yes, it's very beautiful.

– Yes, I'm not a big talker. I like to stay at my house. I just go for a walk with Duque.

– I have two daughters who are already married taking care of their lives, so I don't understand what happened today.

– I was walking with Duque, as I do every day, and suddenly I wanted to sit down. I looked and saw this bench.

Just Beginning

– I sat down and saw that you were not well.

– I wasn't and I'm not yet...

– Well, like I said, I don't really like to talk, but I'm a good listener. If you want to tell me what happened, I promise to listen in silence.

Julia looked at that stranger and didn't understand what was happening. Without knowing why, she began to tell her everything that had happened and ended by saying: – He left without saying a word. He ignored me, he acted like I didn't exist...

Natália, after listening to Julia, began to laugh.

– What are you laughing at? There is no reason to laugh! I'm desperate! I am unemployed and have no chance of getting my previous job back! I was deceived, humiliated! I have nothing else in this life!

I am tired of so much suffering, it seems that I was born to suffer! I am tired of living!

I can't take it anymore, it's better to die!

– Excuse me, Julia. You're right, this is no time to laugh, I just couldn't help it.

– Why?

– Didn't I say it smelled like a man? I was right, right?

– It's true, but how could you know?

Natália laughed again: – Do you think I was born today?

No, Julia. I was a girl, a teenager, a young adult and now I am old. I had an intense life and every time I felt like you are now, the reason was always a man.

– Every time? Was there more than one?

– So many that I lost count.

– You're not telling the truth...

Just Beginning

– I am, and I assure you that if this was the first time you were disappointed with a man, others will come and pass through your life. There will be many and this will only end when you find the one with whom you will live and raise your family. Until then, my daughter, get ready. Men are weak. Of course, there are some who act correctly, but most of them do what Anselmo did, simply, after deceiving the woman, they disappear without saying goodbye.

– They don't have the courage to face a difficult situation.

– Are you sure about that? Wasn't it just Anselmo who acted like this, others do the same?

Natália laughed again: – Many men and women do that, Julia. This has always happened, and I think it will go on forever. So, my girl, raise your head and don't waste time crying for someone who doesn't deserve it.

– I didn't tell you everything.

– Is there more? I am here to listen to you. Do you want to tell me the rest?

I have one more problem. Maybe you can help me meet someone who can help me get rid of this problem.

– What problem?

– I just found out I'm pregnant...

– Since when is pregnancy a problem? I thought you had an incurable disease...

– I really want a son, but not now. Didn't you understand what I said? I don't have a job or a place to live, and now that I'm pregnant, I won't really get a job.

– If I had a place, I would take you to live with me. But I live in a room, where I cook and sleep.

There is no room, but don't worry, God will provide.

Just Beginning

– God? What God? The one who chose me to suffer this way? This God who made me not know my parents, who made me be abandoned by them? This God who made me grow up in an orphanage and now sends me this child that I can't have? I'm sorry, ma'am, but I can't believe in this God. I've always been alone! I've never had anyone take care of me!

Still influenced by Alzira, Natália asked: – Did you say that you were raised in an orphanage?

– Yes, I was abandoned the day I was born.

– This is very sad, but for that to happen, there was a mother who allowed you to be born, right?

– It's true...

– During your life, in difficult times, was there no one to help you? To watch over you?

Julia thought for a moment and replied: – Dona Neide was there. She always treated me with affection, encouraged me to study and have a profession. When I graduated, she found a job for me here in this city.

– You see? She did what I did for my daughters and what any mother does. Even though she wasn't your mother, she acted like she was.

– However, two months after I came here, she suffered a heart attack and died. She also abandoned me...

– Look what happened. She only died after you were referred. Did you say that when you needed a place to live, you found your friend, what was her name?

– Sueli

– She, without knowing you, let you live in her house and is your friend. You were never alone, Julia!

Just Beginning

– Even now, look at what is happening –. Natália said laughing.

– Why are you laughing?

– Look what we're doing now. I'm not sure why, I sat on this bench, we started talking and you're venting. I was never religious. I always thought it was a waste of time, but one thing I am sure, as long as we have faith, everything is fine. Life is in charge of putting things in their place. You will still find a man you will marry and you will be happy with your son.

– That's what scares me.

– Why?

– I'm dying for Anselmo. At times I wish he would die, but I feel that if he came, I would immediately forgive him and forget everything he did. I can't see my life without him.

– Look at life, Julia. As much as it changes, as modernized as it is, certain things are always the same.

Men continue to lie and cheat on women and, for the most part, shirk their responsibilities; women, however, continue to forgive them.

– You're right, but what should be done?

– The day women recognize their value, that will change, Julia. However, that day is far away. Natália got up and smiled, said: – Now, I have to go. I have to make my lunch. Good luck Julia.

I hope everything goes well in your life. Think carefully before taking any action that you may regret later. Tugging at the dog's collar, she said: – Come on, Duke!

Holding the dog, she walked away.

Julia looked and thought: What woman is this, that I don't know and that made me feel so well?

Just Beginning

She got up and started walking. Alzira and Ciro, although they knew that the figures were close, smiling, walked beside her.

Julia walked for a long time, always thinking: even though that lady said all that, I feel like I won't make it. How to have, educate and raise a child? How can I live without a job or a place to live?

I don't want my son to be raised in an orphanage, like I was, or to be adopted by a family that doesn't love him or to grow up thinking that he was abandoned by me like I was. Worst of all is knowing that I won't be able to live without Anselmo. There is no other way, the best thing I have to do is end my life and take my son with me.

Hearing that, the figures came closer and began to spin around her and envelop her with dense energy.

– Ciro, they are back!

– Alzira, they have returned! She changed her mind quickly and attracted them again.

– We're going to throw lights on them so they can escape.

– We can do that, but you know our lights can't cut through this fog.

– It all depends on her wish, only hers.

Julia, without imagining the struggle that was being waged on the spiritual realm, continued walking. She saw a grocery store and went inside. She stopped next to the employee and, in a strong voice, said: – I have problems with mice, do you have any effective poison?

– Yes, I do. Wait, I'll get it. She came back with the poison, gave it to her, and said, You need to put this poison all over the house, especially in the corners. In a few days, all the mice will be

Just Beginning

dead. But, if you have children or animals, be careful, as it is very strong.

She, trying to smile, said: – Don't worry, I don't have children or animals. She paid for the poison and left.

All the way back, she kept thinking about how she was going to take the poison. I'll wait for Sueli to go to work. I need to write a note.

On that note, I'm going to ask Sueli to tell Anselmo what he did to me. I want him to suffer and feel so guilty that he can never be happy again. I will also ask her to find his wife and tell her what happened.

I will die, but he will pay for what he did to me!

She came home and Sueli was still sleeping. She went to her room and went to bed.

She tried to sleep, but the figures would not allow her. They turned and laughed and talked endlessly about how good it would be after her death, as she could rest.

Anxious, Julia decided to leave the house.

Sueli, at the same time every day, got up and saw that Julia wasn't at home: she must be looking for work. Well, I have to go.

She took her bag and left. Júlia, always accompanied by the figures, by Alzira and Ciro, was hiding in an alley from where she could see her apartment because she knew the time when Sueli used to go out.

As soon as she saw Sueli leave, she went home. She went into the apartment and immediately, took a glass, filled it with milk and went into the living room. After placing the glass on the table, she took out a notebook and a pen, sat down.

She wrote why she was doing that. She apologized to Sueli and asked her to send that letter to Anselmo and Suzana.

Just Beginning

She sat down, took the glass, looked at it, and smiled.

The shapes came even closer, making the mist thicker.

Alzira and Ciro, now, accompanied by Neide, crying, tried to throw the lights that didn't reach Julia.

Julia looked at the glass. Suddenly, she remembered what Natália had said. She remembered Neide, Teca, Altair and Sueli.

She remembered how much they had helped her have a happy life.

She thought: what am I doing? How can I kill myself and worst of all, kill my son? How can I end a life that so many have helped me build? No, I won't do that. Even without a family, with everyone's help, I managed to get here!

I have no right to disappoint them ! I'm not going to do that!

She put the glass back on the table and began to cry: I don't know what will happen to my life. But I will try to raise my son and if I am unsuccessful, I will put him in an orphanage or another home.

I have no right to prevent him from being born, from living! Someone will take care of him! I'll get on with my life, I have faith that I will.

Finding a job, a place to live, and trying to be a good mother!

At that moment, the fog cleared and the lights of the friends invaded the entire room, causing the figures to disappear.

Alzira, seeing that they disappeared, smiling, said: – As they say, where there is light, there is no darkness. Thank God, this time, she managed to rescue everything she had done. God be praised.

Julia took the glass, went to the sink and threw it away. She looked around and thought: This house needs cleaning! I want everything around me to be clear and clean!

Just Beginning

She turned on the radio and a song began to play. She took a broom, cleaning products and began to clean the house. A few hours later, everything was clean and in place. Satisfied, she thought: This life, after all, is wonderful! I want to live long! As for Anselmo, as Mrs. Natália said, he doesn't deserve me!

What I have to do is thank this apartment that, for so long, has served as a refuge and I wish that those who come to live here are happy. I am going to take a shower.

So, I'll read one of these Sueli books. According to what I read, everything is always fine and we all have friends who are and will always be by our side and who, as far as possible, help us.

Do I have spiritual friends? I must have, since I have so many here on Earth... When Sueli arrived, she was still reading.

As soon as she entered, she saw that the apartment was clean and, surprised, asked: – Did you spend the day cleaning the apartment, Julia?

– No ! It Just took a few hours.

– I see you are reading one of my books. Are you liking them?

– Actually, they seem a bit fanciful to me.

– Why do you say that?

– It says everything is always fine, that for everything that happens to us there is always a reason, but what I liked the most, although I don't think so, is to imagine that we have spiritual friends who accompany us in all difficult times.

– Why don't you think so?

– I don't know, it would be too good, wouldn't it?

– I don't think it would, I think it is! Today, after everything I've been through with Nilson and now, with all the happiness I feel

Just Beginning

with Eduardo, I think that if I hadn't had help from heaven, I wouldn't have been able to do it.

– Maybe you are right. If it's true, now more than ever, I will need you.

– Why now?

– I'm pregnant...

– What?

– I'm pregnant...

– That's great, Julia! A child should always be welcome!

– It is the opportunity for a spirit to be reborn, rescue and fulfill its mission.

– Apart from that part of reincarnation, I believe what you say, but did you know that I don't have a job and that, being pregnant, I will hardly find another one? When you get married, I will have to move and I won't have the money to pay the rent anywhere. I don't know what to do. I can only wait for my invisible friends to help me. Sueli began to laugh: – What are you laughing at, Sueli?

– It seems that your spiritual friends are already helping you, Julia!

– I'm not understanding.

– Today I had a serious problem in the restaurant. With so much to do, I forgot to pay a bill and will have to pay a fine.

– It's not the first time it happens. I realized that I needed someone to take care of the financial part.

– At the same moment, I remembered you. I like to cook, but when it comes to numbers, I am a failure.

– You are the only person I know in whom I have confidence to be able to do this job.

Just Beginning

– Did you decide that now?

– No! I was going to tell you as soon as I arrived, but our conversation took a different turn. I didn't even know you were pregnant.

– I think, after I found out, everything changed.

– No! This girl will be born and raised with lots of love!

– The strangest thing was that when I decided to hire you to work with me, Rosana called me to talk about the wedding. I told her my decision and that you were moving as soon as I got married.

– She said that you don't have to move, that she doesn't need the apartment and knows that it's well maintained.

– Are you kidding, Sueli!

– No, Julia! It's true! You will work with me, of course, I cannot pay what you received in the other company, but it will be fine.

– Let's have this child, Julia! She will be the happiest in this world!

Julia, unable to stop laughing, happily looked up and said:
– I think I have friends, I do!

– Of course you do! They just aren't at the top! They are by your side and by our side!

– How do you know, Sueli?

– I don't know how, I just know they're here!

– I'm very happy, Sueli! Now, for my happiness to be complete, only Anselmo needs to return.

– Do you want him to come back? Do you want to stay with him?

– Of course. My life will only be complete if he is by my side so that we can raise our son. Sueli looked at her. She wanted to

Just Beginning

criticize, but she remembered what it was like when Nilson left her. She just smiled and said: – That's true. You must go after your happiness. Now let's go to sleep.

– Tomorrow I need to show you the mess in my office.

– Don't worry. Soon everything will be in order.

– You won't regret hiring me.

– I know. Goodnight.

– Good night.

They entered their rooms and soon after fell asleep.

29.– Sensation on the skin

Suzana opened her eyes and looked at her watch. She turned to Anselmo and called him: Anselmo! It's almost ten o'clock, aren't you going to work?

He also opened his eyes and replied smiling: – Today is Saturday, Suzana...

– It's true! I didn't sleep well at night. I was only able to sleep around six o'clock. At that time , I slept so much that I even forgot that today was Saturday.

He, when he got up, said: – Keep lying down. I'll go to the bakery to buy fresh bread.

When I get back, I'll make you a coffee like the one served in a hotel. Then, let's go to the beach.

– I need to bathe in the sea and sunbathe. She looked at him, but remained silent.

– He, without realizing that she was different, got up and left.

Suzana got up too and went to the kitchen. She put water in a kettle and went to the bathroom to bathe. As she bathed, she thought: I can't let it get past today. During the night, I thought a lot and there is no other way. Now is the time to make a decision. I know it won't be easy, but there is no other way.

Just Beginning

Anselmo passed by the lobby, greeted the doorman, and went to the bakery. He bought bread, cold cuts and a cake. He passed a greengrocer, bought some fruit and returned home, thinking: Suzana is strange.

Although more than three months have passed and she is involved in the organization of the cooperative that she is willing to establish, I believe that she has not yet gotten used to living here. I'm doing so well in the company that I need to make her life the best it can be.

He entered the building and, as he passed by the lobby, the doorman said: – Good morning, Mr. Anselmo. Look, this telegram just arrived! It's for Mrs. Suzana.

Anselmo, surprised, took the telegram and went to the apartment.

When he entered, Suzana was finishing setting the table for coffee. Rodrigo was in the shower.

– Suzana, the doorman gave me this telegram. It is for you.
She, surprised, looked at his hand.

– For me? Whose is it?

– You will only know once you open it.

She took the telegram and opened it. It was from Dr. Santana, her old boss. Shivering, Suzana read:

"Suzana

I need you to come talk to me. I'm desperate without you. Everything is a mess, I feel like only you can fix everything here. Call or come. I have a great proposal to get you back to work, including a raise.

Santana. "

With the telegram in hand, Suzana looked at Anselmo, who, seeing her pallor, took the telegram and read it.

Just Beginning

– Who sent this telegram, Suzana? Who had your address?

– When I left my job, I left my address with Olga, my secretary, so that, if she knew about a job, she would write to me.

– With this telegram, I have a lot to think about.

– What does that mean, Suzana?

– It means I'm leaving, Anselmo.

– Leaving, why? I thought you were happy to live here and with the cooperative organization.

– I'm very happy. My mother always said that for everything that happens to us, there is always a purpose that, although at the time we live we do not understand it, over time it shows.

– The purpose of my arrival here was to help those artisans who have always been exploited.

During all this time I was here, I have spoken to many of them and I am getting them to understand that the day they unionize, their pieces will be sold at a fair price.

All works of art will be passed on to the cooperative and it will be in charge of pricing and selling.

I am saying that the parts can be sent to other states and even, why not, abroad.

It's working, Anselmo, many of them already agreed. After some time, others will agree.

– Do you see how everything is going well, Suzana? I don't understand why you said you wanted to leave...

– I have to go. I can no longer be married to you.

– I'm not understanding. Is it because of your job? When we came here, you said it was because you loved me!

You said you wanted to save our marriage!

Just Beginning

– I was lying, Anselmo.

– What?

– I was lying about what you heard. Didn't you understand what's written on that telegram?

– I came here because I was fired!

– Goodbye! Do you get it? If that hadn't happened, I would never have come with you!

– I would never have left my car, my apartment to live in this small apartment, far from my city and the people I know!

Anselmo, hearing that, opened his mouth.

– Were you lying? Were you fired?

– Yes. I was fired the day I thought I was going to get a promotion.

The day that, after being fired, I went to find you to tell you what happened and you were with that girl, remember?

At the same time, Anselmo remembered that day and Julia.

He tried to get the image of her out of his mind. He asked:
– Now that you're going to get your job back, do you want to go back there?

– As I understand it, in this telegram they want me back and I will be able to negotiate a raise.

With that money, I could go back to my apartment. I think I tried so hard enough to sell it now.

I could buy a new car and get back to work!

I just don't want it anymore!

– You don't want it?

– No! I don't want to go back to that life of work, of pressure.

– Although I had money and lived very well, I had a brand new car, I didn't have time to look at the sky, the moon. I didn't

Just Beginning

have time to play with my son, or to bathe in the sea, or to lie on the beach, sunbathing.

– I didn't live, Anselmo!

– Today I live! I had everything I wanted, but nothing I needed!

I learned that happiness is not in what you have, but in the little things. I learned that the size of the house you live in doesn't matter, but how you feel inside. I learned that to be happy, we need little!

– You're driving me crazy, Suzana! Since you found all this here, why did you say you were leaving?

– To have all the happiness that I said I found here, there was only one thing missing.

– What?

– A love, Anselmo. What I also found.

Anselmo, who was sitting, got up and shouted: – What are you saying, Suzana? Did you find a love?

– I found it. A love like never before in my life. Someone who makes me happy just by being by my side.

– Will you leave me for another, man?

–Yes.

– Who is he?

– A boy who lives in the village, who is a painter.

– A painter? Where will you live? In any shack? You who always wanted the best!

– Yes. Didn't I just say that it takes little to be happy?

– You went crazy!

– No, Anselmo! I have never been more lucid. After reading this telegram, I am even happier.

Just Beginning

I'm sure I don't want to go back to that life.

– How are you going to live?

– I have some money saved. I spoke to some merchants here and told them that things were going to change.

That they would have to pay the fair price for the goods. At first, they said they wouldn't buy any more.

However, as time went by, they realized that without the pieces they would have nothing to sell and they accepted the price I asked.

Business is good. When the cooperative is walking alone, I will take these pieces to other states.

– What will happen to Rodrigo?

– He will stay with me, of course. He will be raised in a healthy environment, close to nature.

– You can't do that! He is my son! I will not allow you to raise him without any comfort, living in a hut.

– Several times you said that, for him, it would be better to be raised here, because the air is healthy. I think so.

You will have to decide.

– You know that working the way you work there is no way to take care of him. You will have to hire a maid to take care of him. You know that since we've been here, he has become another child, happy and healthy.

– I want to spend more time with him. I want him to stay with me, but I don't want to fight about it.

– So, if you think it's better for him to be with you, I will not object. If he stays with me, you know that it will be fine and you will be able to see him whenever you want. He is your son and he will always be.

– Are you going to give up your son for a man?

Just Beginning

– No! I am giving up my son, because I don't want you to use him so that I can stay by your side.

I want him to stay away from our possible fights. I'm doing this so that later, when I have to take care of his life, I won't blame him for my unhappiness. I'm trying to make you understand that for me, nothing is more important than my freedom to choose. I don't know how long I'm going to live, but I want that time to be as I choose.

– What will happen to me?

– You haven't been happy with me either.

We had a few good moments at first, but then you know it was all over. It's so true that you found another woman and you're not with her, just because I found out. Go back to her or find another woman. For men, women are never lacking.

– She was going to come with me and she just didn't come because you lied to me and fooled me!

– No, Anselmo! You acted in a way that suited your convenience!

Since she wanted to go with you, she must be waiting now. I feel like there will be no problem.

I have to leave now.

While you think about what you are going to do with your life, I'm going to Vila. I have a lot of work.

When you decide what you want for yourself, for us and for Rodrigo, go there and we will figure it out. She picked up a suitcase. She put in some of his and Rodrigo's clothes.

Then she took the boy and made him kiss his father and silently left.

Anselmo stood there, not knowing what to do. He didn't understand why God was doing this to him.

Just Beginning

He didn't understand why Suzana was abandoning him, changing him for another man, just now that it seemed like everything was fine. He remembered Julia: What happened to her? Is she still waiting for me?

How could I abandon her like I did? I don't know how to live alone...

He lied down staring at the ceiling, began to remember everything that had happened in his life and, mainly, Julia.

30.– The clarification

Some time after falling asleep, Júlia opened her eyes and was again in the garden of María Iné's house, next to Alzira and Ciro. She realized that they were happy. Alzira said: – Congratulations, Julia!

– Do you already know I'm pregnant?

– Congratulations on that too!

– I'm not understanding...

– You, after many incarnations, managed to pass one of the most difficult proofs!

– What proof?

– You chose life! You chose to have your child!

Julia remembered: – It's true, but it was at the last minute.

– Never mind. The important thing is that you did. You used your free will wisely. So from now on, you will only be happy. Everything will work.

– Do you know that I don't need to move and that I'm going to work with Sueli?

– Of course we know and we are happy about it.

– Since the last time we met, I was worried and curious to know what happened to María Inés and Luiz Cláudio. Is she still in

Just Beginning

that horrible place? Was he as demoralized as she wanted? Did he marry Eulalia?

– Take it easy! One question at a time, Julia. Look what happened.

Julia entered and saw when Zefa entered the room and found the body of María Inés.

Desperate, she called Maria Augusta who, as soon as she saw what her sister had done, also began to cry, desperate. María Augusta looked around her and saw the paper where María Inés had written everything that happened between her and Luiz Cláudio and what was the reason for her death, she looked at Zefa and said: Zefa! Let's burn this paper!

Nobody needs to read and know that she committed suicide much less than it was because of a man.

– Was that what she wrote there on this paper?

– Yes, that's what she wrote. We can't let dad or other people know!

– Your father needs to know...

– He doesn't need to and he won't know, Zefa! He just lost mom. He is already suffering a lot.

– I imagine what he will feel when he knows that María Inés also died. He will suffer even more if he knows that she committed suicide.

– We can't tell him, Zefa.

– Okay, my lady, but other people may know.

– If they find out, she cannot be buried in the sacred field.

– When they know that it was for a man and that she was expecting a child, it will be worse.

She will be demoralized and her memory will always be remembered as suicidal and murderous. I can't allow that.

Just Beginning

She is my sister...

– Okay, my lady, what else are you going to do?

– Let's wash her and change her clothes. Then we will put her to bed as if she were sleeping.

– When everything is fine, I'll tell Dad that we don't know how it happened.

Dr. Evaristo will accept what I say. She will be buried with all the pomp and people will regret that she died so young. This secret is ours, Zefa! Only ours! Don't even tell Ignacio.

– No, my lady. I won't. She was my lady, that is, I really liked her.

– I know you liked her, so you will help me. Come on, we have a lot to do.

While Zefa was removing the flowers that were inside a vase, María Augusta lit a candle and set fire to one of the corners of the paper that began to burn and the ashes fell into the vase, where there was water.

In seconds the paper was gone.

– It's done, Zefa. My sister will be remembered with longing and regret. She will have a funeral with all the pomp and will be buried, inside the church, next to my mother.

When Julia saw that, she asked: – Didn't Luiz Cláudio know? Did Maria Inés die for nothing? What happened to him? Did he marry Eulalia?

– Calm down Julia. One question at a time –. Ciro replied, smiling: – Sorry, I know I'm anxious, but I need to know!

– Anxiety is one of the worst evils of the spirit, spiritually or physically, spirits always forget that everything will happen at a certain time. Luiz Cláudio, although he knew the reason for the death of María Inés, continued his life.

Just Beginning

– He married Eulália and, during all the time they lived together, he had several other women.

– He drank a lot and never treated her with affection and respect. Due to the life he led, he died before his time and indirectly committed suicide. For this reason, as with María Inés, he was taken to the same valley of suffering.

– Eulália, although she suffered when she saw what her husband was doing, was always afraid to face him, to be alone.

– At that time, women had little or no value. She had four children and lived for them.

– After death, did María Inés and Luiz Cláudio meet?

– No, although they were in the same valley, their faults were different, so their paths were too.

– María Inés, for a long time, hid from monsters that only she saw. She often relived the moment of her death and saw her body being eaten by worms in the grave. She suffered a lot and several times tried to escape, to return.

– Everyone was worried and hoping that she would finally understand that the reason she was in that place was because she had taken her own life. After suffering a lot, she finally understood and began to cry and ask for forgiveness for what she had done.

– At that moment, rejoicing in happiness, her friends came to her and rescued her. She was taken to a spiritual hospital, where she recovered and regretted what she had done. She said that she needed a new opportunity and that, next time, she would act differently. Luiz Cláudio too, after spending a long time suffering, understood that he was there because of his choices.

– It was because he gave too much value to his power of seduction and because he didn't value the women he seduced and abandoned.

Just Beginning

– He asked for a new chance of redemption. After understanding, asking for forgiveness and help, his friends rescued and treated him. – Eulália also understood that she had allowed her spirit to be imprisoned for her fear of being condemned by society. – Everyone asked for another chance. For this, a meeting was called, where everyone would be present.

– Do you want to attend this meeting, Julia?

– Of course!

– Okay, close your eyes.

Julia smiled and closed her eyes. A few seconds later, Ciro spoke: – You can open your eyes, Julia.

She opened her eyes and saw that she was in a room, where there was a huge table and that María Inés and all those who had participated in her life were sitting around her. At one end of the table, Ciro sat, and at the other, Alzira.

The rest were sitting in the chairs around them.

Ciro, looking at María Inés, asked: – Now that everyone has returned and undergone a treatment, therefore, understood what happened, we are here to prepare for the next incarnation. For that, we need to know what each one wants to achieve and how they want it to be done.

Let's start with Luiz Cláudio.

Looking at Luiz Cláudio, Ciro asked: – What did you learn and what are you, Luiz Cláudio, planning to do? How do you want to be reborn?

– First, I want to thank everyone who tried to help me make good decisions, but since it has been happening for a long time, I made the same bad decisions again. Again, I used my power of seduction to cheat, gain power and have more money. I intend to free my spirit from those mistakes that enslaved me.

Just Beginning

So I want to be reborn as a common man, not so attractive. I promise, this time, I will be the best husband and father I have ever been.

Ciro smiled and turned to Eulalia, asking: – You, Eulalia. What have you learned and what do you plan to do?

– How do you want to achieve your wish?

– I, fearing the comments of society and economic dependence, was afraid of living without Luiz Cláudio, I allowed my spirit to be enslaved and humiliated by him. I intend to be reborn as a strong and independent woman who can make her own decisions without being afraid of what society will say.

So I intend to free my spirit so I can walk.

Once more, he smiled and, turning to María Inés, asked her: – And you, María Inés. What have you learned? What do you want?

How do you want to be reborn?

She, still somewhat embarrassed, replied: – I learned that, because of my pride, because I didn't appreciate my parents, who loved me and gave me everything, I became a proud, intolerant and selfish person. I learned that because of my pride and not accepting that I was abandoned, I made the worst mistake, suicide and that, if that was not enough, I still prevented a spirit from being reborn. Therefore, I intend to be reborn without a family.

Have a poor life and a lot of work. Suffering all kinds of prejudices, and this time, allow my son to be reborn and be happy.

Ciro, looking at the three of them, said: – You know that when we are here, in the spiritual realm, everything seems to be easy.

We feel that we are protected and with the strength to accomplish what we want, but in physical life, everything is different.

Just Beginning

I hope everyone gets what they want. However, you must understand that you will have to meet and go through the same situations and will only be able to walk when you manage to go through them. Often, you will not accept or understand the life you have chosen and will rebel. All of us, your friends, who are here, will be by your side, trying to help. However, we can never interfere with each other's free will.

Now, let's get ready to be reborn. Some, although they have to fulfill their missions and amend their mistakes, will be reborn to help physically. Others will remain here sending light and good thoughts.

Now reborn, try to fulfill what you are saying at this moment and thank God that you can come back victorious.

Julia, hearing this, perplexed, asked: – Is everything you said true? Did they really choose the life they wanted to have in the next incarnation? None of them chose to have money, a good life, why?

– Because, although in physical life, these things attract many spirits, money, most of the time, is a reason to fall, to delay when walking. Money often makes a person selfish, proud, and very powerful.

It doesn't mean that having money is bad, it must serve to make dreams come true and everyone needs to dream, wish happiness for themselves and others. You have to fight for it, through study, work, never through deception, lies and crime.

– Many delay the evolution doing everything possible to always have more money. They steal, they cheat, they kill.

– Everyone has the opportunity to have the money they need to be able to live according to the life they have chosen.

– Did I really choose the life I live today?

– María Inés chose and left that day.

Just Beginning

– Are you saying that I am...

– Look at her.

Júlia looked at the place where María Inés was sitting and saw that she was becoming her own image. Surprised, she asked, Was it me? Was I María Inés? Did I do all those things? It can't be!

– She was and she did all those things. Remember.

Júlia began to remember her life as María Inés. She also remembered the time she spent in the valley. Desperate, she began to cry.

Alzira, touching her arm, brought her back.

– It all happened a long time ago, Julia. We only reminded you so that you could understand the life you lead today.

– Look who comes into this room.

She looked and, to her surprise, saw Eulalia's parents, who became two young men. She, not knowing who they were, smiled.

Alzira continued: – Eulália's parents always liked you and were by your side.

– They just came back so you can be born. They had a work project that will help humanity and that would help them walk a few more steps. However, because of you, they postponed this project. They stayed for a short time on Earth, the time you needed to be engendered, and therefore they could go back to the project they postponed.

Eulalia's mother, now, with the face of a young woman, approached and, smiling, said: – I was reborn with the name of Jandira and my husband, Eulalia's father as Homero. He died a few months after he became a father and I the day you were born. Therefore, you would have what you asked for: to be raised without parents, and we, happy for the mission accomplished, will continue with our project and, whenever possible, by your side.

Just Beginning

Now, we are pleased to see that you passed your tests, so that we can continue our work.

Excitedly, Julia walked over to them, who were with open arms. While they embraced, she said crying : – I thought a lot about you. I wondered what you were like and wondered why you abandoned me.

– We never abandoned you, Julia. We have been on the same walk for a long time and we will stay with you forever, until the day we can walk together.

– Thank you, thank you very much.

Alzira approached and, touching Julia's shoulder, said: – Look at Zefa, Julia.

Julia looked over to where Zefa was standing and saw her face turn to Neide's. Perplexed, she said, Ms. Neide? Were you Zefa?

– I was Zefa, Julia. I couldn't leave my lady.

– In spite of everything, I liked you very well, just like you, Julia.

Alzira interrupted: – Zefa wanted to be reborn so that she could be by your side, when you needed it, and guide you in life.

I wanted to be the director of an orphanage, because besides helping you, I could help other children.

Julia hugged Neide and, still crying, said: – You were my guardian angel.

You were always present in my life. I can never thank you enough.

– You always listened to me and lived up to my expectations.

– You died so early...

Just Beginning

– As soon as you became a professional who could walk alone, my mission ended and I was able to go home.

Alzira spoke again: – Look at María Augusta. Julia looked and saw Sueli appear.

– Sueli? Were you my sister?

They also hugged. Sueli, crying, said: – I needed to apologize...

– Apologize? For what?

– Although I tried to help you, when you said you were expecting a child, I couldn't.

– I always thought it was my fault. If I had been paying more attention, you might not have done what you did.

The least I could do was be reborn by your side so that when you had to pass the same test, I would be there and this time, I would really help you.

– Although I have nothing to forgive, because today I know it was my fault, Sueli, you helped me!

I didn't do the same crazy thing.

– My child is inside me and will be born! You gave me a job and a place to live! Thank you, my sister... – They continued hugging until Alzira spoke again: Look at Luiz Cláudio.

She looked up and saw that he was turning into Anselmo.

– Anselmo?

– Yes Julia. I asked for another chance and I was reborn by your side.

– This time, I should have protected you. I shouldn't have lied or fooled you, but I couldn't resist.

– I went back to doing what I always did. I abandoned you and our son. I also had debts with Eulália. I made her suffer a lot.

Just Beginning

– This time I intended to be a good husband, but I couldn't and I betrayed her again. Julia hugged him: – It wasn't just your fault. I was weak and didn't accept the rejection.

I didn't accept to be abandoned, exchanged for another woman. But this time it was different! Our child will be born!

Eulália, now with Suzana's face, also approached them: – Despite everything, we all walked a little more. Like Suzana, I finally got my freedom. I was able to assess what really has value, I was able to decide my life.

Again, Alzira's voice was heard: – You're right, Suzana. We walked a little more towards the Divine Light.

– This time, we are on our way again and we will not be further. Now, Júlia, look at María Inés's parents.

She looked and began to cry again, because in front of her, María Inés' parents became Teca and Altair.

– Teca? Altair? It can't be!

– Yes, Julia. We have always been by your side.

– I felt your death so much and I never accepted having been abandoned.

– Today you understand the need for that to happen, Julia. We had to step aside so that you could really appreciate your family and understand how important family is. You needed to have one to know what it really was like.

– However, we never left your side. We were together for several incarnations and will continue so for a long time.

– You were the best thing that happened in my life and if it were for me to learn, I can say that I certainly learned.

– Thank you for the wonderful moments you have given me.

Just Beginning

Teca and Altair embraced Julia who, crying, managed to kill the longing she felt for them.

After the hug, walking away, she said: – I never imagined that I had so many friends. I complained a lot about loneliness, not knowing what I had asked and how much I needed it. I don't know how to thank you.

Alzira, smiling, said: Ciro and I, this time, will not be reborn. We'll continue in the spiritual realm trying to help everyone, at times of choice. We have always been by your side. Especially by your side, Julia.

I never imagined that I had so many friends cheering for me. Ciro smiled: – It wasn't just us, Julia, look:

Júlia looked and saw the room full of her old slaves and friends whom she knew as María Inés.

She saw that as they entered, their faces turned into people she had known as Julia.

She saw Natália, Aunt Rosa, Jonás, Margarida and Ignacio and even the taxi driver she met the day she discovered that Anselmo had abandoned her.

Surprised by so many, Julia said: – Not all of them are my friends. Some, like Aunt Rosa, hurt me a lot. Some, I only saw once or some times.

– Like I said, everyone had their own amends , their missions.

They would only find you at a decisive moment. Not everything is what it seems, Julia. Enemies are not always enemies. When they arise, most of the time it's to help us practice forgiveness, humility.

Rosa needed to make you feel the value of a family.

Just Beginning

Rosa approached: – And you taught me that although we have a lot of money, we will never achieve total happiness, if that money was earned at the cost of evil, envy and deception.

Julia, understanding what she meant, hugged her and they both cried.

– Right behind, Paulo Octávio appeared smiling, said: – Although I tried, I could never stay by your side. Luiz Cláudio has always been with us. I hope this time is different.

Julia, without understanding what he was saying, asked: – Did I see you at the dance that María Inés attended? Wait.

– I am remembering! We have known each other in other lives.

– Yes, you saw me at the dance. Once again, I tried to get closer, but you ignored me.

– In this life, I'll try again. Maybe I can do it.

– I hope that as soon as I see you, I'll recognize you.

– I also hope so.

Alzira interrupted them: – You'll see him soon. At Sueli's wedding. Now that everything is cleared up, it's time to wake up, Julia.

– I just didn't understand one thing.

– What was it Julia?

– María Augusta was different from María Inés. She was a girl with good feelings, modest. Why, like Sueli, did she have to meet Nilson and go through all that?

– As I said, everyone, besides helping you, needed to rescue and fulfill their mission.

– Maria Augusta was a modest girl and had good feelings, but, like you, Anselmo and Suzana, through many other incarnations, she was involved with Nilson and his wife. She had

Just Beginning

to choose the path she wanted to walk and make Nilson choose who he wanted to stay with. Today, like Sueli, she is no longer hurt and, therefore, she will be happy with Eduardo.

He has been waiting for her for a long time. Now you really need to wake up, Julia!

– Can't I stay a little longer?

– No, Julia. You need to go back.

– Well, I just wanted to clarify one thing.

– What is the use of knowing all this if I am dreaming and when I wake up I will not remember what I saw here?

– You will have the impression that you don't remember it, but you can be sure that when you need it, you will remember it.

– Maybe not as clearly as it's happening here, but you will always know that you have already lived that, and that this time you need to change the story.

Julia was going to ask one more question, but jumping up, as if she had been pushed into the body, she woke up and thought: What was this crazy dream?

Epilogue

For more than a month, Anselmo tried in every possible way to make Suzana change her mind, without success. He had the firm intention of changing his life and his way of being.

In one of his last conversations, he said nervously: – Don't you know what you're doing, Suzana?

– You are living in a hut and you took my son to live in that poverty! You pushed the boy away from his friends! This is bad!

– First of all, I'm not living in a hut! I live in a simple one-bedroom house, but I am happy, as I never have, and so is Rodrigo! Here he plays in the street with other children.

He lives outdoors and can run as much as he wants! He is not trapped inside an apartment, watching TV!

I know you don't understand like other people won't, but despite studying so much, I didn't know what happiness was. I am happy with my work. The negotiations are going well.

– Don't talk to me! You did it all for one man! You left our house, our life and just for one man!

– It wasn't because of a man, Anselmo! Perhaps he served as an instrument for me to look at the life I had before, but with him or without him, I know that that life didn't bring me happiness!

Just Beginning

– I don't know if I will continue with him or not, I only know that I am free from any bond and that I can choose the life I want for myself. I don't know if it's the right choice, I just know that I chose and that I will bear the consequences.

– You are not thinking about the future of your son! he doesn't need and can not be raised there in that way!

– As long as he is a child, there is no better place to be raised. When the time comes and he needs to study, we will think about how to do it, because even though we are not together, we are still his parents. Meanwhile, he will learn the real values of life. He will learn that what you are must be worth more than what you have, just as I learned.

– You learned what, Suzana?

– I learned that every object of desire loses its value as soon as it is acquired and that we are never satisfied, we always want more things and for that, some work too much, others steal and even kill.

Our son will learn that every dream must be fulfilled, that he can have whatever he wants as long as he doesn't stop living, enjoying life and he doesn't need to do what I did, which was work twenty-four hours, just to have things, without having time to enjoy what I had accomplished.

– You really changed, Suzana...

– I changed and I'm happy about it, Anselmo.

Anselmo, having no arguments left and finally realizing that his marriage was over, said goodbye and left.

Sueli's wedding was two days away. She was excited.

While they had lunch, she said: – Finally, the day is coming, Julia. I'm glad everything is ready and you're working here.

Just Beginning

– I don't know how to thank you. If it wasn't for you, I don't even know what would have happened to my life.

– Don't even think about saying thank you, Julia. I am very happy to have hired you. The accounts are in order and my only concern was organizing everything for my wedding. I hope that even after the child is born, you will not abandon me. I can no longer manage this restaurant without your care –. Julia smiled.

– Don't worry about it. I have no intention of leaving here. I am also enjoying work.

Sueli was going to say something, but for a few seconds she remained silent, staring at the front door of the restaurant. Then she said: Julia, don't look now, but Anselmo has just entered the restaurant.

– What?

– He came in and he's coming this way.

Julia couldn't help it. Although she felt her entire body shaking, she got up and turned to where he was. Anselmo approached and, smiling, asked: – How are you, Julia?

She, still shaking a lot and feeling that the blood was leaking from her face, replied: – I'm fine and you?

– We need to talk.

– I think we really need to talk, Anselmo. Sit down.

– While you're talking, I'm going to the kitchen. Dinner time is getting close and everything must be ready.

– Will you be okay, Julia?

With a trembling voice, Júlia replied: – You can go, Sueli and don't worry, I'll be fine.

Sueli tried to smile and walked away. She knew this was what Julia most wanted, for Anselmo to return. As soon as she left, still shaking, Julia said: – What are you doing here, Anselmo?

Just Beginning

– I went to your building and the concierge said you were working here.

– Yes, I am. Sueli asked me to help her with the bureaucratic part of the restaurant. I'm really enjoying the job.

– I'm here to apologize for what I did to you, Julia.

– It's been more than three months, Anselmo.

– Sorry, Julia. I will never forgive myself for what I did to you, but it was good, because now I know that you are the woman of my life. You're the only one I want to stay with.

Julia began to cry: – You cannot imagine how much I waited for you to come back and tell me what you are saying now, Anselmo.

– Please, Julia. I don't want you to cry or suffer again. I promise that I will make you the happiest woman in the world.

– Like I said, it's been a long time and things have changed.

– I have something important to tell you.

– What is it Julia? What happened that is so important?

– I don't even know how to say it, because I myself don't understand what happened. I've been having some strange dreams.

– Don't ask me what I dreamed, because I don't remember very well. I only know that each time I woke up, that memory became more distant and I felt free. I don't know why you left me with no explanation, but it doesn't matter anymore, Anselmo. – I'm fine and, although, sometimes I thought that everything was over, as Sueli always says, really it was just beginning. I feel that I have a life ahead of me and that it is very far from you.

– What do you say, Julia?

– What you heard. I have one life left and I don't want it to be by your side.

Just Beginning

– You can't be telling the truth, Julia. You always loved me and you always wanted to be with me. Are you getting revenge for what I did?

– No, Anselmo. I'm not trying to get revenge. Until the moment you arrived, I thought that if that happened, I would not say or ask anything and just fall into your arms, but as soon as I saw you, I realized that there was nothing left.

– I don't like you anymore. I am free from your domain.

I will go on with my life, however, alone. Now if you excuse me, I need to go back to work. Never again, Anselmo.

– I need to explain what happened and why I acted that way.

– I'm not interested in your explanations. They don't mean anything to me.

Before he said anything, she got up and went to the back of the restaurant, where the office was.

Sueli was hiding in a place where she could see the two talking, as soon as Julia passed through the kitchen, she saw that Anselmo was still sitting and looking at the door through which she had entered.

As soon as she entered the office, Sueli asked curiously: – What happened, Julia? Did you come to get your bag to go out with him? – Julia sat in her chair and, smiling, said: – No, Sueli. He's already out of my life.

– What are you saying? I thought you wanted him to come back!

– I thought so too, but as soon as I saw him, I remembered some things that I saw in my dreams and I felt that I needed to be free and that, for that, I needed to get away from him. After talking to him, I feel like it happened. I am free, Sueli.

Just Beginning

– I'm free from him and all the bad thoughts I've had about my life. Everything I have suffered is in the past.

– I feel like in the future, I will finally be happy!

– Did he tell you what happened and why is he back now?

– He tried. You may not believe it, but I don't care anymore.

– I want to live life as it comes, without complaining, just living.

– Did you talk to him about the boy?

– No, I didn't.

– He needs to know. He's the father, Julia!

– When my son or daughter grows up and wants to meet his or her father, maybe I will, but not now. This child is only mine.

I know that I have the ability to give her everything she needs plus lots of love and affection.

– None of this will be missing, Julia. I'm here to help you.

Julia looked up and, laughing, said: – You and our friends up there!

Sueli also laughed: – You're right. Now, let's make dinner. Clients will start arriving shortly. Anselmo left there, not believing what was happening in his life. He thought: this can't be happening. What did I do to make all this happen? I don't know what I'm going to do. I don't know how to live alone...

Sueli went to the kitchen and Julia stayed in the office.

She put her hand to her belly and thought: you will be happy and, when you need me, I will always be by your side and our friends too.

She laughed and continued her work.

Just Beginning

When the last customer left, they also left and went home. When they arrived at the apartment, they saw that a car stopped in front of the door of the building. A boy got out of the car.

As soon as she saw him, Sueli asked: – Mario, did you really come?

– Of course! I was happy when I received your wedding invitation. Nothing would make me miss the opportunity to get to know this girl better.

Sueli looked at Júlia and, laughing, said: – This is Mario, Mr. Osvaldo's son, who helped me take you to the hospital –. Julia, a little embarrassed, said: – I'm sorry for the work I made you do that day.

– You don't need to apologize. If that hadn't happened, I probably wouldn't have met you.

– According to our friend here, everything is always fine and it's always beginning.

– I hope this is a new beginning for both of us.

Julia looked at Sueli who laughed and said: – It's not my fault. I just said what I thought. Now shall we go up? When they entered the apartment, Sueli, laughing a lot, said: – Do you know that Mario didn't lie?

– About what?

– He came only to talk and meet you. That day, he was impressed by your beauty.

– Are you kidding, Sueli?!

– It's true, Julia! Since that day, we have talked a lot about you! He knows everything that has happened to you.

– Everything?

– Everything! Even about the child you are expecting.

– How could you do that, Sueli?

Just Beginning

– I needed to help you and since he showed interest...

– It's okay. He's kinda cute...

– Kinda? He is cute! I hope Eduardo doesn't hear us.

– There is no danger, Sueli. He won't come until tomorrow, will he?

– Yes. After the wedding, he won't travel anymore. As soon as we return from the honeymoon, we will move into our house. Júlia remembered Mario's face and, smiling, said: – He's really handsome!

– Yes, he is, Julia. Now shall we go to bed? I'm exhausted...

– Me too.

When she lied down, Julia looked at the ceiling of the room and spoke softly: – Thank you, my friends.

– I hope to have a dream like that again. She smiled and stretched out on the pillow, and fell asleep.

Alzira and Ciro also smiled. She said: – Decisions were made and everything bad was left behind. Now, she is on the right path. We will wait to see what happens.

Embraced, they disappeared.

The End

More from Eliana Machado Coelho and Schellida

Aimless Hearts

The Shines of Truth

The Right to be Happy

The Return

The Silence of Passions

Force to Start Over

The Certainty of Victory

Lessons that Life Provides

Strongest than Ever

Without Rules to Love

A Dairy in Time

A Reason to Live

ELISA MASSELLI

Just Beginning

There is Always a Reason

Encounters with the Truth

Just Beginning
Books by
MÔNICA DE CASTRO & LEONEL

Despite Everything

Love is not to be played with

Head on with the truth

From my all being

Desire

The price of being different

Twins

Giselle, the lover of the Inquisitor

Greta

Till Live do us part

Heart Impulses

The Actress

The Force of Destiny

Secrets of the Soul

Memories that the wind brings

World Spiritist Institute
https://iplogger.org/2R3gV6

www.ingramcontent.com/pod-product-compliance
Lightning Source LLC
LaVergne TN
LVHW041616060526
838200LV00040B/1312